Ann—

May the Lord bless you as you
study His Word.

Ashley Day

Exploring Revelation

A Devotional Commentary

By

Ashley Day

authorHOUSE™

1663 LIBERTY DRIVE, SUITE 200
BLOOMINGTON, INDIANA 47403
(800) 839-8640
WWW.AUTHORHOUSE.COM

First published by AuthorHouse 09/28/05

ISBN: 1-4208-7893-X (sc)
ISBN: 1-4208-7892-1 (dj)

Printed in the United States of America
Bloomington, Indiana

This book is printed on acid-free paper.

Seed-Time Ministries, Inc.,
5110 N. 4th Street,
Coeur d'Alene, Idaho 83815

Tel: (208) 765-3714
admin@seed-time.org
http://www.seedtime.net

God Bless. Jan 2006

Ashley Day

Dedicated to the members of
the Seed-Time Board:

Larry and Linda Runkle, Al and Judy Hassell,
Edna Day, Andrew Day, Kenneth Vaughn,
Roger Tinkey and Nicola Rowe,

in gratitude for their consistent direction,
support and encouragement
over the past many years.

"The sower sows the Word" (Mark4:14)

TABLE OF CONTENTS

EXPLORING REVELATION

As significant current events unfold all around us and voices are heard everywhere, saying "look here" and "look there", it is important that we keep our feet firmly grounded on the Word of God. Outside God's Word there is no stability and it is easy to be alarmed or sidetracked by spectacular forecasts that have very little substance to them. Our primary task as Christians is to know what God's Word says about the last days and to refuse any information that may be hearsay and which cannot be reconciled with the Scriptures.

CHAPTER 1

AFFIRMATION

When information of the magnitude of this book is presented it is essential that the source be well-documented. Anyone could write a book about last things, and many do, but it's wise to take much of what is written with a pinch of salt.

However, when, as in this case, the author is God Himself, it is necessary that the facts be well affirmed. And here, in the opening verses of Revelation, John takes pains to impress upon his readers the accuracy and reliability of what he is about to write. The information did not originate with him. It came from God the Father to God the Son and was then communicated to John by an angel. In light of parallel experiences by Daniel in the Old Testament, this angel was probably Gabriel, though John doesn't say so.

So John's opening phrase in verse 1 gives the subject for the whole book together with the source of his information:

> "The revelation of Jesus Christ, which God gave him to show to His servants."

The title in the King James Bible ("The Revelation of St. John the divine") misses the mark and is correctly missed out in most modern translations. It is not part of the inspired word but was put there by ancient scribes to provide a title for the manuscript.

This book is not about John, nor his revelation. It is about Jesus Christ in His role as ruler, conqueror and controller of all things, spiritual and temporal. When Jesus said to His disciples, *"All power is given unto me in Heaven and on earth"* that is precisely what He meant, namely, *ALL* power, total control over all things.

This book is the revelation of Jesus Christ in all the power and glory given to Him by God the Father. Dr. Moffat wrote that Jesus Christ is the medium for all revelation, which is true. The writer to the Hebrews wrote that

> *"God has in these last days spoken unto us by His Son, whom He has appointed heir of all things, by whom He also made the universe, who, being in the brightness of His glory and the express image of His person, and upholding all things by the word of His power, when He (Jesus) had by Himself purged our sins, sat down at the right hand of the majesty on high."*

It all speaks of God the Father working through the Lord Jesus as the sole executor of all matters concerning the created universe. At least eight times in John's Gospel alone, reference is made to the passing of revelation from the Father through the Son, to us. (John 3:34-35; John 5:20-23; John 7:16-17; John 8:28; John 12:49; John 14:10, 24; John 17:8).

This is important because here in Revelation 1:1 it clearly states that the revelation of Jesus Christ was given by God to Jesus to pass on to His servants. In other words, it comes directly from the throne of the universe. No wonder we are cautioned to take these words seriously and to pay special attention to what they say.

Verse 1:1 again:

> *"The Revelation of Jesus Christ, which God gave unto him, to show unto his servants things which must shortly come to pass; and he sent and signified it by his angel unto his servant John."*

The word "shortly" does not mean "soon", but "suddenly". It meant that the events of this book were not necessarily going happen immediately (which, of course, they did not) but when their time comes they will happen suddenly.

Verse 2:

> *"Who bare record of the word of God, and of the testimony of Jesus Christ, and of all things that he saw."*

In these two verses (Revelation 1:1-2) is affirmation of the importance and the accuracy of what we are about to study. It originated with God the Father, was given to the Lord Jesus Christ, who, in turn, sent it by an angel to the John, the disciple whom Jesus loved, to be passed on to you and to me.

Verse 3:

> *"Blessed is he who reads, and they who hear the words of this prophecy, and keep those things which are written therein: for the time is at hand."*

Not all people would have had access to the manuscript itself and so the blessing was promised, not only to those who read it out loud but to those who listened to it being read, and more important, to those who took heed to what it says.

This is the only book in the Bible that promises a special blessing to those who study it, yet it is possibly the most neglected book in the New Testament. Because it contains pictures and types that are not very easy to apply to the present day, many people avoid it. They assume that it is impossible to understand. However, that is sadly wrong. If that were true, why would this prophecy be called *"Revelation"*? The very word, "revelation", means "to reveal, to make something clear". And why would God promise a special blessing to those who study it? Obviously it was intended to convey valuable information to those who took the trouble to examine it. It is specifically called here "a prophecy" because it deals with things that have not yet come to pass and the Holy Spirit is able to speak to us through it, just as clearly as He does through any other book of the Bible. This is the inspired Word of God.

AUTHENTICATION

This paragraph deals with the same general subject but develops it a little further.

3

Verse 4:

"John to the seven churches which are in Asia: Grace be unto you, and peace, from him which is, and which was, and which is to come; and from the seven Spirits which are before his throne."

Here, the human writer takes his place. Up until now he has been writing about God, the Lord Jesus and angels but now John is writing what he has been told and is beginning to communicate with the churches.

Some have questioned that the writer was the Apostle John because he calls himself a "servant". That objection seems rather weak to me because Paul, Peter, Jude and even Jesus' half brother, James all called themselves "servants" in their letters. There is no valid reason for doubting that the same John who wrote the fourth Gospel and the three letters in the New Testament was the writer here in the book of Revelation.

He was writing to seven specific churches, located in the western part of Asia Minor, which is present-day Turkey. The remains of these places are still in existence and real people with real names and faces made up their congregations. They must have received this prophecy with awe.

Can you imaging how we would feel to receive a message from God via the Lord Jesus Christ, through the mediation of an angel, written by a great apostle, addressed specifically to your church and dealing with intimate problems that existed within it? How would you feel under those circumstances? These seven ordinary congregations received these messages. They must have made a profound impression on them.

So John introduces himself first as the human writer. Second, comes the source of the prophecy. As before, this was God the Father. *"Grace be unto you, and peace, from him which is, and which was, and which is to come."* The Father's eternal nature is stressed first. He is now, He always was and He always will be the Almighty.

Thirdly, we are introduced to an additional party of this writing, namely, *"the seven Spirits which are before his throne."* Nobody knows for certain who these seven spirits are. Some believe that they have reference to the Holy Spirit of God and that the expression means "sevenfold Spirit", indicating perfection. They base their belief not only that the Godhead is in focus here but also that in Isaiah 11, the Word speaks of a sevenfold Spirit of God (The Spirit of the Lord, the Spirit of wisdom, the Spirit of understanding, the Spirit of counsel, the Spirit of might, the Spirit of knowledge and of the fear of the Lord).

Others claim that the seven spirits here refer to seven powerful angels who stand in the presence of God. Nobody knows for sure and if someone comes and tells you that they do know, you should not listen to them because they are mistaken. However, whoever it is, or they are, they seem to co-author the message which is about to be delivered. This gives added weight to the belief that the Holy Spirit is intended.

Fourthly, the beginning of verse 5:

> *"And from Jesus Christ, who is the faithful witness, and the first begotten of the dead, and the prince of the kings of the earth."*

On earth, Jesus faithfully spoke fourth God's Word, and He is now about to do it again in this letter. First, He is the *"faithful witness"*, and the Greek word *"witness"* is the word, *"martyr"*. Second, He is the *"firstborn from the dead"*. Quite a number of people, in both Old and New Testaments were raised from the dead but they all had to die again. Only Jesus was raised from the dead in a permanent resurrection body in which He still dwell today. He is the first born because millions of other will follow Him as the result of His atoning work upon the cross. That is why in Romans 8:29 Paul refers to Him as *"The first born among many brethren."* The many brethren are, of course, people like you and me, who have been saved through His blood and will be raised the dead also.

Finally, He is referred to as *"The prince of the kings of the earth"*. "Prince", in the King James Bible, means "ruler", as the modern translations renders it. Whether they realize it or not, Jesus is the ruler of the kings of the earth. World leaders may think they are in charge but they are mistaken. Jesus has been in control of all history from the beginning. He is, right now, in the process of bringing the world empires into position for the cataclysmic events that are described in this book.

ACCLAMATION

The second part of verse 5 and verse 6:

> *"Unto him that loved us, and washed us from our sins in his own blood. 6 And hath made us kings and priests unto God and his Father; to him be glory and dominion for ever and ever. Amen."*

John is now speaking as the messenger and he identifies himself with the churches to whom he will be writing. The words, "loved *us*", "washed *us*", *"our* sins" and "hath made *us*" include John in the blessing, indicating that he is numbered among the recipients.

Were it not for the atoning work of Christ, we would all be heading straight for the judgments described in this book. If you want to know what you've missed, read Revelation!

At this point, the prophecy begins but only by way of announcement. The mood is still one of praise and acclamation. In verse 7 John writes:

> *"Behold, he cometh with clouds; and every eye shall see him, and they also which pierced him: and all kindreds of the earth shall wail because of him. Even so, Amen."*

I am sure John vividly remembered the day when he had stood on a hill near Bethany, along with the other disciples, gazing up into the sky, and saw Jesus lifted up by some invisible force, defying gravity. They'd watching Him until he disappeared into the clouds and then suddenly an angel had stood beside them and had told them that this same Jesus, whom they had seen taken up into heaven, would so come in like manner as they had seen Him go. No timetable was given. They had no idea whether His coming was close or distant but they knew He would come eventually.

The years since then had passed by and John had faithfully carried out his mission but now, in his old age, he was able to confirm with unimaginable authority that Jesus would indeed come in the clouds and that when He did it would be a global event. Every eye will see Him – even those who were responsible for His death.

Of course, as Zechariah 12:10 makes clear, this did not mean people like Caiaphas and Herod and Pilate. They were probably all dead by this time anyway. It refers to the House of David and the inhabitants of Jerusalem. For the moment, John is being general and is not speaking of the details. Apparently he is not referring to the rapture here, which will take place before these judgments fall. There is no evidence that every eye will see the rapture. That will be an instantaneous thing, when the church will be snatched away, prior to the judgments of this book. Here in Revelation, the church dominates the scene until the end of chapter 3, when it disappears suddenly with the words, *"Come up hither"*. It is not referred to any more until chapter 19, when the marriage of the Lamb is described. So the "coming" described here in verse 7 is Christ's coming at the end of the Tribulation period to set up His kingdom on earth. It is the coming described in Matthew 24.

In Exodus 3, when Moses asked for God's name, God replied, *"Tell them I AM has sent you."* That is the first person singular of the present tense of the verb "to be", the verb of existence. In the New Testament, when the unbelieving Jews protested that they had Abraham as their forefather, Jesus said, *"Before Abraham was I AM."* Here in Revelation, the Lord, whose revelation is about to follow, reveals Himself in all His power through John. In verse 8 He says *"I AM."*

Verse 8:

> *"I am Alpha and Omega, the beginning and the ending, saith the Lord, which is, and which was, and which is to come, the Almighty."*

These are incredible words and they sum up the unimaginable power and majesty of the Lord Jesus Christ as He is today. Some texts add "God" to "Lord" there but that is a doubtful and unnecessary addition. This statement introduces, more clearly than any other phrase, the subject of the book of Revelation.

It was Jesus who lived originally in unapproachable light; it was He who deigned to take upon Himself human flesh and suffer rejection and the cross to pay the penalty for the world's sin; it was He who was raised to glory; He who has controlled history ever since that time, He who will come for His bride before the judgment begins, and He who will come again in great glory at the end of the age. He has always been and always will be the Almighty and this book is about Him. It is *"The revelation of Jesus Christ"* to you and to me. It originated from the very throne of the universe, was revealed to the Lord Jesus, who called an angel to send it to John who, in turn, is now writing to you and me, and a blessing is promised to those who read these words and do them!

In John chapter 21 there is an interesting incident that ties Peter and John together. In John 21:18, Jesus says,

> *"Verily, verily, I say unto thee, When you wast young, you girded yourself, and walked wherever you wished: but when you are old, you will stretch forth your hands, and another shall gird you, and carry you where you do not wish to go. 19 This he said, signifying by what death Peter should glorify God. And when he had spoken this, he said to him, Follow me. 20 Then Peter, turning about, saw the disciple whom Jesus loved following; who also leaned on his breast at supper, and said, Lord, who is he who betrays you?"* (That was John, of course). *21 Peter seeing him, said to Jesus, Lord, and what shall this man do? 22 Jesus said to him, If I will that he tarries till I come, what is that to you? You follow me. 23 Then a rumor went around among the brethren, that that disciple should not die: yet Jesus did not say to him, 'He shall not die'; but, 'If I will that he tarries till I come, what is that to you'?*

Now obviously the rumor concerning John was started by Peter, who misinterpreted what the Lord said, but it is interesting to see how things turned out. According to the earliest tradition, Peter was indeed crucified by Nero about the same time that Paul was executed. However, unlike most of the other apostles, John was not killed. Instead, he was exiled in his old age to the small island of Patmos, just off the coast of Turkey, where he was forced to work in the mines.

Today, visitors to Patmos discover a small community nestled round the harbor and are then taken up a long steep hill, to the cave where John is said to have lived. Unlike the pictures some writers paint of the island, it is quite green and pleasant, with spectacular views of the bay, but we must not forget that John was not there as a tourist. He was a prisoner of Rome and lived there under Spartan conditions, cut off from friends and family.

But it was in those stark and primitive surroundings that John received the greatest vision of the risen Christ afforded to any man. He did not live to see the historical return of Christ to this earth. That is still future today, but he did live to see it all played out before his eyes, in vision form.

We should remember that God inhabits eternity and in eternity the principle of sequence has no meaning. Sequence (past, present and future) presupposes time. Therefore, because John was briefly transported into eternity in his vision, he saw the *actual events* take place, even though, in time, they have not yet occurred. *John saw the Lord return.*

It is doubtful that the contents of the book were all revealed at the same time. More likely, it was in the form of a series of visions, each following on the previous one. Here, John is about to describe the opening scenes of this spectacular revelation.

The Patmos Vision

Verse 9:

> *"I John, who also am your brother, and companion in tribulation, and in the kingdom and patience of Jesus Christ, was in the isle that is called Patmos, for the word of God, and for the testimony of Jesus Christ."*

John was a "brother" to his readers because he was a fellow child of God, through faith in the Lord Jesus Christ. He was a companion in tribulation because he was suffering right along with them for his testimony. Together with his readers, John was looking for the kingdom of Jesus Christ and enduring with patience the tribulation which the world imposed upon those who identified with it.

Verses 10-11:

> *"I was in the Spirit on the Lord's day, and heard behind me a great voice, as of a trumpet, 11 Saying, I am Alpha and Omega, the first and the last: and, What thou seest, write in a book, and send it unto the seven churches which are in Asia; unto Ephesus, and unto Smyrna, and unto Pergamos, and unto Thyatira, and unto Sardis, and unto Philadelphia, and unto Laodicea."*

It is difficult to know exactly what John meant by *"the Lord's day"*. Many consider it to be a reference to the first day of the week. Maybe it is but as Dr. Walvoord points out, although the first day of the week is often called the Lord's Day *now*, it was never called the Lord's Day in the Bible. It was always referred to as "The first day of the week". Personally, I prefer the view that John was transported, in his spirit, to a different time frame, to The Day of the Lord, which is used in the Scriptures to denote the tumultuous times just prior to, and including, the Lord's return to this earth in great power and glory.

John's first indication that something unusual was happening was not visual but audial. He *heard* a voice behind him, but it was no ordinary voice. It was a voice like nothing he had ever heard before, and here we find the first indication in this book that John was dealing with experiences that defied human description. Many times during this prophecy, John uses phrases like "as it were", "as of", "like", "as if", which indicate that the things he saw and heard were so far beyond human comprehension that he was unable to find adequate words to describe them. He had to try to find familiar things, with which people could identify, and say "well, it was a bit like this, or that, or something else". Here, the voice was so clear and penetrating that the nearest he could come to describing it in words was that it was "like a trumpet".

The Alexandrian text omits the next few words but the majority of manuscripts agree that the voice said, *"I am alpha and omega, the first and the last."*

Now if God the Father was speaking in verse 8 and the Lord Jesus was speaking in verse 11, we have another instance of the oneness between the Persons of the Godhead. Both inhabited eternity, before the creation of the universe, and both will live on eternally after the present universe has come to an end. Therefore, both were "alpha" (the beginning) and both will be "omega" (the end).

As John remained transfixed by the indescribable sound of the voice, it continued, *"Write what you see in a book* (on a scroll) *and send it to the seven churches in Asia."*

That could be confusing because John knew there were more than seven churches in Asia. By this time, the Roman province of Asia contained many churches. But the voice clearly specified which churches were to receive this prophecy, namely, Ephesus, Smyrna, Pergamos, Thiatyra, Sardis, Philadelphia and Laodicea. All of these were situated in the western part of the province, each within a few miles of the next, and together they formed a kind of loop, with Pergamos at the northernmost point and Ephesus and Laodicea at the two southern ends.

However, these churches were not singled out at random. There was a purpose in their selection. First, the number seven signifies completion and it can therefore be assumed that the seven churches of Revelation were intended to represent the church as a whole. The text of the second and third chapters makes it clear that, put together, the messages to these local bodies are applicable to all fellowships everywhere. These congregations had internal problems of various kinds, which have been repeated in other forms throughout the history of the church. At any given time it would be possible to find all of them causing trouble within the body of Christ. You wouldn't find the specifics now, of course, because we live in a different era and the problems that hit those churches were different from those which hit us today. Nevertheless, the principles remain.

Second, the order in which the problems within these churches are presented can be seen to clearly parallel the history of the church from apostolic times to the present day. These truths are not spelled out in the text but they are evident from the course of history and from simple observation in our own time.

Third, the truth emerges from this section that Christ has an intimate knowledge of what goes on within each local body. He is just as well aware of everything that is said and done in your local congregation as He was of what was happening in Sardis, Ephesus or Laodicea. He is perfectly aware of everything that takes place in every board meeting, every private conversation, every Sunday school class. That should be a caution to us.

Confrontation

It is one thing to *hear* the revelation of truth but to *see* it is sometimes much more difficult to bear.

> *"And I turned to see the voice that spoke with me. And being turned, I saw seven golden candlesticks (lamp stands); 13 And in the midst of the seven candlesticks one like unto the Son of man, clothed with a garment down to the feet, and girded about the breast with a golden girdle."*

Immediately, Christ is revealed in two roles which John never saw Him take during His ministry here on earth. The first is that of priest and the second is that of judge. Jesus did not come into this world as a priest. He chose to enter the world through the tribe of Judah, whereas the priests all came from the tribe of Levi.

During His earthly life, Jesus never saw the inside of the Holy Place in the temple. He never saw the golden altar of incense, or the golden table of showbread, or the great veil, embroidered in blue and scarlet that hung before the Holy of Holies. Nor did He see the golden menorah, which shed light upon the gleaming furniture within the Holy Place. Only the priests saw those things and Jesus was not a priest. But Hebrews tells us that now He is "a priest for ever", not after the order of Levi, but after the order of Melchizedek (Hebrews 7:9-21). Here Christ is revealed in priestly robes, walking amidst the seven golden lamp stands. The only purpose of a priest is to represent sinful people before a holy God and therefore Christ's role spoke of mercy, compassion and forgiveness. That is ever His nature.

The second aspect of Christ's appearance spoke of His role as Judge.

Verses 14-17:

> *"His head and his hair were white like wool, as white as snow; and his eyes were as a flame of fire; 15 And his feet like unto fine brass, as if they burned in a furnace; and his voice as the sound of many waters. 16 And he had in his right hand seven stars: and out of his mouth went a sharp two-edged sword: and his countenance was as the sun shines in his strength. 17 And when I saw him, I fell at his feet as dead."*

Obviously, the whiteness of His hair spoke of wisdom. The fiery gaze of His eye spoke of His ability to penetrate into our very souls and read what is there. His feet, like burning bronze spoke of judgment. Bronze was the metal used for the altar of sacrifice and its implements. Now His voice sounded to John more like the sea crashing on the shore, or a great waterfall rushing over its precipice. In His right hand He held seven stars (which will be explained later) and from His mouth issued a sharp two-edged sword. This represented the Word, by which the universe was called into existence from nothing in the very beginning; by which the flood came in the days of Noah, and by which the present universe is held together until the final judgment, when, by the same Word, it will be destroyed by fire.

Finally, John saw that Christ's countenance was *"as the sun shines in his strength"*, that is, at midday, directly overhead. When Saul saw the face of Jesus on the Damascus road, he was struck blind. Some say he never recovered fully. John, even though he was in a spiritual trance, fell at His feet as one dead. The sheer majesty of this One was so overwhelming that even the disciple whom Jesus loved, and who knew Jesus so well, could not stand the sight of Him.

In Revelation chapter 6, we read that when Jesus returns to this earth, the kings, the great men, the rich men, the captains and the mighty men, along with rest of the populace, will hide themselves in the rocks and the caves of the mountains and will cry to them, *"Fall on us and hide us from the face of Him who sits upon the throne and from the wrath of the Lamb!"* (Revelation 6:15-16). He won't even have said anything. The people will plead to be hidden just from the *face* of Him who sits upon the throne!

In Revelation 20:11 we are told that the heavens and the earth themselves will flee away from the face of Him who sits upon the throne, and there will be no place found for them. Such is the power and the majesty of our God that one look into His face would be sufficient to strike terror into the hearts of any who have rejected Him.

Commission

Verse 17 again:

> *"And when I saw him, I fell at his feet as dead. And he laid his right hand upon me, saying unto me, Fear not; I am the first and the last: 18 I am he that lives, and was dead; and, behold, I am alive for evermore, Amen; and have the keys of hell and of death."*

It is easy to imagine John's first encounter with the glorified Christ as if it took place at a distance, as if John were in some kind of theater and this pageant was being played out before him on a stage or on a screen. But verse 17 makes it clear that this was not so. John fell at Jesus' *feet* and the Lord reached out and laid His *hand* upon Him. This was a face-to-face encounter, just two or three feet away.

John turned round to see who was speaking to him and he looked straight into the eyes on the One who ruled the universe! No wonder he fainted! But the Lord was merciful. Understanding John's distress, He comforted him and told him not to be afraid. So many times, the words of Jesus to His disciples were the same – *"Be not afraid"*, *"Fear not, it is I"*. And here He says, in effect, *"John, don't be afraid. You know me. I was dead but now I am alive for ever more."*

The Lord's next statement was a little more obscure. *"I have the keys of Hades and of death."*

In His death and resurrection, Jesus stripped Satan of the power he once had over death. You see, all along Satan's ace card had been two-fold. It had been man's sin and the holiness of God that gave Satan his power. He knew that God's holiness could not allow sinful men to enter into His presence and he knew that God in no way could overlook the fact that man was a sinner. Therefore, having deceived man into sinning, Satan could effectively guarantee that death would prevail because God's holiness would ensure it.

However, when Jesus died on the cross, the price of that sin was fully paid and a way was opened whereby God could be reconciled with sinful man without violating His holiness. That meant that Satan's power was neutralized. He could no longer claim God's holiness as the guarantee of man's death because God's holiness had been satisfied. The demands of God were now fully satisfied in the death of His Son. Thus Jesus now held the keys of death, not Satan. Whoever trusted Him and the salvation He had won would live. Whoever refused would die.

Hades (Hell in the King James) does not refer to the Lake of Fire, the final abode of the dead, but to the intermediary place where lost souls are kept awaiting judgment. This is described in Luke 16, where Jesus told the story of Lazarus and the rich man.

Jesus holds the keys of both death and Hades. Judgment is under His control. God has delivered all judgment into His hands and He will decide when the inhabitants of Hades will be brought forth, to stand before the Great White Throne.

Key Verse

Now we come to perhaps the most important verse in the book of Revelation because it provides an outline for the entire prophecy and we can divide the book into its sections according to this verse.

In verse 19 Jesus says:

> *"Write the things which you have seen, and the things which are, and the things which shall be hereafter."*

The things John had seen were obviously the contents of chapter 1. He had seen the risen and glorified Christ as priest and as judge, standing amidst the seven golden lamp stands. He had witnessed Christ's glory. He had been overwhelmed by His power. Those were the things that John had *"seen"*.

"The things that are" follow in chapters 2 and 3. They concern the spiritual condition of the seven churches in the western part of Asia Minor during this present age. They are what *"is"*. They are what exist during the church age.

"The things that shall be hereafter" obviously concern what follows when the church age closes, described in Revelation chapter 4 to the end of the book.

Thus, we have now completed our study of the first section, *"the things John saw"*, and now we can move into the second section, *"The things that are"*.

However, one verse remains before we close this chapter, and this explains a little more of what John *"saw"*.

Verse 20:

> *"The mystery of the seven stars which you saw in my right hand, and the seven golden candlesticks. The seven stars are the angels of the seven churches: and the seven candlesticks which you saw are the seven churches."*

That is self-explanatory. The golden lamp stands represented the seven churches and the fact that Jesus stood in their midst symbolized His presence and control over them. We may think we run our own affairs but we should never forget that Christ is Head of the church and that we are answerable to Him in everything we do.

The word *"angel"* ("angelos") simply means *"messenger"*. We naturally think of angels as being supernatural beings, and some are. Those who surround the throne of God in Heaven are supernatural but they are not called "angels" because they are spirit beings. They are termed "angels" only because they are God's heavenly messengers. Human beings can be messengers also, which makes them "angels".

Each of the messages in chapters 2 and 3 was given to the "angel" of the church being addressed. We could take this to be the pastor or leader of that particular congregation, not a heavenly being.

However, the fact that the seven stars, representing the pastors or leaders of the seven churches, were in the Lord's right hand signified both His control over them and His protection of them. Certainly, there can be no safer place.

CHAPTER 2

THE SEVEN CHURCHES OF ASIA

"The things that are" consists of seven messages given to seven specific churches that existed and flourished at the time of John in the western part of the Roman province of Asia Minor (western Turkey today).

Like churches today, no two were alike. They each had their own personality, their own strengths and weaknesses, and as we examine them we should ask ourselves, "Do any of their characteristics apply to us?" The messages differ considerably from church to church but generally speaking their pattern remains more or less constant. In most cases there is a greeting, a commendation, a warning and a promise. One message lacks a commendation and two lack warnings but they are exceptions.

Not only were these churches historical assemblies, which actually existed in John's day, but also they represent the chronological development of the church as a whole throughout history. The characteristics of the first church (Ephesus) correspond to conditions prevalent during the first hundred years of the church's existence, the "Apostolic Age". The second church (Smyrna) corresponded to the next two hundred years, which began with Nero's reign and ended with Constantine's endorsement of Christianity in AD 312. The third church (Pergamos) represents the next five hundred years of history, during which the church was infiltrated by pagan customs and its previous purity was adulterated. The word *"Pergamos"* means *"thoroughly married"* and it fits this period perfectly.

At the time when the Roman emperor, Constantine, saw a vision of a cross in the air and consequently embraced Christianity, he was at that time the head of the pagan religious cults, known as the *"Etruscan mysteries"*. They had originally come from Babylon. Instead of giving them up, he mixed them with Christianity, bringing many of the heathen customs and beliefs into the church. So although the church was spared the terrible persecutions it had suffered under preceding emperors but in a spiritual sense it actually suffered more from Constantine on.

Christ's Message to Ephesus

Verse 1:

> *"Unto the angel of the church of Ephesus write; These things saith he who holds the seven stars in his right hand, who walks in the midst of the seven golden candlesticks (lamp stands)."*

Ephesus was the capital of Asia Minor and one of the most important cities in the Roman Empire. Its harbor and strategic commercial position brought it great wealth and, as is usual, also a great amount of vice and immorality. The temple of Diana, or Artemis, as the Greeks called her, was one of the seven wonders of the ancient world and the church there had been particularly blessed and privileged. It had been founded by Paul, who preached there personally for three years and who had seen its influence spread throughout that region. After Paul, the pastorate passed to Timothy and after Timothy to the apostle John himself. There is also evidence that the great Apollos ministered there at some time.

In consequence, few assemblies could claim to have had such exalted leadership. Undoubtedly Ephesus was known as a center in the Christian world at that time. Although his name is not disclosed, the "angel" or leader of the church was certainly an influential figure. Quite probably John knew him by name. He certainly knew the church well enough and many of the people who made up its congregation.

The fact that Jesus introduced Himself as the one who *"holds the seven stars in his right hand and walks amid the seven golden lamp stands"* was important. It signified, as we saw at the end of chapter 1, that the man who received this message, whoever he was, was both secure and accountable. That should be enough to daunt anyone who teaches the Word to a local body, or to anyone who assumes leadership. The Lord is present, and He is aware, not only of our words and actions, but of the motives behind them.

Verses 2-3 and 6:

> *"I know your works, and your labor, and your patience, and how you cannot bear those who are evil: and you hast tried those who say they are apostles, and are not, and have found them to be liars: 3 And have borne, and have patience, and for my name's sake have labored, and have not fainted."*
> *"6 But this you have, that you hate the deeds of the Nicolaitanes, which I also hate."*

This church was well above average. First, they were industrious. The words, *"works"* and *"labor"* in the King James Version, or *"deeds"* and *"hard work"* in the NIV, seem at first glance to mean the same thing but they don't. *"Works"* or *"deeds"* refer to the action itself, the effort put forth, while *"labor"* or *"hard work"* refer to the weariness that such effort produces. The same word is translated *"weariness"* in 2 Corinthians 11:27.

These people were obviously putting their backs into their service for Jesus Christ and experiencing fatigue as the result. Only a small percentage of church members today serve the Lord to that degree. Many become weary trying to meet the demands of secular society but comparatively few become fatigued service the Lord.

Second, these people were patient. That doesn't mean that they were placid but that they were enduring, persevering. The road had not been easy but they'd kept on keeping on just the same and Jesus put that down as a plus.

Third, the Ephesians were morally upright. They could not bear or endure those who were evil, which suggests that they dealt firmly with any who caused disharmony in their midst. No doubt Paul had taught them well on that issue because his letters are very clear on that subject.

Fourth, they were discerning. In his first letter, John cautioned his readers not to believe every spirit but to "try" the spirits, whether they are of God because many false prophets have gone out into the world. John was not referring to direct communication with the spirit world but to who or what was behind the messages of those individuals who came by and wanted to preach. If it was the Holy Spirit working in them the message would be in harmony with revealed truth and it would glorify the Lord Jesus Christ. On the other hand, if the devil were behind it, then the message would undermine the Lord's authority and weaken, rather than strengthen the church's faith.

So the Ephesians had tested those who claimed to be apostles and were not and they'd found them to be false. These people were on their toes. They knew their theology. Jesus gave them an "A" for that part as well.

Fifth, the Ephesians were doctrinally sound. Verse 6 states that they *"hated the deeds of the Nicolaitanes"* and in so doing they came down firmly on the side of Jesus Christ. The Nicolaitanes were a sect of people in Ephesus, and in Pergamos and probably other places also, who believed and taught that Christians were free to indulge in all kinds of pagan excesses. The result was moral and licentious behavior, which brought discredit upon the name of Christ. The Ephesian Christians rejected that teaching.

So, on a scale of 1 to 10, we could probably give the church in Ephesus an 8 or a 9. It was the kind of church to which you'd want to belong. It scored high for involvement, for perseverance and for doctrinal purity, which could not be said for every church today. These were the things the Lord looked for in a church.

I wonder what His reaction is to some of the things people get excited about in the church today. Things like "hymns versus praise songs", "to clap or not to clap", or "the sanctuary is too hot or too cold". If we take our eyes off the real issues and we major on the minor, we shall get off track. Jesus does not evaluate a church on that basis. He looks at the service record, and He examines our hearts.

However, there was still a serious problem.

Verses 4-5:

> *"Nevertheless I have somewhat against you, because you hast left thy first love. 5 Remember therefore from whence thou art fallen, and repent, and do the first works; or else I will come unto thee quickly, and will remove your candlestick from its place, except thou repent."*

There are three main factors in that section, namely, the problem, the remedy and the consequence of ignoring the remedy. The problem was lack of love; the remedy was repentance and the consequence of ignoring the remedy was eradication.

The problem was that they had "left their first love". Love, here, is our old friend *"agape"*, which, according to the Scriptures, comes only from God Himself. It is not something we can switch on. We can't say, "OK, I'm going to love with agape love", because that would not be possible. Agape comes from God. Therefore the problem in Ephesus was deeper than it appeared to be on the surface. In an imperceptible way, this body of believers, who were so active in their Christian work, doctrinally sound and spiritually correct, had drifted from their original closeness with Jesus Christ.

What we learn here is that it is possible for a church to do all the right things, say all the right things and believe all the right things, and yet at heart still wander from the Lord. That's scary! When that happens, the fellowship tends to become long on rules and short on love. The work goes on just the same, programs continue, but the underlying love is missing. What happens is that control has been subtlety transferred from God to man. And this is always a recipe for failure.

When Paul wrote to the Corinthians, he told them that no matter what heights of excellence a body might attain in gifts or service, if it lacks love it amounts to nothing. The reason for this is that God

IS agape love and to the degree that agape love is missing, whether in a home or in a church, *God* is missing! That doesn't mean He is missing in presence. That would not be possible because He is omnipresent, but He is missing in control and influence. Human logic has taken over.

That is evidently what had happened in Ephesus. Everything continued as usual. Everyone was busy, the doctrine was jealously guarded, they were theologically correct but a cataract had quietly grown over their spiritual eyes and consequently their view of God had become dimmed.

What was the remedy? Repentance! Start again! They had taken a deviant course and their remedy was to recognize the problem, to turn about, and to get back into their original path. Repentance always presupposes recognized sin and in this case, the sin was a drifting away from the true faith in, and commitment to, the Lord Jesus Christ. There needed to be confession, forgiveness and restoration.

Jesus said if they failed to heed His warning, they would be removed from their place. Individual members would not lose their salvation but the church as a whole would lose its witness eventually.

There's nothing left of Ephesus today except a beautiful Roman ruin. The city itself is a wonder to behold. The streets where Paul walked and many of the buildings still stand in their places. The theater where the riot took place is still there for all to see. But the church's witness has long since been extinguished. The light was removed long ago.

Verse 7:

> *"He who has an ear, let him hear what the Spirit says to the churches; To him who overcomes will I give to eat of the tree of life, which is in the midst of the paradise of God."*

Christ's reference to what the *Spirit* says to the churches is another indication of the oneness of the Persons of the Godhead.

What, then, *does* the Spirit say to the churches? In the Garden of Eden there grew two very special trees, the tree of life and the tree of the knowledge of good and evil. Nobody knows what they looked like. To eat of the tree of life would bring eternal life, while eating of the tree of the knowledge of good and evil would bring death. Adam and Eve chose to eat of the wrong tree and as the result of their disobedience the whole human race was plunged into spiritual darkness. It remained in that darkness until Calvary. But in the fullness of time, Jesus came into the world to remedy the problem. The Garden of Eden disappeared, along with its trees, leaving no trace whatsoever.

However, in the Garden of God the tree of life still grows. In Revelation 22: 2 John records seeing it in his vision. In this verse Jesus promises that He personally will give overcomers access to this tree. Can you imagine what Safeway would charge for one of its fruits if they could get hold of it? But they can't. The fruit is reserved for overcomers and it's under the personal control of God.

The only remaining question is "What is an overcomer?" It is certainly not someone who has enough courage and willpower to defeat the enemy because no ordinary man exists who could do that. There really has only ever been one overcomer in the history of the human race and that was Jesus. Therefore, an overcomer has to be one who is totally identified by faith with Him.

In Revelation 12, Satan is described as a great dragon, a dragon with which Michael and his angels fought in the heavenlies. Then, in verse 11 of that chapter, we are told how the saints overcame him. *"They overcame him by the blood of the Lamb and by the word of their testimony, and they loved not their lives unto death."* Their faith and their commitment were not in themselves, not in a system, not in a church. It was founded squarely upon what Christ had done. To be an overcomer is to have an unshakeable trust in the finished work of Jesus Christ, no matter what the devil may choose to throw at us.

1 John 5:5 sums it up beautifully:

> *"Who is he that overcomes the world, but he that believes that Jesus is the Son of God?"*

Christ's Message to Smyrna

The name, *"Smyrna"* is fitting for the church selected by the Lord Jesus to receive the second of His seven messages. *"Smyrna"* means *"myrrh"* and myrrh is associated with suffering and death.

Smyrna was located about 40 miles to the north of Ephesus and, like its neighbor, it was an important seaport and center of trade. It had a long history. Its roots went back many centuries before Christ but it became important under the Ionians in about 900 BC. Eventually it was destroyed by the Lydians and lay in ruins for some two hundred years until Alexander the Great recognized its potential and planned to rebuild it. Unfortunately, he died before the project started but his successors carried out the restoration and Smyrna soon became an important commercial center.

When Rome conquered the territory, they recognized Smyrna's importance, due to its position on the trade routes to India, Persia and Rome, and it became part of the province of Asia in 133 BC. Many Jews lived in Smyrna but it was overwhelmingly pagan. It was the center of "emperor worship" for the entire Roman Empire and boasted a temple dedicated to Tiberius Caesar. Zeus and other gods were worshipped there also, and the struggling Christian community found itself in a very vulnerable position. Unlike Ephesus, which is now uninhabited, Smyrna is still a flourishing city of some 200,000 people and its church remains intact.

The letter opens, as do all the other letters in this section, with a greeting.

Verse 8:

> *"And to the angel of the church in Smyrna write; These things saith the first and the last, who was dead, and is alive."*

The main characteristic of the church in Smyrna was its suffering, and Jesus introduced Himself not only as one who also had suffered, but as one who had conquered. He understood their predicament and yet He was above it. He had been there in the beginning and He would still be there when the story came to an end. He had suffered and died at the hands of those who even now were the masters of Asia Minor and yet here He was, victorious over the worst that men could do.

This greeting must have caused great encouragement to the people who first received the letter. Jesus knew. He understood, and yet at the same time He was in total control.

Verse 9:

> *"I know your works, and tribulation, and poverty, (but you are rich)..."*

Part of the persecution of Christians in those days consisted of the confiscation of their property. Anyone betraying or reporting a Christian to the Roman authorities was rewarded with a percentage of the confiscated property. Consequently, most believers in Smyrna were reduced to abject poverty. That is what the word translated "poor" or "poverty" signifies. Christians were reduced to nothing and Jesus knew it. Yet there was nothing the authorities could do to rob the Christians of their real wealth. Despite their poverty on this earth, they were still "joint heirs with Jesus Christ" and Christ was "heir of all things". You can't get much richer than that!

Verse 9 again:

> *". . and I know the blasphemy of those who say they are Jews, and are not, but are the synagogue of Satan. 10 Fear none of those things which you shall suffer: Behold, the devil will cast some of you into prison, that you may be tried; and you shall have tribulation ten days."*

Not only were the Roman authorities a problem but some members of the Jewish community were active in the persecution of Christians also. We must understand that true Jews were persecuted along with the Christians because they could not recognize Caesar as lord,

27

either. However, some of them were active in betraying Christians in an attempt to save themselves but by doing so they betrayed their own faith. Consequently, Jesus refused to acknowledge them as Jews and referred to them as "the synagogue of Satan".

When Paul wrote to the Romans, he told them,

> *"For he is not a Jew, who is one outwardly; neither is that circumcision, which is outward in the flesh: 29 But he is a Jew, who is one inwardly; and circumcision is that of the heart, in the spirit, and not in the letter; whose praise is not of men, but of God."* (Romans 2:28-29

God looked on the heart and He considered those whose hearts were far from Him as not being Jews at all.

Some believe that the "ten days" that Jesus refers to in this verse refers to ten periods of oppression under successive Caesars. That may be so but it is only a guess. The periods don't work out very accurately and there is nothing in Scripture to suggest Jesus meant that. The only sure thing to be gleaned from the phrase is that the period to which Jesus referred would eventually come to an end. It ended in AD 313, when Constantine brought the persecution of Christians to a close throughout the empire.

Unlike the letter to Ephesus, and most of the other letters in this section, this letter to Smyrna contains no criticism and no warning for them to change their ways. However, like the others, it ends with a promise.

Verse 10b:

> *"Be faithful unto death, and I will give you a crown of life. 11 He that hath an ear let him hear what the Spirit saith unto the churches; He that overcomes shall not be hurt by the second death."*

Violent death was to be the lot of many of the people who received this letter, and many of them were faithful to the end. Just to become a Christian in those days took great courage because everyone knew what a profession of faith was likely to lead to. This was a pure period in the church's history, during which only those who were prepared to suffer and die for their faith identified with Christ.

The church in Ephesus, although a real church in the time of John, represented the Apostolic Age, the first 100 years of the Christian church after Pentecost. It began with great power and excitement as the apostles spread across the world preaching the Gospel but by the end of the period the fires were beginning to grow just a little cool.

Smyrna on the other hand, symbolized the 200 years following the Apostolic Age, when the great persecutions from Nero to Constantine took place. Some five million Christians died for their faith during that period.

To this persecuted church Jesus made two promises. The first was *"If you are faithful to the end I will give you a crown of life"* and the second was *"he who overcomes will not be hurt by the second death."*

The word for crown there is *"stephanos"*, just a wreath of leaves, twined together, made into a crown and given to victors in the games. Its value lay not in its intrinsic worth but in what it represented. Nobody knows what the crown of life will be like. It may not be a material crown at all. But we do know that it will stand for the unending spiritual victory over physical death.

The *"second death"* is defined very clearly in Revelation 20:14, where John sees the Lake of Fire and says, *"THIS IS the second death."*

When the Lord returns to this earth, living Christians will not die at all. They will be caught up alive to meet the Lord in the air (1 Thessalonians 4:13-18). All other generations of Christians will have to die once. They will die physically. But those whose names are not found written in the Book of Life will have to die twice - physically, when their natural life on this earth comes to an end and spiritually when they are banished forever from the presence of God.

God is the source of everything worthwhile – love, joy, peace, light, happiness and beauty. Separation from Him will amount to an unending, conscious existence, devoid of all blessing and pleasantness. That will be the second death.

Christ's Message to Pergamos

It is no secret that churches within close proximity to one another are often widely different. Each church has its own personality. That's why people choose one church over another, why we don't all attend the same one. Therefore it should not come as a great surprise to discover that Smyrna and its neighbor to the north, Pergamos, were quite different from one another.

Pergamos (Pergamum) was located about seventy miles north of Smyrna. Both cities were strong but for different reasons. It has been said that Smyrna was the great commercial center, Ephesus was the great political center and Pergamos was the great religious center.

Sir William Ramsey said that Pergamos was the one city that deserved to be called a "Royal city". It had a temple dedicated to Caesar Augustus and because of the area's beauty and pleasant climate, Augustus made Pergamos his Summer home. It was a wealthy city, totally given over to idol worship. Temples and statues and altars and sacred groves abounded everywhere. There was great beauty but great wickedness also. At least four major cults were prominent there.

Pergamos was built on a mountaintop about 1000 feet high. It was skirted by rivers that completely surrounded the mountain's base and was heavily fortified. At one time it boasted a library of over 200, 000 volumes, which Mark Anthony gave to Cleopatra. She removed it to Alexandria and there it became known as one of the world's greatest libraries.

Such was the site of the third church to receive a dictated letter from the Lord Jesus.

Verse 12:

> *"And to the angel of the church in Pergamos write; These things saith he which has the sharp sword with two edges."*

Immediately we sense danger because, as we saw earlier, the sword which in John's vision protruded from the mouth of the Lord spoke of judgment.

Verse 13:

> *"I know your works, and where you dwell, even where Satan's seat (throne) is: and you hold fast my name, and have not denied my faith, even in those days wherein Antipas was my faithful martyr, who was slain among you, where Satan dwells."*

Apparently times had already been rough for Christians in Pergamos. No doubt many had already died. But Jesus singled out just one of their number, named Antipas as an example of their faith. We don't know much about him but according to legend, he boldly refused to denounce the faith and was eventually roasted alive by the Roman authorities. The savagery and cruelty of those who were determined to stamp out all Christian witness was boundless. But no wonder, when we see who the principle resident of Pergamos was. It was, at that time, where Satan dwelt and where his throne was!

Some might raised their eyebrows at that and say, "Well isn't Satan *everywhere?*" And the answer to that question is "No, he is not." His angels or agents are everywhere. He commands a highly organized army of demons, who carry out his bidding. They are the *"principalities and powers and the rulers of this world's darkness"*, referred to in Ephesians 6, but only God is *everywhere*. Satan is not omnipresent; he is a created being and is limited. He can be in only one place at one time. We can't tell where he is because we can't see him, but Jesus knows. At that particular time Satan's headquarters were evidently right there in Pergamos.

Some scholars believe that this was a reference to the great altar of Zeus, which stood in the acropolis of the city at that time (and can now be seen in Berlin, incidentally). However, the word translated *"seat"* in verse 13 means *"throne"*, not *"altar"*.

Others point to the serpent worship that was strong in the city. But the fact THAT Jesus referred twice to the fact that Satan *"dwelt"* in Pergamos and that his *"throne"* was there seems too obvious to explain away.

In his famous book, "The Two Babylons", Dr. Hislop does a masterful job of tracing the spread of occult activity across the ancient world. It began in Babel, at the time of Nimrod (Genesis 10). From there it spread to Phoenicia, to Egypt, Greece, and to Italy. And everywhere the successive and national idolatrous systems were all variations of the same original theme. The various deities had different names in different places and at different times. But the same identity and purpose was behind them all.

From Babylon, the headquarters of these mysteries (the Etruscan mysteries) eventually moved to Pergamos, and later still to Rome. Apparently, in John's day Pergamos was the center.

Jesus said He understood how difficult times were. He knew more clearly than they did what they were up against. It is still the same with you and me. However difficult or frightening things become we must never fall into the trap of thinking that God doesn't understand our circumstances. Of course He understands. We must also never imagine that because things are rough that God is somehow absent or disinterested. Some times He allows us to experience hard things for our own good.

Jesus said to these people, "I know where you live and I know who your neighbor is. I also see what happens to you and I keep the record. I saw what happened to Antipas. Nothing happens without my knowledge because I am there with you!"

The world was a very difficult place for these early Christians. They suffered terribly for their faith but they stood firm, claimed the crown and passed the torch of faith to future generations, until, in the fullness of time, it reached us. If you are a Christian, you have a spiritual pedigree that could be traced right back to the time of Christ. Through the centuries people have been faithful, some have died, but they kept the trust that was committed to them. Now it is our turn. Christianity is always only a generation old and it is for us to pass it on to the next generation. The torch is in our hands. Now it is our turn to run. Will we drop it or will we carry it on?

However, despite the struggle in Pergamos, there were also problems.

Verse 14:

> *"But I have a few things against you, because you have there those who hold the doctrine of Balaam, who taught Balac to cast a stumbling block before the children of Israel, to eat things sacrificed unto idols, and to commit fornication."*

The story of Balaam is well-known. It is found in Numbers 22–25. When Israel was approaching the borders of Moab, on their way to Canaan, Balac, the king of Moab, hired Balaam to curse Israel because he was afraid that Israel was about to invade his land. Balaam, greedy for the reward that Balac offered, attempted to comply, but the Lord would not allow him to do so. Every time he tried to curse Israel a blessing came out of his mouth instead.

Balaam therefore had a new idea. He suggested to Balac that Balac should invite Israel to the licentious feasts to Baal, the Moabites' god, in order to draw the people into sin and cause God to judge them Himself. Balac followed Balaam's advice and it worked like a charm. 42,000 people perished as the result. Now Jesus said that the same thing was happening in Pergamos.

Peter, in his second letter, referred to "the *way* of Balaam" (his greed), Jude wrote about the "the *error* of Balaam" (the false notion that God somehow be a party to corruption) and Jesus refers here to "the *doctrine* of Balaam" (which was his deliberate seduction of God's people, to draw them away from the truth).

The next phrase begins with the word, *"thus"*, meaning that the conclusion is assumed.

Verse 15:

> *"Thus, or so you also have those who hold the doctrine of the Nicolaitanes, which thing I hate."*

We looked at that when we were discussing verse 6 and we saw that these Nicolaitanes were guilty of exactly the same thing – immorality. Once again, Jesus said, "I hate their teaching". There was only one thing to do if the church in Pergamos was to survive.

Verse 16:

> *"Repent; or else I will come to you quickly (suddenly), and will fight against them with the sword of my mouth. 17 He who has an ear, let him hear what the Spirit saith unto the churches."*

Notice that Jesus did not say "I will fight against *you*." He said, "I will come to you suddenly and fight against *them*." The Lord never threatens His true church. He threatens those who would undermine its purity and lead its members astray.

There is a strong warning here against sexual immorality. Where Satan is most active, sexual looseness is most rampant.

Verse 17:

> *"To him who overcomes will I give to eat of the hidden manna, and will give him a white stone, and on the stone a new name written, which no man knows except he who receives it."*

Reference to the "hidden manna" immediately makes us think of the Ark of the Covenant. During the wilderness wanderings the manna was a very public thing. It came down every night and covered the ground, so that people could go out and gather it. The *hidden* manna was to be found only in one place, namely, inside the Ark of the Covenant (Hebrews 9:4). God told Moses to place one day's ration of manna inside the Ark as a testimony to future generations. Whereas the ordinary manna would perish very quickly, this must have been preserved miraculously by God.

The Ark of the Covenant, standing behind the veil in the Tabernacle, was a picture of the Lord Jesus and the hidden manna inside represented the bread of life. In John 6:31-33 we read that the people said to Jesus:

> *"Our fathers did eat manna in the desert; as it is written, He gave them bread from heaven to eat. 32 Then Jesus said to them, Verily, verily, I say unto you, Moses gave you not that bread from heaven; but my Father gives you the true bread from heaven. 33 For the bread of God is he who comes down from heaven, and gives life unto the world. 34 Then said they to him, Lord, evermore give us*

> *this bread. 35 And Jesus said unto them, I am the bread of life: he who comes to me shall never hunger; and he who believes on me shall never thirst."*

In other words, the manna that God gave to the people every morning was a picture of the Christ who would one day come and redeem them. So the hidden manna spoke of the saving life of Christ, promised to everyone who receives Him.

The white stone has been variously explained. Some say it was a reference to one of the stones in the high priest's breastplate, on which names were engraved, others claim it was a reference to stones given to people accused in the courts of law (a black stone if guilty and white stone if innocent). Others say it stood for friendship, still others that it stood for victory in the games. The truth is that nobody knows. It is all imagination. In any case, it doesn't really matter. Whatever the white stone stood for, it represented the reward for faithfulness and it is permanent in nature. God's law was written in stone and it was never changed. Here, our new name is written in stone and it is written by the finger of God. That should satisfy our curiosity.

Christ's message to Thyatira.

Thyatira was situated about 40 miles south east of Pergamos, on the borders of ancient Mysia. Like the other cities addressed by Christ in this section, Thyatira had a long and turbulent history. Unlike the others, it was important more for its strategic military position than for its commercial value. It was originally founded as a Macedonian colony by Alexander the Great after the destruction of the Persian Empire, but by the time John came along it had been under Roman control for about two hundred years.

The city was well known for its production of purple dye, favored by the Roman aristocracy. Lydia, one of the founding members of the church in Philippi, was a seller of purple cloth and came from Thyatira.

Verse 18:

> "And to the angel of the church in Thyatira write; These things saith the Son of God, whose eyes are like a flame of fire, and his feet are like fine brass (bronze)."

As we saw earlier, bronze represented judgment and the Lord's fiery eyes suggest His penetrating gaze that burns through all hypocrisy and pierces the most cunning façade. When the Lord sits in judgment there will be none of those "smoke and mirrors" that we witness in some of the prominent trials today. The truth will be as clear as crystal and the issue will be either guilty or not guilty. There will be no technicalities or plea bargains.

The church in Thyatira parallels the period of history between AD800 and the Reformation in the early 1500's. This was the period during which papal corruption dominated the church and controlled the minds of the people. It was during this time, between AD 73 and AD 1085 that the Catholic Church gained secular power as well as religious dominance under Pope Hildebrand. Rituals and doctrines were introduced which supplanted personal faith in Jesus Christ. Worship of the mother and child, which is not Christian, came from Babylon and was introduced into the church. The mass was introduced and the unscriptural doctrine of purgatory began to be taught. Also indulgences began to be sold, generating great wealth for the church. Bulls and decrees from the pope began to have more sway on the people than the Scriptures themselves and those who opposed these teachings were subject to being tried for heresy. Later, in that same period, the terrible Inquisition arose when thousands of Christians were imprisoned and tortured. Many were put to death by being burned at the stake.

However, during that time, as in all other periods of history, there were those who remained faithful, which brings us to the next part of Jesus' message to Thyatira.

Verse 19:

> *"I know your works, and love, and service, and faith, and your patience, and your works; and the last to be more than the first."*

Not all Christians in Thyatira were corrupt. Many served faithfully. According to this verse, it seems as though their good works were improving. We don't know what these works were but they were evidently generated out of love and were acknowledged by the Lord Jesus.

Verses 20-21:

> "*Notwithstanding I have a few things against you, because thou suffer that woman Jezebel, who calls herself a prophetess, to teach and to seduce my servants to commit fornication, and to eat things sacrificed unto idols. 21 And I gave her time to repent of her fornication; and she repented not.*"

We have no idea whether or not this woman was actually named Jezebel but the name given to her is enough to identify her character. Jezebel was the heathen wife of King Ahab of the Northern Kingdom, back in the days of Elijah. She brought her immoral Baal worship from Tyre with her, killed all the priests of the Lord she could find in Israel and soon caused the nation to turn to idolatry. Later, through her daughter, Athaliah, to Jehoram the King of Judah, she even managed to cause the Southern Kingdom to turn to Baal worship also.

Whoever this woman in Thyatira was, she represented a similar trend to that in Jezebel's day. Over time it had been carried on and added to, so that the corruption already mentioned in the church at Pergamos was being perpetuated and made worse. As a prophetess, she placed herself above the Word of God and taught the people to follow their own lusts instead of obeying the clear teaching of Scripture.

In 1 Corinthians 8, Paul writes that meat is just "meat", whether it has been offered to idols or not. But Christians could be made to stumble very easily if they were to eat it with a guilty conscience. These people had been steeped in idolatry before becoming Christians. It was therefore very unwise to get involved in anything to do with the old practices. It was the spiritual connection that made it bad.

Evidently the Lord had given this woman time to repent but she had failed to do so. His charge against the church amounted to apathy.

He was accusing them of being so apathetic that they had allowed this Jezebel to operate without intervening, so that gradually she had gained power and virtually taken over control.

Church leaders should never be party to a witch hunt, but nevertheless they should be diligent in protecting the local body from exposure to false and damaging doctrines. Nothing could be more important. It is one of the main responsibilities of the Elders but evidently in Thyatira they had fallen down on the job. Since they had failed to take action, Christ was about to do so.

Verses 22-23:

> *"Behold, I will cast her into a bed (a sick bed), and those that commit adultery with her into great tribulation, unless they repent of their deeds. 23 And I will kill her children with death; and all the churches shall know that I am he who searches the reins (minds) and hearts: and I will give to every one of you according to your works."*

Some have read the threat to cast Jezebel and her followers into "great tribulation" to mean "THE Great Tribulation". They take the view that this is a warning that the unrepentant part of the professing church will go through the seven-year tribulation in the end times.
However, we should remember that true Christians will not be included in that number. They will be *"kept from the great tribulation that shall come upon all the world"* (Revelation 3:10).

However, there are *professing* Christians who are not saved at all (Matthew 7:21-23). I feel more comfortable accepting this statement on its face value and believing that people who teach false doctrine are heading for real trouble further down the road, if not in this life, certainly in the next.

The Lord has been very patient with false teachers and systems through the years and certainly the final generation of the apostate church (those who profess to be but are not) will experience the Great Tribulation period. The phrase, *"all the churches"* , in verse 23 confirms that it will be a universal thing.

Verses 24-25:

> *"But to you I say, and to the rest in Thyatira, as many as have not this doctrine, and who have not known the depths of Satan, as they say; I will put upon you no other burden. 25 But that which you have already hold fast till I come."*

All God asks for is faithfulness!

Verse 26:

> *"And he who overcomes, and keeps my works to the end, to him will I give power over the nations: 27 And he shall rule them with a rod of iron; as the vessels of a potter shall they be broken to shivers: even as I received of my Father. "*

This is obviously a promise for the future. The people who originally received this letter have been dead for centuries and the Lord still hasn't come back! They never did rule over the nations but they will, one day.

Verse 28:

> *"And I will give him the morning star. 29 He that has an ear, let him hear what the Spirit says to the churches."*

The morning star is a designation specifically of the Lord Jesus Christ. Jesus said, *"I am the root and offspring of David, the bright and morning star"* (Revelation 22:16). In other words, if we remain faithful, He will give us Himself!

CHAPTER 3

Christ's Message to Sardis.

Sardis was situated about 30 miles south east of the city of Thyatira. Like the other cities referred to by Jesus in this section, Sardis was an ancient community with a history that went back into the legendary past. It was once the capital of the kingdom of Lydia, which rose to power about 700 BC and it held sway over that area for about 140 years. It became very wealthy, known for its gold and silver and its last king, Cresus, was proverbial for his great riches.

Cyrus the Great eventually defeated the province, and Lydia became a Persian province. However, by the time of John, the Romans had controlled the area for about 150 years.

Verse 1:

> *"And to the angel of the church in Sardis write; These things saith he who has the seven Spirits of God, and the seven stars."*

The Lord was obviously not very pleased with this church and His introduction simply affirmed that he and not they was in control. The "seven" Spirits seem to describe not a multiplicity of Spirits but the fullness of *the* Holy Spirit. Seven always speaks of fullness and completion. Chapter 1:20 also told us that the seven stars in Christ's right hand represented the seven angels or messengers of the churches receiving these messages.

So Jesus introduced Himself to the church in Sardis as the One to whom these leaders were held accountable. All church leaders are held accountable to Him. There was no commendation for this church and so we have to go directly to the warning, which is the second part of verse 1 through verse 3:

> *"I know your works, that you have a name that you live, but are dead. 2 Be watchful, and strengthen the things which remain, that are ready to die: for I have not found your works perfect before God."*

Outwardly this church appeared to be alive and active. Everything was going well. It had a good name and a good tradition but in God's eyes it was dead.

Barclay writes:

"A church is in danger of death when it begins to worship its own past, when it is more concerned with forms than with life, when it loves systems more than it loves Christ and when it is more concerned with material things than with spiritual things."

I think we could add another section to that in the present day, namely, "When it is more concerned with numbers than with spiritual quality".

Jesus doesn't look at the outward appearance of a church. Our organization or our numbers, programs or activities do not impress him. He looks through all that and reads our hearts. To Him, life does not reside in our activity but in our relationship with Him and in our obedience to His Word.

It is sad to see how far some of the old-line churches have moved from their original position. We had a friend in England who was the Archdeacon of the Diocese of Exeter, where we lived. He was an evangelical and enjoyed preaching a Gospel message when visiting the various churches in the diocese. He told us that on one occasion, after he had presented the way of salvation at a service in one of these churches, an old lady came up to him and said, "Thank you Archdeacon for that new doctrine!" This was the denomination that gave us Bishop Moule and C. S. Lewis, yet many of its vicars now deny the very foundation upon which the church was built. The truth of God's Word is no longer taught from their pulpits. There is plenty of activity – often aggressive social involvement and good works – but nothing that could not continue uninterrupted if the Holy Spirit were to be removed completely.

This had evidently happened in Sardis and the Lord was warning them of the precarious nature of their position. He told them, *"I have not found your works perfect before God"*. Good works please God, provided they are carried out for His glory and in the energy of His power but religious activity, done in the energy of the flesh, is unacceptable to Him because it is dead spiritually.

Verse 3:

> *"Remember therefore how you have received and heard, and hold fast, and repent."*

There is always a remedy for deadness. That remedy is confession and repentance (1 John 1:9). However, first we have to recognize what we are doing, or not doing, as sin. We have to face up to the fact that some of the things we are doing amount to sin. Good things, done in the energy of the flesh, can amount to sin.

The second part of verse 3:

> *"If therefore you will not watch, I will come on you as a thief, and you shall not know what hour I will come upon you."*

This was an obvious reference to the future, a reference to the Lord's sudden return. In Matthew 24:42 He says,

> *"Watch therefore, for you do not know what hour your Lord is coming. Watch therefore: for ye know not what hour your Lord doth come. 43 But know this, that if the master of the house had known in what watch the thief would come, he would have watched, and would not have allowed his house to be broken into. 44 Therefore be also ready: for in such an hour as you think not the Son of man will come."*

He will come suddenly. This is no time for slumbering. It is a time to examine our hearts and to make sure that we are in the faith.

It is a well-known fact that twice in its history Sardis fell due to the over-confidence of its defenders. Sardis was built at the top of a precipitous cliff, about 1000 feet above the valley floor. It was thought to be impregnable. However, in 549 BC Persian soldiers climbed the cliffs under cover of darkness and succeeded in taking the city. They caught the Lydians off-guard. They were not watching.

However, Sardis failed to learn from their own experience. Three hundred years later, in 214 BC, the forces of a Syrian king, Antiochus lll, did exactly the same thing. Once again, the city fell due to the inattentiveness of its defenders.

Verse 4:

> *"You have a few names even in Sardis who have not defiled their garments; and they shall walk with me in white: for they are worthy. 5 He who overcomes shall be clothed in white raiment; and I will not blot his name out of the book of life, but I will confess his name before my Father, and before his angels. 6 He who has an ear let him hear what the Spirit says to the churches."*

The Lord knows those who are His. He makes no mistakes. Even in the midst of apostasy, He knows those who are faithful to Him. Elijah thought he was the only one left, but God revealed to him that there were 7,000 others who had not bowed the knee to Baal.

In the Scriptures, salvation is spoken of as a garment to be worn. It is not something that we achieve, or earn. It is something that we wear.

Isaiah wrote,

> *"I will greatly rejoice in the LORD, my soul shall be joyful in my God; for he hath clothed me with the garments of salvation, he hath covered me with the robe of righteousness."* (Isaiah 61:10)

The same picture is painted in Zechariah 3, where the high priest, Joshua, is seen on earth wearing filthy garments. It was a picture of his natural sin as a human being. These garments were taken from him and replaced with the white robes of righteousness. These robes covered his natural unrighteousness.

The righteousness we receive, as Christians, is not our own but Christ's, and we are given the privilege of wearing that righteousness, like a spotless robe.

Paul wrote to the Philippians,

> *"Not having my own righteousness, which is of the law, but that which is through faith in Christ. (Philippians 3:9)."*

The "Book of Life", which is mentioned here, is the record that decides who will enter Heaven and who will not. I can find no reference in Scripture where names are being *entered into* the Book of Life. However, there are numerous verses that speak of names being *blotted out* of it. This leads me to believe that everybody's name is there at birth, and continues to be there until death. The names only of those who have trusted Jesus Christ as their Savior are allowed to remain in the book. The rest are blotted out.

That means that your name is written in the Book of Life at this moment, whether you are a Christian or not. The question is, will it remain there or be blotted out? The names of those who leave this earth without trusting Christ will be blotted out at death.

Historically, the church in Sardis seems to parallel the period following the Reformation, from the early 1500's, when Martin Luther rebelled against the apostasy and tyranny of the church, until about 1750, when the time of John Wesley came along and things began to heat up spiritually. Although the great doctrine of Justification by Faith had been re-discovered at the Reformation and great light was thrown upon the Scriptures during those years, it was a period of bitter theological argument and contention. The church as a whole was cold, self-satisfied, legalistic and dead.

Christ's Message to Philadelphia

The city of Philadelphia lay about 28 miles south east of Sardis and was named after a man named Atillus Philadelphus, who was the brother of a king of Pergamos, who built in around 160 BC. Most people know that the word, *"philadelphia"* means *"brotherly love"*. It was given to the city due to the unusual bond between these two brothers.

Verse 7:

> *"And to the angel of the church in Philadelphia write; These things saith he who is holy, he who is true, he who has the key of David, he who opens, and no man shuts; and shuts, and no man opens."*

Unlike the other letters, this greeting has only a veiled reference to the description we find in chapter 1. The others are all lifted right out of that chapter but this one is not. Certainly the Lord is holy and true, and I am sure the people of Philadelphia recognized that. However, the fact remains that whereas the other letters drew their greeting directly from chapter 1, this one does not.

Here, Jesus quotes from Isaiah 22:22, which had specific reference to a man named Eliakim. He was a scribe in the court of King Hezekiah. He was chosen to replace a corrupt treasurer named Shebna, at the time of peril to the nation, in order to restore hope and security. As treasurer, Eliakim was to be given *"the key of David"*, that is, the key to the royal treasury of Hezekiah and to be responsible for its safe keeping.

Here, Jesus applies those same words to Himself. He says, *"I have the key of David"*. The inference is that He would take personal responsibility for the safe keeping of His treasure, which, in this case was the church in Philadelphia.

Verse 8:

> *"I know your works: behold, I have set before you an open door, and no man can shut it: for you have a little strength, and have kept my word, and have not denied my name."*

Jesus doesn't describe the works of the Philadelphian Christians but they did evidently please the Lord. This assumes that what they did was in accordance with His will and was carried out in dependence upon His power.

The term, *"you have a little strength"* carries the meaning, *"you have ONLY a little strength."* However, they had used what they had to the glory of God, and that is all that mattered. God never asks more than that. He never demands what we do not have. He simply asks us to use what we have faithfully.

The open door about which Jesus speaks would seem to be the door to effective ministry. The Lord always opens ways and means whereby those who remain faithful to His Word can share the message with others.

Verse 9:

> *"Behold, I will make those of the synagogue of Satan, who say they are Jews, and are not, but who lie; behold, I will make them to come and worship before your feet, and to know that I have loved you."*

We came across the expression, *"the synagogue of Satan"* in chapter 2:9, when we were examining Christ's message to Smyrna. These two churches (Smyrna and Philadelphia) were the only two which drew no criticism from the Lord, yet they suffered the greatest opposition. It suggests that opposition was stirred up most violently by those who stood upon God's Word and were faithful in their witness. That is still true today.

Obviously, the Jewish opposition in Philadelphia never did worship at the feet of the Christians there. The Lord's reference was obviously to the end times that are still future today. Jesus did not mean that the Jews would one day worship the Christians. That could never be. He meant that they would one day worship Christ as their Messiah in the presence of those whom they had persecuted.

Verse 10:

> *"Because you have kept the word of my patience, I also will keep you from the hour of temptation (trial), which shall come upon allthe world, to try them that dwell upon the earth."*

This is a very important verse. Jesus did not keep those Christians in Philadelphia from being persecuted. Until comparatively recently, an arena stood in Philadelphia where Christians were put to death for their faith in Romans times. No, Jesus specifically refers to a time of trial, which will be universal in scope. It will come upon the whole world. There never has been such a time in all history and there never will be, except for one period, namely, the Great Tribulation period, which will close out this present age.

In Matthew 24:21, Jesus said,

> *"For then shall be great tribulation, such as was not since the beginning of the world to this time, no, nor ever shall be. 22 And unless those days are shortened, no flesh will be saved."*

The slaughter during that period of time will be so great that if God were not to step in and bring it to a close the human race would cease to exist.

"But", He adds, *"For the elects' sake, those days shall be shortened."* The "elect" are the remnant, and for their sake, God will step in.

Obviously, this did not happen to the church in Philadelphia, and it still has not yet happened. Therefore, this verse tells us that those who are faithful to God's Word and persevere in their faith, when the end times do come will be brought out from the Great Tribulation.

Verse 11:

> *"Behold, I come quickly (suddenly): hold that fast which you have, that no man take your crown. 12 Him who overcomes will I make a pillar in the temple of my God, and he shall go no more out: and I will write upon him the name of my God, and the name of the city of my God, which is new Jerusalem, which comes down out of heaven from my God: and I will write upon him my new name. 13 He who has an ear let him hear what the Spirit says to the churches."*

Jesus is not promising here to turn faithful Christians into pillars. In any case, in Revelation 21:22 John says clearly, concerning the Heavenly Jerusalem, that there was no temple there. The Lord's meaning is that those who are faithful in this life will be rewarded with a position of responsibility and honor in the Heavenly kingdom.

The church in Philadelphia seems to correspond to the period of history from about 1730 to the end of the age. In the 1700's, the great revivals began. John and Charles Wesley, and Whitefield, then later, Finney, Moody, Spurgeon and many others all blazed their ministries across the stage of humanity. The period also saw the great missionary awakening, with William Carey sailing to India and a host of others who found open doors to China, Africa and the islands of the sea.

From the time of the great revivals until the present day, the movement has continued. Faithful men and women have carried on the work. But side by side with their dedication there has co-existed an apathy within the church that has tended to choke out the fires of evangelism. That brings us to the final message of Christ to the churches.

Christ's Message to the Church in Laodicea

The city of Laodicea lay about 45 miles SE of Philadelphia and about 100 miles east of the first church we looked at, which was the church in Ephesus. So we have now traveled in an elongated loop and have ended up more or less where we began.
No doubt when John saw Christ standing amidst the seven golden lamp stands, which represented these seven churches, they would have been arranged in this same oval shape.

Laodicea was a very wealthy trade center and, as is often the case, its wealth had led to a preoccupation with sports and other leisure activities.

Hal Lindsay describes it as a wealthy banking center with a medical school, noted for a healing eye ointment. The city was very pleasure conscious, with a huge race track and three lavish theaters, one of which was half again the size of a football field.

In all probability, the church was wealthy also and its comfortable circumstances had evidently led to apathy, which is always a danger.

When Paul wrote to the church in Colossae, he evidenced a deep burden for this church in Laodicea. He wrote in Colossians 4:16:

> *"When this epistle is read among you, see that it is read also in the church of the Laodiceans; and you likewise read the epistle from Laodicea. 17 And say to Archippus, Take heed to the ministry which you have received from the Lord, that you fulfill it."*

"Fulfill" means to *"fill it up"*, *"carry it through"*. Maybe Archippus, who was the angel of the church in Laodicea at that time, failed. We don't know, but there is a suggestion that Paul could see trouble brewing within the church there.

Verse 14:

> *"And to the angel of the church of the Laodiceans write; These things saith the Amen, the faithful and true witness, the beginning of the creation of God."*

Once again, the three attributes of Christ in this verse did not come directly from chapter 1. None of them is mentioned there. Nevertheless, they are all true. First, the Lord Jesus is the *"Amen"*, the *"So be it"*. Often in the King James Bible we see the words, *"verily, verily, I say unto you"* and the word translated *"verily"* is *"amen"*. (*"Amen, amen, I say unto you."*)

Jesus is truth and therefore His Word is truth. When a church loses its commitment to Christ it has invariably first moved away from its belief in the infallibility of the Scriptures. When the Bible ceases to be a church's foundation it has nothing to stand upon but the philosophy of men. That is a slippery slope, leading to all kinds of conflicting ideas because the philosophers never agree with one another. They all say, "I'm right and all the others are wrong".

When Paul wrote to the Colossians (which he expressly commanded them to share with the Laodiceans) he warned them:

"Beware, lest any man spoil you through philosophy and vain deceit, after the tradition of men, after the rudiments of the world and not after Christ." (Colossians 2:8)

So as Jesus opened this letter, He first reminded the Laodiceans that He was the "Amen", "the Truth". Second, He is *"the faithful and true witness"*.

The writer to the Hebrews wrote:

"God, who at sundry times and in divers manners spoke in time past to the fathers by the prophets, 2 Has in these last days spoken unto us by his Son, whom he has appointed heir of all things, by whom also he made the worlds; 3 Who being the brightness of his glory, and the express image of his person, and upholding all things by the word of his power, when he had by himself purged our sins, sat down on the right hand of the Majesty on high."

What other witness could offer those qualifications? None exists, nor ever has existed, nor ever will do!

Third, Jesus said He was *"the beginning of the creation of God."* When a church moves away from its position of faith in the inspired Word of God, it is but a small step to deny the truth of creation and embrace the theory of evolution. Evolution has so many holes in it that the only people still clinging to it are those who refuse to accept the Biblical account of creation. The reason for this is simple: If creation is true, then we are created beings, and as created beings we are morally answerable to our Creator for our actions. That is not acceptable to the unregenerate heart of man. He therefore clings to a worn and discredited theory rather than submit to the authority of God.

Like the letter to Sardis, this letter contains no commendation. Jesus found nothing good to say about the church in Laodicea, so we move directly to the warning in verse 15-19.

Verse 15:

> *"I know your works, that you are neither cold nor hot: I would you were cold or hot. 16 So then because you are lukewarm, and neither cold nor hot, I will spue you out of my mouth."*

In other words, *"You make me sick!"* My question is this: What did Jesus really mean by "cold" or "hot" when He applied it to a church? We seem to know, don't we, without even putting it into words, but everyone who writes a book or preaches a sermon on this passage seems to come up with a different idea. Some think that the formal churches are cold while the charismatic churches are hot, but the style of worship is not in view here. Congregations are not graded on their spirituality by the noise they make, or by the energy they may extend. God looks upon the heart, not on the outward appearance. So these terms have to be *"heart* terms", don't they?

The church in Laodicea was still functioning. Jesus was still there with them. Their lamp stand had not been removed from the circle, and no doubt fine men and women were present within their congregation. But *as a church* they were lukewarm.

It seems to me that a church that is neither hot nor cold is trying to be neutral and a neutral church will not take a stand on anything. It wants to be everybody's friend, accept everybody's view, make everybody comfortable and avoid teaching anything that might cause ripples. In order to do that, the whole counsel of God can no longer be taught because God is just a little insensitive when it comes to some of the more personal issues. He calls sin "sin" and He puts His finger on uncomfortable areas that could cause people to leave the church. A neutral church could not risk that.

The *love* of God is still taught in a lukewarm church. All the benefits of being a Christian are presented, but the *justice* of God and the need for repentance are discreetly avoided. And although the angel or messenger of the church must take primary responsibility, it is also invariably what the congregation wants. Therefore the whole body comes into condemnation.

Verse 17:

> *"Because you say, I am rich, and increased with goods, and have need of nothing; and know not that you are wretched, and miserable, and poor, and blind, and naked... "*

That is the sadness of such a group. They think they are alright. They don't see there is anything wrong. They attend church regularly, pay their tithes, sing the songs, even pray occasionally, but they want to be left in peace, unhindered by issues and unconvicted by passages of Scripture like this one.

The desire for worship, the power of prayer and missionary zeal were all characteristics of the church in Philadelphia but they are all missing in Laodicea.

What, then, is the remedy for a situation such as this? Verse 18:

> *"I counsel you to buy from me gold tried in the fire, that you may be rich..."*

In other words, *"You imagine that your material prosperity will buy you security, but it won't. You need to turn back to me!"*

Verse 18 again:

> *". . and white garments, that you may be clothed, and that the shame of your nakedness does not appear."*

As we discussed earlier, the righteousness of Christ is given to believers as a garment, to wear as a covering. People like these Laodiceans are usually very respectable folk. They pride themselves on the excellence of their theological correctness and of their moral standards. They often bemoan the condition of the society around them. But ethical respectability alone is like filthy rags in God's sight. We need to be covered by the robe Christ's righteousness and that is granted only in exchange for faith. *"Abraham believed God and it was accounted to him for righteousness."* (Romans 4:3)

Verse 18 again:

> *"...and anoint your eyes with eye salve, that thou may see."*

Laodicea was famous for its eye salve but the Lord Jesus was not referring to that. He was speaking of spiritual sight, which they lacked. Jesus told the Pharisees (who were extremely religious people), *"Because you say, 'we see', therefore your sin remains"* (John 9:41). They could not see. They only thought they could. Only the Holy Spirit can supply that kind of sight. None of these spiritual benefits is available to those who "try" to be a Christian but avoid the issues.

Jesus is not being mean here. He takes no pleasure in making people feel bad or giving people guilt trips. The next verse clarifies that.

Verse 19:

> *"As many as I love, I rebuke and chasten: be zealous therefore, and repent."*

True love is not always "nice". Sometimes it has to be stern; sometimes it inflicts pain. But always it has the welfare of the other person in view. Jesus loved these people, just as He loves you and me, regardless of what we've been doing or the state we happen to be in at the moment. Which would be the most loving thing to do – to allow these Laodiceans to go on their way thinking they were alright, when all the time they were heading for judgment, or to warn them of their danger and counsel them to repent? The answer is obvious. The "you're OK, I'm OK" kind of church does not really love at all. They allow people to walk a path that leads to disaster without warning them of their peril. They say, *"We don't want to upset these people. We won't say anything that offends them. We'll let them go on their way to hell!"* That's not love.

Verse 20:

> *"Behold, I stand at the door and knock: if any man hears my voice, and will open the door, I will come in to him, and will sup with him, and he with me."*

This has been used by generations of people as a salvation verse but it's not a salvation verse at all. It is addressed to a church and Christ is in the midst. Jesus still recognized it as a church, but He had been pushed outside. The Laodiceans no longer recognized Him as their master. They had assumed that role themselves. Now He was on the outside, asking permission to come back in! What grace, that the Creator and Maintainer of the universe, who could destroy them with a word, should ask *them* for permission to take His rightful place in their midst! May we never reach that place, either as a fellowship or as individuals.

Verses 21-22:

> *"To he who overcomes will I grant to sit with me on my throne, even as I also overcame, and am set down with my Father in his throne. 22 He who has an ear let him hear what the Spirit says to the churches."*

As we have seen before, we overcome only by placing our confidence in Christ. Any other way is false. Even if we *think* we are overcoming we are being duped. The promise here is given to the same people whom Jesus addressed up in verse 17, people who were lukewarm, who thought they were alright but were not. He didn't care how far off track they had wandered, how apathetic they had been, or how long they had been pushing Him away. He didn't care how much they had grieved Him. He loved them still and was ready, not only to restore them to fellowship but to elevate them to such an honor that they could not even imagine.

Jesus has not changed since that time. He offers the same grace to you and to me. All He asks is that we "open the door" of our hearts and allow Him to reclaim His rightful position.

Laodicea represents the church at the end of this age. Because we are living at the end of this age, it refers to us. So might Philadelphia. That is for us to decide. Mixed up together are representatives of all seven of those churches. In any cross section of Christian society, individuals will be found that would fit into any one of the seven. However, the predominant characteristics of the end-time church will be those of Laodicea, lukewarm, neither hot nor cold.

Our aim should be to identify with the church in Philadelphia, which was neither cold, like Sardis nor lukewarm, like Laodicea. The Lord opened a door of service to them that nothing on this earth could close. Laodicea is a long way from us, both in terms of time and geography, but we should ask ourselves how close it comes to us on the personal level.

CHAPTER 4

THE THINGS THAT SHALL BE HEREAFTER

Since the seven churches represent *"the things that are"* (the church age), *"the things that shall be hereafter"* describe events that will take place after the church age ends. So as we open chapter 4, we are looking into the future and seeing what will happen after the church has been removed from this earth.

At this point, there are some ground rules that will govern our study from this point on:

1. Wherever possible, we will take God's Word literally. If John says that he saw a horse, we will not suggest that really saw a stealth bomber. He knew what a horse looked like, just as we do today, and we can therefore accept what he says he saw as fact.

2. We shall reject the "historical view" of Revelation, which claims that chapters 4 through 22 have really already been fulfilled in history. Those who take this view assign the various events in Revelation to the rise and fall of past nations and various other events that took place in history. They all disagree with one another and they end up in confusing world of their own imagination because they are forced to spiritualize Biblical statements and interpret them as meaning something other than what they clearly say they are.

3. Wherever possible we shall compare Scripture with Scripture, type with type. The Bible is often its own best interpreter. The Old Testament sheds a great deal of light on the New and vice versa.

4. In this book, John is often confronted with scenes that he finds impossible to describe in words. Many times he uses phrases like, "as it were", "as if", "like", because the nearest he could come to a description of the things he saw was to compare them with what was familiar to him in those days. It is only at this point that we have license to suggest that what he saw *may* have been things familiar to *us today* but which to him were incomprehensible - things like tanks and rockets and bombs that would have baffled his powers of description.

The Rapture

Verse 1:

> *"After this I looked, and, behold, a door was opened in heaven: and the first voice which I heard was as it were of a trumpet talking with me; said, Come up hither, and I will show you things which must be hereafter (literally, 'after these things'). "*

This verse begins and closes with exactly the same phrase, *"after these things"*. Question: After *what* things? Answer: After the church age (chapters 2-3). In his vision, John saw a door opened in Heaven and heard a voice that sounded to him like a trumpet say, "Come up here" i.e. into Heaven.

When we compare this verse with 1 Thessalonians 4:16-18, the likeness is startling. In that passage it says,

> *"For the Lord himself shall descend from heaven with a shout, with the voice of the archangel, and with the trumpet of God: and the dead in Christ shall rise first: 17 Then we which are alive and remain shall be caught up together with them in the clouds, to meet the Lord in the air: and so shall we ever be with the Lord."*

The *"dead in Christ"*, plus those *"who are alive and remain"* obviously embrace the entire church. 2 Thessalonians makes it clear that this event will *precede* the rise of the Antichrist. It will therefore precede the Tribulation period also, just as it does here in Revelation. The church, which has been the sole subject of discussion for the last two chapters, disappears at this point and is not seen again until chapter 19. At that point the Tribulation period will have come to an end. In accordance with the rest of Scripture, Revelation places this event before the judgments of chapters 6-20 begin. This agrees with Revelation 3:10, where Jesus tells the faithful church of Philadelphia that He will take them out of the *"hour of trial that will come upon the entire world."*

God's Throne

Verses 2-3:

> *"And immediately I was in the spirit: and, behold, a throne was set in heaven, and one sat on the throne. 3 And he who sat was to look upon like jasper and a sardius stone."*

What shall we see when the rapture takes place? We shall see God upon His throne, just like John did. We could not be in Heaven without seeing Him because He is the very purpose and reason for it being there. He is its light and its temple. John did not attempt to describe the One who sat upon the throne, because He was indescribable. It is unlikely, even in a vision that John looked upon the *face* of God. According to 1 Timothy 6:16, God dwells in *"the light into which no man can approach; whom no man has seen, nor can see"*. More likely, John saw the glory that emanated from God's throne. It struck him with its color and beauty. John describes Heaven as being full of color. To John, the One who occupied the throne was like jasper and sardius. By that he meant to convey that God's brilliance and light reminded him of those jewels. Jasper was clear as crystal (Revelation 21:11). It was found in a variety of colors but the principal color was a violet purple. Sardius was a precious red stone, better known today as carnelian and it gained its name from Sardius, the city, where the mines were located. It was also found in Babylonia and Arabia.

According to Exodus 28:20, jasper and sardius were the first and last stones in the high priest's breastplate.
The high priest was to be a type of Christ and carry the nation on his heart before the Lord. The twelve stones imbedded in the

breastplate were each engraved with the name of one of the tribes. The sardius stone carried the name of Rueben (the eldest) and the jasper stone carried the name of Benjamin (the youngest). The same two stones will also feature in the foundations of the New Jerusalem in Revelation 21.

Ezekiel 28:13 tells us that both stones were worn by Lucifer in the Eden of God before he fell. Nobody knows for certain what specific significance jasper and sardius were intended to carry in this passage but it may suggest that God was appearing to John in His covenant relationship with Israel and that although judgment was impending He still carried them close to His heart.

I suspect that John was simply trying to describe the luminous beauty coming from the throne, while the throne itself spoke of the government that had always been. The voice didn't say to John, *"Come up hither and help us set up a throne."* John was summoned into Heaven to witness a scene that was eternal. God had always been on the throne.

Verse 2 again:

> *"… and there was a rainbow round about the throne, like an emerald."*

A rainbow is a symbol of mercy following judgment. It reminds us of the covenant God made with Noah after the flood. It stands for His promise that, *"whiles the earth remains, seed-time and harvest, and summer and winter, and cold and heat, and day and night shall not cease."* (Genesis 8:22). The rainbow is composed of light, refracted by the raindrops into its seven primary colors. And I think it is interesting to notice that violet, the color of jasper is at one end, red, the color of sardius, is at the other, while green, the color of emerald, is bang in the middle! Here John saw violet and red light emanating from the throne, while an emerald green halo or iris encircled it. In his first letter, John wrote that *"God is light"*, and if He is light He must also be all the colors of which light is composed.

Verses 4-5:

> *"And round about the throne were four and twenty seats (thrones): and on the thrones I saw four and twenty elders sitting, clothed in white robes; and they had on their heads crowns of gold. 5 And out of the throne proceeded lightnings and thunderings and voices: and there were seven lamps of fire burning before the throne, which are the seven Spirits of God".*

Some claim that these elders were angels but the word "elder" in the Bible is always used to describe a man. Elders were always chosen representatives of the people, both of Israel and of the church. When Isaiah and Ezekiel saw visions of God's throne, no elders were present. This was due to the fact that before the resurrection, the Old Testament saints were confined to Paradise (Sheol, "Abraham's bosom") and they were awaiting their victorious release to Heaven after Jesus died and rose again.

Here, in John's vision, the elders wore white robes, the symbol of Christ's righteousness, and gold crowns. The word used for crown is "stephanos", a victor's reward. The stephanos is never connected with angelic beings but is promised on several occasions to faithful believers. It therefore becomes obvious that these elders were not angels but glorified men.

We might ask," *Why were there twenty-four elders?"* The correct answer to that question is *"Nobody knows"*. Some identify them with the twenty-four courses of priests that David appointed under the direction of God. Others think they were the twenty-four patriarchs listed in Abraham's line in the book of Genesis. Still others believe they were godly men who were appointed to this exalted position because of merit. There is credit to each one of these ideas but however brilliant they may be, they are still only theories or guesses. The only things we know for certain are that they were *there* and that they must have been representatives of a much wider group. An elder is always a representative, much like our senators or members of parliament are today. Their principal service in Heaven was to participate in worship.

Once again, the seven burning lamps represented the fullness of the Holy Spirit. In chapter 1, Jesus told John that the group of lamp stands he saw represented the seven churches, to which Jesus was about to write. He also mentioned the seven-fold Spirit of God, but in that chapter the lamp stands were on earth, whereas here they are in Heaven and the Holy Spirit is actually identified with them.

Verse 6:

> *"And before the throne there was a sea of glass like unto crystal."*

Some texts say that it "looked" like glass. Glass was rare in John's time and glass of the brilliance and consistency of this would have been completely unknown to John. It must have filled him with wonder to see it.

Not only did John see the twenty-four elders but he saw another group before the throne.

Verse 6 again:

> *"...and in the midst of the throne, and round about the throne, were four living creatures full of eyes before and behind."*

John could not give them a name. He had never seen anything like them in his life before. For want of a better description, he just called them *"living creatures"*.

Verse 7:

> *"The first was like a lion, and the second like a calf, and the third had a face as a man, and the fourth was like a flying eagle. 8 And each of the four living creatures had six wings; and they were full of eyes within..."*

The fact that these living creatures were not only around the throne but also in the midst of the throne, tells us that whoever they are, they are the highest angelic beings in Heaven. They are the closest to God.

The point to remember regarding these creatures is that God is the creator of all beauty. Everything that fills us with wonder and admiration, everything that moves us to tears with its beauty - the sunset, the mountain, the snow, the butterfly, the rose - are His creation and He is perfect in all His ways. It is therefore unthinkable that He would surround His Person with anything ugly or grotesque.

As we read the description of these living creatures, we are inclined to imagine them as monsters. But in reality, they must be absolutely beautiful. Although we are unable to picture them adequately they must be surpassingly beautiful for God to create them to occupy a place of such unequalled intimacy with Himself.

Many commentators have seen a parallel between their four faces and the four Gospels. The first was like a lion, the king of beasts, and Matthew's Gospel portrays Jesus as the King. The second was like a calf, or ox, the obedient servant of man, and Mark's Gospel portrays Jesus as the Perfect Servant. The third was like a man, and Luke's Gospel; portrays Jesus as the Perfect Man. The fourth was like an eagle, that soars above the realms of earthbound men and John's Gospel reveals Jesus as God.

John's description of these creatures identifies them as the cherubim. Ezekiel saw them in the first chapter of his prophecy and he also mentions their likeness to man, lion, ox and eagle. However, he thought they all had all four of those faces. Cherubim were stationed at the entrance to the Garden of Eden after man fell and golden cherubim bowed over the mercy seat above the Ark of the Covenant. In Ezekiel 28, the prophet describes Satan as being originally *"the cherub who covered"*, before he sinned and was cast out of Heaven.
Ezekiel wrote in chapter 1 of his prophecy,

> *"As for the likeness of the living creatures, their appearance was like burning coals of fire, and like the appearance of lamps: it went up and down among the living creatures; and the fire was bright, and out of the fire went forth lightning."*

Isaiah may have seen them in his prophecy, only he calls them *"seraphim"*, which means *"fiery one"*. Their many eyes suggest a constant alertness but their primary function was evidently to participate in the worship.

Heavenly Worship

Verses 8b-11

> ". . *and they rest not day and night, saying, Holy, holy, holy, Lord God Almighty, who was, and is, and is to come. 9 And when those living creatures give glory and honor and thanks to him who sits upon the throne, who lives for ever and ever, 10 The four and twenty elders fall down before him who sits on the throne, and worship him who lives for ever and ever, and cast their crowns before the throne, saying,*
>
> *11 Thou art worthy, O Lord, to receive glory and honor and power: for thou hast created all things, and for thy pleasure they are and were created.*"

Notice that the stream of praise is focused on two main things. First, that God is eternal and second, that He is the Creator. God does not reign over one colossal accident, as some people suggest. He reigns over a carefully crafted plan, which demanded unimaginable genius and power to devise and carry out. It is mathematically perfect. He was, is and always will be the Almighty.

The victors crowns, awarded to the twenty-four elders and the thrones upon which they sit seem totally out of place in the presence of such majesty. So they come down from their thrones and they cast their crowns before Him as they sing His praise.

The word *"cast"* sounds in our ears rather like *"sling"*, doesn't it? One therefore gets a picture of twenty-four dented crowns rolling all over the sea of glass and being retrieved by linesmen, who are stationed for that purpose! But the sense seems to be more dignified than that. It describes an impulsive reaction, stimulated by the glory of the One upon the throne, making His creatures realize that He alone is worthy of praise and honor.

CHAPTER 5

The Book with Seven Seals

This chapter opens onto the same scene that left in chapter 4. The throne of God still stands in its place, with a mixture of beautiful colors radiating from it and lightening, thunder and voices coming from within. The Sea of Glass still stretches out from the throne's foot and the twenty-four elders, wearing white robes and golden crowns, still occupy their places around the throne. The seven lamps of fire still burn, signifying the presence of the Holy Spirit, and the four living creatures, which so amazed John, still occupy their places in attendance upon the Almighty.

However, John now notices something he had not seen before.

Verse 1:

> *"And I saw in the right hand of him that sat on the throne a book written within and on the backside, sealed with seven seals."*

The focus changes from the throne and its surroundings to the One who sits upon the throne. This is the first time that any reference has been made to His Person and it is significant that the reference is made to His right hand. In Scripture, the right hand always signifies power and strength. Here, the power and strength of God is being highlighted.

Further than that, attention is drawn not to the hand itself but to something grasped in it, namely, a scroll, written on both sides and sealed with seven seals. The King James Version translated the word *"biblion"* as *"book"* but books, as we know them, were not invented until much later. John's attention was drawn to a scroll, rolled up tightly and held in the hand of the One who sat upon the throne. Obviously the scroll was very important and contained powerful information. As we shall see, all the secrets of this prophecy of the book of Revelation were hidden within it.

Where did it come from and what was its identity? As is so often the case with the book of Revelation, there are many different solutions offered to the questions, some of which have merit and others are pure imagination. Clarence Larkin, whose views on prophecy are very sound, believed that the scroll was in fact the title deed to the earth. Others, such as J. Vernon McGee and John Walvoord would agree with him. Larking wrote:

> "When Adam sinned, he lost his inheritance of the earth and it passed out of his hands into the possession of Satan, to the disinheritance of all of Adam's seed. The forfeited title deed is now in God's hands and is awaiting redemption. Its redemption means the legal repossession of all that Adam lost by the fall. Adam was impotent to redeem the lost possession but the Law provides (Leviticus 25:23-24) that the kinsman may redeem a lost possession."

That is the basis for the book of Ruth, where Boaz plays the role of the kinsman and secures Ruth as his wife. It is a picture of Christ as our kinsman redeeming the church as His bride. Redemption, in this case, is not the salvation of souls. That was secured over two thousand years ago. This is the redemption of man's earthly inheritance, which was given to Adam when he was created but forfeited when he sinned.

However, there are other points to notice also:

First, the seven seals binding this scroll will soon be opened, one by one, and when they are they will reveal that the document in God's hand is, in fact, not so much a title deed as the map of the Tribulation period, during which sin and Satan will have their final fling and be brought to an end. It will contain a timetable for God's judgments, which be poured out upon this earth.

Second, Christ will have no further work to do when He comes, in order to defeat Satan and take full possession of His kingdom. Satan was defeated at the cross and Jesus could have claimed His inheritance at any time since then.

Third, the title never was, and never shall be, claimed or won by war, famine or pestilence. There was only one price sufficient to defeat Satan and was the shed blood of the Lord Jesus Christ. When we see Christ return in glory in Revelation chapter 19, He will not have to fight His way to the throne. He will merely say the word, and it will be done.

Fourth, In Daniel 12:4, after the prophet had been shown a panorama of the end times, the angel Gabriel said to Daniel, *"But thou, O Daniel, shut up the words and seal the book until the time of the end."* Then, in verse 8 of the same chapter, Daniel says, *"My Lord, what shall be the end of these things? And he said, Go your way, Daniel, for the words are closed up and sealed until the end times."* I know of no passage in the Bible that speaks of the scroll bearing the details of the Tribulation period being reopened, other than here in Revelation.

There may be overtones of the "title deed theory" in this book. Henry Morris cites the case of Jeremiah, who purchased a tract of land, to which he had the right as a kinsman. But knowing that the Babylonian invaders would soon bear down upon them, he caused the sealed deed of the transaction to be buried in the ground, believing that the rightful owner would one day return and claim the land. (Jeremiah 32:8-15) Thus it was purchased but not claimed until much later. Similarly, Jesus purchased the title at Calvary but will not come to claim it until the end of the Tribulation period.

I don't argue with that, but personally I feel more comfortable looking at the scroll in the right hand of God as being the very same one that was shut up in by Daniel, back in the days of Darius the Mede. Here in Revelation 5, we come to the end times and God is preparing for the scroll that Daniel saw to be opened.

Verse 2:

> *"And I saw a strong angel proclaiming with a loud voice, 'Who is worthy to open the book, and to loose the seals thereof?' 3 And no man in heaven, or on earth, neither under the earth, was able to open the book, nor to look thereon. 4 And I wept much, because no man was found worthy to open and to read the book, or to look thereon."*

It is interesting to see the adjectives there. A *strong* angel proclaimed with a *loud* voice. We gather something of the pageantry of this scene from those words. *"Strong"* means *"mighty"* and this mighty angel posed the question of all time to all living creatures, namely, *"Who is worthy to open the scroll and to break the seals?"* Twice, the word *"worthy"* is cited as the qualification required. Although search was made throughout the entire universe, no-one was found who could meet the standard. Whoever qualified would preside over a period of history when the judgments of God would fall upon the earth and Satan's bid for power would come to a final, devastating end. The candidate would have to be perfectly righteous, totally free from the sin that had plunged the earth into its present state. Obviously, no created being could meet those qualifications. This upset John and he wept because he wanted to see the scroll opened and its contents revealed.

The Lion

Verse 5:

> *"And one of the elders said unto me, Weep not: behold, the Lion of the tribe of Judah, the Root of David, has prevailed to open the scroll, and to break the seven seals thereof."*

Word was out that "the Lion of the Tribe of Judah" had qualified. Judah was the fourth son of Jacob (Israel). Just before he died, Israel gathered his twelve sons around him and gave each one the blessing God had laid upon his heart. To Judah he said,

> *"Judah is a lion's whelp (cub). From the prey, my son, thou art gone up. He stooped down; he crouched like a lion and as an old lion. Who shall rouse him up? The scepter shall not depart from*

Judah, nor a lawgiver from between his feet, until Shiloh comes, and unto Him shall the gathering of the people be." (Genesis 49:9-10).

The lion has been recognized from the beginning of time as the symbol of kingship and the Lord Jesus came from the tribe of Judah, through Mary. He above all others was qualified to rule and preside over the final cataclysmic events of this age. It has been pointed out that since only Christ had conquered sin, death, hell and Satan himself, only He could be trusted with the world's future. The expression "the root of David" speaks of the fact that Jesus sprang from David's family line, thus fulfilling the promise of the Messiah in the Old Testament. The lion of the tribe of Judah had prevailed to open the scroll!

The Lamb

Verse 6:

> *"And I beheld, and, lo, in the midst of the throne and of the four living creatures, and in the midst of the elders, stood a Lamb as it had been slain, having seven horns and seven eyes, which are the seven Spirits of God sent forth into all the earth. 7 And he came and took the book out of the right hand of him that sat upon the throne."*

John turned to see the lion and he saw a lamb! The diminutive for of the word *"lamb"* in this verse pictures a *little* lamb, emphasizing its gentleness. Christ was led as a lamb to the slaughter. He was the Lamb of God who took away the sins of the world. Like a lamb, He died without a struggle, yet in doing so He won the greatest victory the universe has ever seen. His victory made it possible for sinful men and women to be forgiven and cleansed. Yet they rejected Him and wanted to hear nothing about Him. They nailed Him to a cross!

Now He stands in preparation for the final show down, which is about to begin.

Although John saw Jesus as a Lamb, He was not defenseless. The horns spoke of power. Horns played a prominent part in the Old

Testament prophecies. God communicated the rise and fall of nations to Daniel by showing him succeeding empires as fierce animals with horns - two for Medo-Persia, one for Greece, ten for the final empire and even one notable horn for the Antichrist. In Zechariah 1:18, the prophet wrote, *"I raised my eyes and I looked and there were four horns. And I said to the angel who talked with me, 'What are these?' And he answered me, 'These are the horns that have scattered Judah, Israel and Jerusalem."* In other words, they stood for the nations that had attacked the land.

Here, the lamb had seven horns, which symbolized absolute power. Similarly, the seven eyes represented absolute knowledge. Seven always speaks of completeness. We must keep in mind that what John saw was a vision, in which a great deal of symbolism was used. Jesus is spoken of as a lion but John sees Him as a lamb. Dr. J. Vernon McGee suggests that the lion speaks of Jesus at His second coming, while the lamb refers to Him at His first coming. He wrote: "The lion is symbolic of His majesty, while the lamb is symbolic of His meekness. As a lion, He is sovereign; as a lamb, He is Savior. As a lion He is a judge; as a lamb He is judged. The lion represents the government of God; the lamb represents the grace of God."

As John watched, the lamb took the scroll from the right hand of God and prepares to break the seals which have held it closed and unread since the time of Daniel. He may be a lamb that was slain but He is also the maker and maintainer of the universe, and His hand is firmly on the wheel of history.

The Song

Verses 8-10:

> *"And when he had taken the scroll, the four living creatures and the four and twenty elders fell down before the Lamb, each having a harp, and golden bowls full of incense, which are the prayers of saints. 9 And they sang a new song, saying, Thou art worthy to take the book, and to open the seals thereof: for thou wast slain, and hast redeemed us to God by thy blood out of every kindred, and tongue, and people, and nation; 10 And hast made us unto our God kings and priests: and we shall reign on the earth."*

The NIV follows a different text and substitutes the words, "You purchased *men* from every tribe, language, people and nation." This eases the difficulty caused by the living creatures including themselves in the song of redemption. They, of course, were eternal creatures and not included in redemption.

The scene is reminiscent of the one in Daniel chapter 7, where the prophet probably sees the same drama enacted. In Daniel 7:13-14, Daniel wrote:

> *"I saw in the night visions, and, behold, one like the Son of man came with the clouds of heaven, and came to the Ancient of days (God), and they brought him near before him. 14 And there was given him dominion, and glory, and a kingdom, that all people, nations, and languages, should serve him: his dominion is an everlasting dominion, which shall not pass away, and his kingdom that which shall not be destroyed."*

Here, Christ's dominion over the earth is about to be enforced, as the seals on the scroll are broken, one by one. John heard the chorus and recognized it as a hymn of praise to the Lion of the Tribe of Judah, the Lamb who had taken away the sins of the world.

Worship

Verses 11-14:

> *"And I looked, and I heard the voice of many angels round about the throne and the living creatures and the elders: and the number of them was ten thousand times ten thousand, and thousands of thousands; 12 Saying with a loud voice, Worthy is the Lamb that was slain to receive power, and riches, and wisdom, and strength, and honor, and glory, and blessing. 13 And every creature which is in heaven, and on the earth, and under the earth, and such as are in the sea, and all that are in them, heard I saying, Blessing, and honor, and glory, and power, be unto him that sits upon the throne, and unto the Lamb for ever and ever. 14 And the four living creatures said, Amen. And the four and twenty elders fell down and worshipped him that lives for ever and ever."*

What a scene! John says, "I looked" and "I heard". Forty-four times in this book John declares what he saw and twenty seven times what he heard. These scenes must have made an impression on John's mind that nothing could ever erase or even dim. Dr. Woolvard writes,

> *"In concentric circles, with the Lamb in the center, surrounded by the living creatures and the four and twenty elders, the angelic host is seen on every side, numbering ten thousand times ten thousand; an innumerable throng in one mighty symphony of praise!"*

John was being shown one of the most spectacular events in the history of the universe. The earth had been under the domination of Satan ever since Adam's fall in the Garden of Eden. He is referred to in the Scriptures as "the god of this world", meaning he has held sway over the affairs and minds of men. At the cross, his power was cancelled. If men and women turned in faith to Christ, they could now be delivered from his grip. Nevertheless, he has continued to function, and will be allowed to continue until the "Times of the Gentiles" have been fulfilled. The curse of God was placed on the earth at Eden and it will continue until the Lord removes it. (See Romans 8:19-23).

As the Lord Jesus took the scroll from the Father's hand and prepared to break the first seal, the heavenly multitude lifted their voices in praise. There must have been a most intense sense of excitement. John was privileged to see a scene, which has not yet taken place. But when, in real time, this event finally does take place, *you will be there*! You will see it and hear it and you will join in this chorus. By the sheer grace of God He provided a savior and it will be by His merits alone that we shall be present. We owe Him absolutely everything!

CHAPTER 6

THE SEAL JUDGMENTS

The First Seal: A White Horse (The Antichrist)

Verses 1-2:

> *"And I saw when the Lamb opened one of the seals, and I heard, as it were the noise of thunder, one of the four living creatures saying, 'Come and see'. 2 And I saw, and behold a white horse: and he who sat on him had a bow; and a crown was given to him: and he went forth conquering, and to conquer."*

When we see a conqueror wearing a crown and riding a white horse, as we do in this first scene, we naturally think of Christ Himself. But this horseman is not Christ. The Lord will return at the *end* of this period of judgment, not at the beginning, and the armies of heaven will accompany him. Whoever this horseman is (and there is nothing in the text to tell us) he represents the first stage of the cataclysmic, seven-year period of history at the close of this age. This has been called "The Tribulation Period".

This rider wears a crown, which is a *"stephanos"*, and we have already seen in an earlier chapter that the "stephanos" is not a kingly crown but a victor's wreath. When Jesus comes, in chapter 19, we are told that He will be wearing *"many diadems"*, the "diadem" being the crown of kings. He will come to reign. This rider seems to be setting the stage for the evil to begin. I believe he represents the Antichrist, the world ruler who will dominate the earth during the Tribulation Period. He is the one Daniel called "the prince that shall come". Daniel wrote of him:

> *"And through his policy he shall cause craft to prosper in his hand; and he shall magnify himself in his heart, and by peace shall destroy many."* (Daniel 8:25)

In other words, the Antichrist will not gain his power by military force, but by public acclaim. He will come as a deliverer. He will begin his reign as a negotiator of peace and the nations will settle down under his shadow, relieved that at last peace has been achieved on the earth. Even now the stage is being set for such an event. Across the world there is a shortage of real leadership. The United Nations is weak and indecisive. There is nobody to follow. No great leader exists to unite the world, and people everywhere are wishing that a strong man would arise to bring peace, order and prosperity.

When a leader arises with supernatural charisma and an outstanding ability to pull opposing parties together, the international community will hail him as a savior. However, their rejoicing will be short-lived because they will awaken one day to the realizing that this one in whom they have placed their trust is in fact a monster! He will demand total obedience and even worship for himself.

As Paul wrote in 1 Thessalonians 5:3:

> *"When they shall say, Peace and safety; then sudden destruction shall come upon them, as labor upon a woman with child; and they shall not escape."*

This is a picture of the Tribulation Period. They will imagine themselves to be safe; they will think they are at peace, but that is the very time when sudden destruction will fall. In 2 Thessalonians 2:3-4 Paul wrote:

> *"The man of sin shall be revealed, the son of perdition; 4 Who opposes and exalts himself above all that is called God, or that is*

worshipped; so that he as God sits in the temple of God, showing himself to be God."

In verses 9-11 of the same chapter, Paul continues:

"...whose coming is after the working of Satan with all power and signs and lying wonders, 10 And with all deceivableness of unrighteousness in those who are perishing; because they received not the love of the truth, that they might be saved. 11 And for this cause God shall send them strong delusion, that they should believe a lie."

I believe that this first horseman's likeness to Christ is intentional. His great desire is to take the Lord's place. He once said, *"I will be like the Most High."* (Isaiah 14:12-24). His aim is to be a counterfeit Christ, and when he comes, the world will be deceived into believing him.

Daniel prophesied that he will make a seven-year peace treaty with Israel, guaranteeing their sovereignty and freedom of religion, but will break it mid-term and demand worship for himself.

The Second Seal: A Red Horse (War)

Verse 12:

"And when he had opened the second seal, I heard the second living creature say, Come and see. 4 And there went out another horse that was red: and power was granted to him who sat thereon to take peace from the earth, that they should kill one another: and there was given unto him a great sword."

One of the reasons why we should reject the idea that the first horseman is Christ is that when He brings peace it will be permanent, whereas here it is short-lived. Immediately following the brief period of peace and prosperity, a war will break out, unlike anything man has ever seen. All history has been marked by wars but this will be the granddaddy of them all. The rider of the red horse will "take peace from the earth". That means that as a commodity, or principle, peace will be withdrawn from the society of men. The whole planet will be thrown into a frenzy of violence and conflict, both nationally and personally.

Note the words, "it was *granted*, or *given*, to the one who sat on it to take peace from the earth". All control is in the hands of the One who sits upon the throne and he is obviously coordinating events on the earth from Heaven. It is God who gives authority to these terrible horsemen to carry out their assignments.

The third Seal: A Black Horse (Famine)

Verses 5-6:

> *"And when he had opened the third seal, I heard the third living creature say, Come and see. And I beheld, and lo a black horse; and he who sat on him had a pair of balances in his hand. 6 And I heard a voice in the midst of the four living creatures say, 'A measure of wheat for a penny, and three measures of barley for a penny; and see you hurt not the oil and the wine'"*.

The color black speaks of two things, namely, mourning and famine. Both of these logically follow war. We need only look at the situation in nations where hostilities have erupted to see the condition into which the population has been plunged.

According to Matthew 20:2, a penny (denarius) represented a day's wage for a normal working man and according to Herodotus, the Greek historian, a quart of corn was a soldier's daily supply of food in the army of Xerxes. At the inflated prices quoted in verse 6, it would be almost impossible for a man to feed his family. Famine would occur and there would be a great shortage of food. Widespread hunger would result. Oil and wine were luxuries, enjoyed only by the rich. Oil corresponded to beauty aids, which would still be available at a price. That is not unusual. In the most difficult times luxuries have been available for those who could afford them.

The fourth Seal: A Pale Horse (Death)

Verses 7-8:

> *"And when he had opened the fourth seal, I heard the voice of the fourth living creature say, Come and see. 8 And I looked, and*

> *behold a pale horse: and his name that sat on him was Death, and Hell followed with him. And power was given unto them over the fourth part of the earth, to kill with sword, and with hunger, and with death, and with the beasts of the earth."*

The word *"pale"* is *"chloros"*, from which we get our words chlorine or chlorophyll. It represents a ghastly pale green, which suggests sickness. Here is a picture of death on an unprecedented scale. We are talking about 25% of the earth's population who will die! That is about 750 million souls. Some have suggested the use of biological warfare during that time, which is a distinct possibility. It has been pointed out that the death toll at that time will be far larger than that of the Great Flood because the population is so much greater. Treated geographically, it will amount to more than the entire population of Europe.

The Lamb calls the horseman forth, and power is given to him from the throne. From a humanistic point of view, the problem of pestilence, famine and violence is merely the logical results of war but here they are clearly seen to be the direct judgments of God upon a race that has rebelled against Him. Ezekiel warned of this. In Ezekiel 14:21 we read:

> *"For thus saith the Lord GOD; How much more when I send my four sore judgments upon Jerusalem, the sword, and the famine, and the noisome beast, and the pestilence, to cut off from it man and beast?"*

Jesus referred to the same four judgments. In Matthew 24 the disciples asked Him, *"What will be the sign of your coming and of the end of the age?"* And Jesus replied:

> *"Take heed that no man deceive you. 5 For many shall come in my name, saying, I am Christ; and shall deceive many. 6 And you shall hear of wars and rumors of wars: see that you are not troubled: for all these things must come to pass, but the end is not yet. 7 For nation shall rise against nation, and kingdom against kingdom: and there shall be famines, and pestilences, and earthquakes, in divers places."* (Matthew 24:4-7)

All four of the judgments mentioned by Jesus (false Christ's, war, famine and pestilence) are represented by these four horsemen of Revelation 6.

The Fifth Seal: Tribulation Martyrs

Verses 9-11:

> *"And when he had opened the fifth seal, I saw under the altar the souls of them that were slain for the word of God, and for the testimony which they held: 10 And they cried with a loud voice, saying, How long, O Lord, holy and true, dost thou not judge and avenge our blood on them that dwell on the earth? 11 And white robes were given unto every one of them; and it was said unto them, that they should rest yet for a little season, until their fellow servants also and their brethren, that should be killed as they were, should be fulfilled."*

According to Exodus 29:12, the blood of the sacrifice was poured out at the base of the altar (under the altar of sacrifice). It is therefore significant that the souls of those who have died for their faith during the Tribulation period are temporally in that place in Heaven. Here again, symbolism is obviously being used. These souls had not been shoved under the altar to keep them out of mischief. They were there because of the nature of their death. They had died for their faith and their position under the altar was one of dignity and privilege. When they asked how long it would be before their persecutors were brought to justice, they were given robes, signifying their received righteousness and told to rest a little longer because others would soon be joining them, at the end of the Tribulation period. Justice would eventually be done when Christ set up His kingdom.

The judgment of Matthew 25, coming as it does immediately following the Tribulation of Matthew 24, bears this out. There the nations will either enter the millennial kingdom or be consigned to the Lake of Fire, depending on their treatment of those whom the Lord calls "My brethren". This is a passage of Scripture that is constantly taken out of context, especially by missionaries who want to use it for their purposes. But it is a *Tribulation* passage and has to do with the judgment of the nations at the close of the Tribulation.

The Sixth Seal: Terror

Verses 12-17:

> *"And I beheld when he had opened the sixth seal, and, lo, there was a great earthquake; and the sun became black as sackcloth of hair, and the moon became as blood; 13 And the stars of heaven fell to the earth, even as a fig tree casts her untimely figs, when she is shaken by a mighty wind. 14 And the heaven departed as a scroll when it is rolled together; and every mountain and island were moved out of their places. 15 And the kings of the earth, and the great men, and the rich men, and the chief captains, and the mighty men, and every bondman, and every free man, hid themselves in the dens and in the rocks of the mountains; 16 And said to the mountains and rocks, Fall on us, and hide us from the face of him that sits on the throne, and from the wrath of the Lamb: 17 For the great day of his wrath is come; and who shall be able to stand?"*

This speaks of the worldwide terror of the presence of God and I believe it describes the final end of the Tribulation period. Jesus painted exactly the same picture in Matthew 24:29-31. He said:

> *"Immediately AFTER the Tribulation, the sun will be darkened, the moon will not give its light, the stars will fall from Heaven and the powers of the heaven shall be shaken. For then the sign of the Son of Man will appear in Heaven and all the tribes of the earth shall mourn and they shall see the Son of Man coming in the clouds of Heaven with power and great glory."*

That is exactly the same thing as we have just read in Revelation, but rather than accept this awesome picture as a literal description, some have tried to spiritualize it. They have made it mean the collapse of society, or the breakdown of order; the destruction of political and religious life. I believe it would take a lot more than that to induce wicked men to beg the rocks to fall on them, to shield them from the face of Him who sits upon the throne and from the wrath of the Lamb. There is only one thing that would cause them to do that, namely, the visible return, in power and glory, of the Lord Himself.

The prophet Joel also spoke of these same phenomena in His prophecy. In chapter 2:30 and 31 God spoke to Joel and said:

> *"And I will show wonders in the heavens and on the earth, blood, and fire, and pillars of smoke. 31 The sun shall be turned into darkness, and the moon into blood, before the great and terrible day of the LORD come."*

Many commentators consider the book of Revelation to be chronological in nature, and claim that this event merely marks a point of increased intensity in the Tribulation period. I find that difficult to accept because obvious references are made in later chapters to the very same events we have just been discussing, only in more detail. It is more logical to take this chapter as a brief overview of the entire Tribulation period in capsule form, beginning with the peaceful rise of the Antichrist and concluding with its climax, when the Lord returns in power and glory. Subsequent chapters will fill in the details in more detail.

If we were to dwell upon the horror of these scenes, we could easily become depressed and gloomy. But that is the bad news. The good news is that nobody need be here on the earth when they are taking place on the earth. The decision is ours to make. The Lord said very clearly, *"Whosoever will, may come"*. In other words, if you don't come, then evidently you don't want to; and if you don't want to, then this is what you must be prepared to face. There is an insurance policy into which every one of us may enter, and the premium has already been paid by Jesus Christ!

CHAPTER 7

An Interlude

The opening verses of chapter 7 describe a delay in the process of divine judgment. Whereas chapter 6 seems to cover the entire Tribulation period, chapter 7 goes back to the beginning and traces the same period through in greater detail. The interlude or delay marks the boundary between the two narratives.

Verse 1-3:

> *"And after these things I saw four angels standing on the four corners of the earth, holding the four winds of the earth, that the wind should not blow on the earth, nor on the sea, nor on any tree. 2 And I saw another angel ascending from the east, having the seal of the living God: and he cried with a loud voice to the four angels, to whom it was given to harm the earth and the sea, 3 Saying, Harm not the earth, neither the sea, nor the trees, till we have sealed the servants of our God in their foreheads."*

There is something very suggestive about the wind being completely still. We talk about the calm before the storm but these calms are only local. The great global wind systems continue, controlling many aspects of life here on earth. They transport moisture from the oceans to the land, they cool the surface of the earth and aid in the reproductive systems of many creatures, plants and trees. Here is pictured the greatest clam the world has ever known; the dreaded doldrums enveloping the face of the entire planet and producing a stifling sense of impending doom. God great purpose in judgment is held up in order that 144,000 Israelite believers might be protected from its fury. They are described as the servants of God and are to be placed under the direct protection of the Lord Himself.

This is not a new thing. In the book of Genesis the Great Flood was delayed for 120 years, while Noah built the ark. Later in the same book, God delayed the judgment of Sodom and Gomorrah in order to rescue Lot and his family from judgment. In the book of Joshua, God delayed the destruction of Jericho while the spies made contact with Rahab and arranged for her family to be rescued when the fall came.

Peter wrote, *"The Lord knows how to deliver the godly out of trial and to reserve the unjust unto the Day of Judgment, to be punished."* (2 Peter 2:9)

However, there is a difference here. Noah and Lot and Rahab were removed *out* of the judgment, just as Jesus promised the church in Philadelphia to remove them from the Tribulation. However, these witnesses will remain *through* it.

The 144,000 Witnesses

Verses 4-8:

> *"And I heard the number of them which were sealed: and there were sealed an hundred and forty and four thousand of all the tribes of the children of Israel. 5 Of the tribe of Juda were sealed twelve thousand. Of the tribe of Reuben were sealed twelve thousand. Of the tribe of Gad were sealed twelve thousand. 6 Of the tribe of Aser were sealed twelve thousand. Of the tribe of Nepthalim were sealed twelve thousand. Of the tribe of Manasses were sealed twelve thousand. 7 Of the tribe of Simeon were sealed twelve thousand. Of the tribe of Levi were sealed twelve thousand. Of the tribe of Issachar were sealed twelve thousand. 8 Of the tribe of Zabulon were sealed twelve thousand. Of the tribe of Joseph were sealed twelve thousand. Of the tribe of Benjamin were sealed twelve thousand."*

This paragraph tells us a number of important things about the Tribulation period. First, the twelve tribes of Israel will still be in existence. People talk about the "ten lost tribes of Israel" but that is a misnomer. They are not lost at all! Man may not know where they are but God does. For the most part, Jewish people today are unable to know which tribe they belong to but God knows. He has not lost sight of His people. Some point to the fact that the word "Jew" comes from the word "Judah" and claim that the name applies only to descendents of that tribe. That is technically true but in the Scriptures, the term *"Israelite"* and *"Jew"* are used interchangeably. Jesus was from the tribe of Judah but He specifically came to the *"lost sheep of the house of Israel"* (Matthew 15:24). Paul was a Benjamite but he called himself a Jew (Romans 11:1, Philippians 3:5). Anna came from the tribe of Asher but she recognized her identification with the Jewish race (Luke 2:36).

The Scriptures are clear that one day, all twelve tribes will be re-gathered. The claim by the British Israelites, that with some variations, Britain and the United States are the lost ten tribes, is both anti-Semitic and make-believe. There is no basis for it in the Scriptures. The promises made by God to Israel were unconditional and they will be fulfilled in His good time. Otherwise His holy name could be called into question.

In these verses, the tribes are not listed in the order of their birth. In fact they are thoroughly jumbled up. The order goes 4, 1, 7, 8, 6, 2, 3, 9, 10, 11 and 12. The tribe of Dan is missing altogether; Manasseh, one of Joseph's sons, is listed but Ephraim, the other, is not mentioned. Nobody knows the reason for this, though there are many theories. Dan was the northernmost tribe of the twelve, one of the first to go into idolatry and also to be swallowed up by the Assyrian invaders. Ephraim was prominent in idolatry but so were all the others. There was not one tribe that was not involved in idol worship and it would be only supposition to say that this was why Dan and Manasseh are not named in verses 4-8.

This is an example of many areas in the book of Revelation where a great deal of time and effort can be wasted on what seems to be investigative Bible study but which is completely unfruitful because no clear answers are ever forthcoming. Such activities produce only theories, most of which are wrong. If God does not choose to tell us why He does certain things, it is far more productive to accept His judgment and move on than to waste time confusing ourselves with dubious possibilities.

Here God has confirmed that twelve tribes will still exist at the end of the age. That means they must exist today because God will not create them afresh. All the stock of Israel descends from one or other of the twelve sons of Jacob and God knows who is who.

The second thing illustrated in this passage is that Israel is quite distinct from the church. That might be obvious to some but there is a strong movement today, which claims that God rejected His ancient people when they rejected Christ, and that God's promises to Israel were all transferred to the church. That comes under the same heading as the British Israelites!

The church is not in view here. The church on earth disappeared at the end of chapter 3. It is true that during the church age God set Israel aside as the center of His program but He never forsook her. He never cast her off. She is very much a part of His over-all plan for the ages and when the last and when the last days come He will restore all twelve tribes living at that time.

The Innumerable Multitude

Verses 9-14:

> *"After this I beheld, and, lo, a great multitude, which no man could number, of all nations, and kindred, and people, and tongues, stood before the throne, and before the Lamb, clothed with white robes, and palms in their hands; 10 And cried with a loud voice, saying, Salvation to our God who sits upon the throne, and unto the Lamb. 11 And all the angels stood round about the throne, and about the elders and the four living creatures, and fell before the throne on their faces, and worshipped God, 12 Saying, Amen: Blessing, and glory, and wisdom, and thanksgiving, and honor, and power, and might, be unto our God for ever and ever. Amen. 13 And one of the elders said to me, 'Who are these who are arrayed in white robes? And whence did they come?' 14 And I said to him, 'Sir, you know.' And he said to me, 'These are they who came out of great*

tribulation, and have washed their robes, and have made them white in the blood of the Lamb."

This has troubled many people. They say, "If the Holy Spirit is removed with the church at the beginning of the Tribulation period, how come so many people are saved?" Their reasoning is based on 2 Thessalonians 2:3-7, which reads,

"Let no man deceive you by any means: for that day shall not come, unless there come a falling away first, and that man of sin be revealed, the son of perdition; 4 Who opposes and exalts himself above all that is called God, or that is worshipped; so that he as God sits in the temple of God, showing himself that he is God. 5 Remember not, that, when I was with you, I told you these things? 6 And now you know what withholds that he might be revealed in his time. 7 For the mystery of iniquity already works: only he who now lets (restrains) will continue to let until he is taken out of the way."

The word "let" in verse 7 (KJV) is an Old English word and has a very distinct meaning. Until he died a few years ago, a friend of ours operated an old mill, one of the oldest working mills in England. It is an ancient stone building, nestled in a green valley and worked by a water wheel. The water is brought to the wheel along a narrow channel connected to a nearby stream and it is controlled by a wooden sluice gate, which is raised to allow the water to run underneath and thus turn the wheel. As the wheel turns, the machinery inside the building revolves ancient millstones that grind the grain brought there by farmers round about.

The sluice is called the "leat" or "let" because it holds back the water until the owner wants the mill to turn. When he is ready, he pulls down a lever, which raises the sluice gate and allows the flood to flow under the water wheel. Then the grinding begins. It is a wonderfully pictorial illustration of what will happen in the last days. Something, or someone will restrain, or let, until he is taken out of the way, and then the flood will begin to turn the mill of judgment.

This restrainer is referred to as "he". Thus it is not a force or a principle or an organization that holds back the flood of evil, but a person. We may not realize that the flood of evil is being held back because we see so much of it around but what we see today is merely a shadow of what will take place in the end times.

Obviously no human being would live long enough or command sufficient power to hold back the tide of spiritual wickedness throughout all the ages of time. Therefore the restrainer has to be a spirit being. The only two spirit beings even approaching that kind of power would be either God or Satan. And since the restrainer must be stronger than the one being restrained, and since it is obviously Satan and his influence being restrained, the Restrainer has to be God Himself.

From Pentecost to the present day, the Spirit of God has indwelt every believer and Jesus promised that He will abide with them for ever. In Ephesians 1:13-14 the Holy Spirit is identified as the seal of our salvation, our security and the down payment on our inheritance *"until the redemption of the purchased possession"*. Therefore, when the church is removed, He also will be removed.

The question is, "If the Holy Spirit has been removed, how come all these people in verse 9 are saved?" The answer is that His withdrawal will be the canceling out of what happened at Pentecost. The Holy Spirit did not come for the first time at Pentecost. He had been on the earth since the beginning of creation. During the years of the Old Testament, the He guided and filled and empowered men and women for His purposes. *"Holy men of God spoke as they were moved by the Holy Ghost."* (2 Peter 1:21) Multitudes of men and women, whose names we don't know, were not only drawn to belief in God but were empowered for service by the Holy Spirit. At Pentecost something new took place. The atonement of Christ made it possible for the Holy Spirit to permanently indwell believers and the church was born. This will be the relationship withdrawn in the last days. The Holy Spirit will revert to the Old Testament principle. Those who are saved after the rapture will not be part of the church. The church will have already departed.

Here in Revelation 7 an innumerable multitude, from all nations, is seen to have eternal life. They are no doubt the same people pictured in Revelation 6:9-11. How do they hear the Good News? Not from the church. The church age is over. Apparently the 144,000 Israelites will be the evangelists.

The coming of the Lord for His church does ***not*** depend on the Gospel being preached to every nation. Some say that the Lord cannot return until we have finished that work. That is not true. That activity is placed by Christ in the Tribulation period, after the church has departed. Jesus said, in Matthew 24:14, *"The Gospel of the kingdom shall be preached to the entire world, for a witness to all nations, and then shall the end come."* The *"end"* in that passage is not the rapture of the church but the coming of Christ in power and glory to set up His kingdom at the end of the age.

It is significant that Jesus did not say "The Gospel of *salvation* shall be preached to all nations." He said "The Gospel of *the kingdom* shall be preached." This agrees with Matthew 25, where the nations at the close of the Tribulation period will be judged. On that occasion, Jesus will say to the good nations, "Inherit the *kingdom* that was prepared for you from the foundation of the world."

However, there is danger here of inferring that those who neglect salvation in this present age will have a second chance during the Tribulation. The Scriptures clearly teach that this idea is false.

2 Thessalonians 2:9-10a:

> *"Even him, whose coming is after the working of Satan with all power and signs and lying wonders, 10 and with all deceivableness of unrighteousness in those who perish."*

That is a description of the antichrist, who will rise to power during the Tribulation. He will be energized by Satan and will completely delude those who are called here *"those who perish (are perishing)"*. The next phrase explains who these people will be and why they are deluded.

2 Thessalonians 2:10b:

> " . . *because they receiv__ed__* (past tense*) not the love of the truth, that they might be saved."*

These people will have heard the way of salvation while the door was still open but will have failed to take advantage of it.

Verse 11a:

> *"For this cause"…* (Present tense)

What cause? *"Because they received not the love of the truth"* when they had the opportunity.

Verse 11 again:

> *"For this cause God shall send them strong delusion, that they should believe a lie: 12 that they **all** might be damned."*

There will be no exceptions to those who fall into this group.

Verse 11b:

> *"who believ**ed** (Past tense) not the truth, but **had** (Past tense) pleasure in unrighteousness."*

It becomes obvious that this innumerable multitude of saved people from all nations, who will come out of the Great Tribulation, will not be those who heard the Gospel of salvation during the church age but rejected it. They will be those who do not hear the Gospel before the Tribulation begins.

The last part of Revelation 7:14 makes it clear that these people will have been saved by the blood of Christ, just as all others are today. We must remember that all salvation, in all ages, has relied on the blood of the Lamb. There has never been any other remedy for sin. The Old Testament saints looked *forward* to the cross. They waited for the price to be paid before their salvation became operative. The church looks *back* to the same atonement, and so will the Tribulation saints.

The Eternal State

Verse 15:

> *"Therefore are they before the throne of God, and serve him day and night in his temple: and he who sits on the throne shall dwell among them. 16 They shall hunger no more, neither thirst any*

more; neither shall the sun light on them, nor any heat. 17 For the Lamb which is in the midst of the throne shall feed them, and shall lead them to living fountains of waters: and God shall wipe away all tears from their eyes."

One day He will take possession of His inheritance and we shall see Him as He is. Then we shall be able to sing the song as never before:

"All hail King Jesus!
All Hail Immanuel!
King of kings, Lord of lords,
Bright Morning Star!
And throughout eternity I'll sing your praises,
And I'll reign with you throughout eternity!"

CHAPTER 8

The Seventh Seal (Silence)

In chapter 6 we saw the Lord Jesus take the seven-sealed scroll from the hand of God and open six of its seals. As He did so, a series of judgments fell upon the earth. Chapter 7 then pictured a delay in the process, while God set 144,000 witnesses, selected from each of the twelve tribes of Israel, aside for protection. Now, as we come to the 8th chapter, the Lord Jesus is about to open the seventh seal and as He does so, seven further judgments are released. Each of these is introduced by the sounding of a trumpet in Heaven. Consequently, they are known as "The Trumpet Judgments".

These trumpet judgments are not a progression beyond the seal judgments because the seals control the whole book of Revelation. The Trumpet Judgments are what lie hidden under the seventh seal. Later, in chapter 11, when we reach the seventh trumpet we shall discover a further set of judgments, known as "The Bowl Judgments" and they will flow from the seventh trumpet. Thus we have three sets of judgments, namely, the seals, the trumpets and the bowls. However, the last two sets (the trumpets and the bowls) are actually hidden under the seventh seal. This boils down to the truth that the events described in the remainder of the Revelation, from now to the end of the book, are actually released by the breaking of this final seal.

The Prelude

Verse 1:

> *"And when he had opened the seventh seal, there was silence in heaven about the space of half an hour."*

Here is a scene full of suspense. There is an atmosphere of foreboding, brooding, like the heavy calm before a storm. Sounds are muffled, even the birds stop their singing, and all Heaven waits in hushed expectancy for the next scene to unfold.

Half and hour is not very long when compared with months and years, even centuries, but it represents an eternity when its pause marks the awful contemplation of the judgment of God.

Verse 2:

> *"And I saw the seven angels which stood before God; and to them were given seven trumpets."*

We are not told who these seven angels are but they are described specifically as *"THE seven angels who stand before God."* A clue to their identity might possibly be found in Luke chapter 1, where the angel Gabriel appeared to Zacharias in the temple. He came to announce the birth of John the Baptist, which would be a miracle in itself because both John and Elizabeth were past the age of bearing children.

When Zacharias had trouble believing the angel's message, Gabriel said to him, *"I am Gabriel, who stands in the presence of God, and I am sent to speak to you and to give you these glad tidings."* There may be no connection between the two passages but there does seem to be some significance to the phrase, *"who stands in the presence of God"*. If these seven angels, who are described the same way here, include Gabriel, they are among the highest ranking beings in the whole universe. This gives an idea of the importance of the judgments about to fall.

Verse 3:

> *"And another angel came and stood at the altar, having a golden censer; and there was given unto him much incense, that he should offer it with the prayers of all saints upon the golden altar which was before the throne."*

The trumpets were *given* to the seven angels and the incense was *given* to the eighth. They were not acting independently. These were not judgments brought about by angels. God Himself brought them about. All the power came either from the throne or from the Lamb. Control of every event was squarely in the hands of God.

The scene before us is obviously the sanctuary of God in Heaven. The earthly tabernacle and temples were not original designs, later copied by God. They were designs given by God to be modeled on the Heavenly pattern.

In the earthly tabernacle, the golden altar of incense was considered to be part of the furniture of the Holy of Holies but for the protection of the priests who tended it, a veil hung between it and the Ark of the Covenant. When Jesus died this veil was ripped from the top to the bottom because the barrier of sin had been removed. Here in Heaven there is no veil. The veil is missing and the golden altar of incense stands directly before the throne of God. The Ark of the Covenant was a picture, or representation, of God's throne in Heaven, which explains its awful holiness.

Verse 4:

> *"And the smoke of the incense, which came with the prayers of the saints, ascended up before God out of the angel's hand."*

Several times in Scripture, incense is associated with the prayers of the saints - not a Catholic kind of saints, who are set apart by the church for special veneration, but all believers through all periods of time. If you are a believer, then you are a saint. Your prayers are included in this scene.

Verse 5:

> *"And the angel took the censer, and filled it with fire of the altar, and cast it into the earth: and there were voices, and thunder, and lightning, and an earthquake. 6 And the seven angels who had the seven trumpets prepared themselves to sound."*

The action is about to begin and it is heralded by atmospheric and seismic disturbances upon the earth. The prayers of the saints are not cast to the earth. They remain before God, but fire from the altar is cast upon the earth. It is almost as if the power of God, coming into the close proximity of the earth, causes violent reactions in the realm of nature. The atmosphere is over-charged with electricity; the molten layers beneath the earth are stimulated to agitated action.

THE TRUMPET JUDGMENTS

The First Trumpet

Verse 7:

> *"The first angel sounded, and there followed hail and fire mingled with blood, and they were cast upon the earth: and the third part of trees was burnt up, and all green grass was burnt up."*

Many commentators have attempted to spiritualize this scene and make it mean something other than what it clearly says. This is dangerous because it launches us into a world of imagination, in which man takes the place of God and decides what God's Word means. If *"holy men of God spoke as they were moved by the Holy Spirit"*, and if *"all Scripture is God-breathed"*, we must remember that God, not John, was causing these words to be written.

As we saw previously, whenever we come across words such as *"as it were"*, *"like"*, or *"as if"*, we have a certain authority to look around for possible solutions. But when clear statements are made, as they are here, concerning everyday things, which John knew, as well as we do, we should accept the fact that what he says is literal. John knew what hail looked like, and what fire and blood were, just as well as we do. He also recognized trees and grass. It therefore seems naive to suggest that the first trumpet really means the wars of the Goths and Vandals against the Roman Empire, or that the trees and the grass really represent the rich and the poor. These so-called "historical" interpretations are actually a thin covering for unbelief. If we don't believe that God is capable of sending unprecedented weather conditions upon the earth, we have no alternative but to come up with our own substitutes. These are usually more difficult to believe than the straightforward acceptance of God's Word.

Here God's Word says that John saw a global storm of hail, mixed with fire and blood. It did devastating damage to the trees and pastures of the world. The hail would break down crops and damage property, the fire would cause huge forest and city conflagrations and the blood would bring terror to all who witnessed it. Joel (Joel 2:30) and Ezekiel (Ezekiel 38:22) both foretold the falling of hail mixed with blood and fire in the last days. In Exodus 9, the seventh plague was not symbolic. It really happened. *"The Lord rained hail upon the land of Egypt; so there was hail and fire mingled with the hail very grievous, such as there was none like it in all the land of Egypt since it became a nation."*

The Second Trumpet

Verse 8:

> *"And the second angel sounded, and as it were a great mountain burning with fire was cast into the sea: and the third part of the sea became blood; 9 And the third part of the creatures which were in the sea, and had life, died; and the third part of the ships were destroyed."*

Here we do find a qualifying clause, *"as it were"*- *"As it were a great mountain burning with fire."* That tells us that it was not a great mountain but that it resembled one. No man-made missile could be that large, or do that amount of damage. John almost certainly saw some kind of meteorite hit the earth. As it entered the earth's atmosphere it would have signaled its arrival by a fiery and terrifying display. Probably scientists will know of its coming before it arrives but they will be able to do nothing about it, and when it finally hits the earth, the impact will be like nothing this globe has ever experienced before.

According to this account, the point of impact will be one of the oceans, though it doesn't tell us which one. The devastation will be enormous. All the ships in the area and all marine life will be blotted out. The tsunami will itself wreak unprecedented damage.

Notice that John does not say that a third part of the sea became *"as it were"* blood. He said *"it became blood"*, just as the waters of Egypt became blood during the plagues.

The Third Trumpet

Verses 10-11:

> *"And the third angel sounded, and there fell a great star from heaven, burning as it were a lamp, and it fell upon the third part of the rivers, and upon the fountains of waters; 11 And the name of the star is called Wormwood: and the third part of the waters became wormwood; and many men died of the waters, because they were made bitter."*

There is no qualifying clause here. John recognized what he saw; a star fall from Heaven. Again, it burned fiercely as it entered the earth's atmosphere but unlike the previous visitor, which impacted in one place only, this will apparently break up and spread out over a large area, polluting the water supply in the process. John gives no details. He simply states that it happened. There is no point in attempting to explain the phenomenon. It would not help us to know *how* an extra-terrestrial body striking the earth would poison the water supply. God's Word says it will and that should be good enough for us.

The Fourth Trumpet

Verse 12:

> *"And the fourth angel sounded, and the third part of the sun was smitten, and the third part of the moon, and the third part of the stars; so as the third part of them was darkened, and the day shone not for a third part of it, and the night likewise."*

There is no way man can take any credit for these happenings. He can have no control over heavenly bodies crashing into the earth's atmosphere. Bearing in mind the infinitude of outer space and the immense period of time it takes for even light to travel from one star to another, these two judgments could well be on their way even now. If we knew they were coming, there is nothing we could do to avoid the collisions. No earthly power could prevent or control them. God is demonstrating His unquestionable sovereignty in these areas. He is teaching man that despite all his arrogance and pride, he is absolutely helpless before the mighty hand of God.

Some have attempted to soften the blow by suggesting that the light is reduced by a third for a period of time, rather than a third of the bodies themselves being struck. This might be explained by thick clouds of ash flooding the heavens as the result of seismic activity. However, the last part verse 12 makes that theory difficult to support because John states that as the result of a third part of the sun being darkened, it failed to shine for a third part of the day. Presumably the clouds of ash would not come and go according to the clock. They certainly didn't when Mount St. Helens blew in 1980! They remained until they eventually disbursed and the heavier particles fell to the earth.

Dr. Henry Morris suggested that in some way unknown to man the internal reactions of these heavenly bodies might be slowed down for a limited period of time, so as to reduce their output by a third. God, who placed them in space, is certainly able to adjust their workings for a day or so. Moonlight, of course, is reflected, so if the sun's power were to be turned down, the moon would respond automatically.

Jesus spoke of cosmic disturbances in the last days. In Luke 21:25-26 He said,

> *"And there shall be signs in the sun, and in the moon, and in the stars; and upon the earth distress of nations, with perplexity; the sea and the waves roaring; 26 Men's hearts failing them for fear, and for looking after those things which are coming on the earth: for the powers of heaven shall be shaken."*

The Woe Judgments

Verse 13:

> *"And I beheld, and heard an angel flying through the midst of heaven, saying with a loud voice, Woe, woe, woe, to the inhabitants of the earth by reason of the other voices of the trumpet of the three angels, which are yet to sound!"*

Most translations have *"eagle"* in place of *"angel"* flying the midst of heaven. However, the impact is in what it says rather than what it was. Due to this verse, the last three judgments have been called *"the woe judgments"*, signifying their greater intensity.

"In the midst of Heaven" is one word in the original, and it means *"mid-heavens"*, not necessarily the dwelling- place of God but more likely the atmospheric heavens, (the sky). The message seems to be directed to the people on the earth. John does not reveal whether this event will be visible or audible. If it is, its impact upon the earth's inhabitants will be dramatic.

CHAPTER 9

The Fifth Trumpet

The last three trumpet judgments are different from the other four in one very obvious aspect. The first four judgments deal with elements we can understand, even if we cannot control them - things like hail, fire, blood and pollution. The last three introduce elements we do not understand and which we cannot explain. We have never seen anything like them. They are supernatural in origin, which adds to the horror of their presence.

The fifth angel is now about to sound.

Verses 1-2:

> *"And the fifth angel sounded, and I saw a star fall from heaven to the earth: and to him was given the key of the bottomless pit. 2 And he opened the bottomless pit."*

The Bible does not describe the "bottomless pit", or the "abyss", as it is translated in some places. It never speaks of its location. It simply refers to it as a fact. It exists in another dimension and is obviously feared by the spirit world. Today we are inclined to think of a pit as being a bowl-shaped affair but the abyss is more like a shaft or well and it is the prison house of evil spirits. It is mentioned nine times in the New Testament and on all occasions it is referred to in that context.

In Luke's Gospel we read the story of Jesus, when He visited Gadara, on the eastern shore of the Sea of Galilee. There He confronted a man possessed by evil spirits.

Luke 8:28-31:

> *"When he saw Jesus, he cried out, and fell down before him, and with a loud voice said, 'What have I to do with you, Jesus, Son of the most high God? I beseech you, do not torment me.' 29 (For he had commanded the unclean spirit to come out of the man. For oftentimes it had seized him and he was kept bound with chains and fetters; and he broke the bonds, and was driven of the demons into the wilderness.) 30 And Jesus asked him, saying, What is your name? And he said, Legion: because many demons had entered into him. 31 And they besought him that he would not command them to go out into the deep."*

The word translated *"deep"* in verse 31 is *"abyss"*, the same word referred to as *"the bottomless pit"* in Revelation. Obviously this place was, and still is, well known to the spirit world and viewed with terror by the spirits. The demons were terrified that Jesus would send them there.

There is no qualifying clause before the word "star" in Revelation 9:2. John does not say, *"as it were, or like* a star" but the context makes it clear that this was not an actual star; it is a person because it is referred to as "him" and "he". He is given the key to the abyss, which he opens. He has intelligence and volition and is entrusted by God to carry out His will. He is most likely to be an angel, since angels are referred to as stars in other Scriptures.

Verse 2b:

> *". . and there arose a smoke out of the pit, as the smoke of a great furnace; and the sun and the air were darkened by reason of the smoke from the pit."*

Here we have the first reference to the earth's physical atmosphere being affected by emissions from a spirit location. It is as if God were opening one dimension into another.

Verse 3:

> *"And there came out of the smoke locusts upon the earth: and to*
> *them was given power, as the scorpions of the earth have power. 4*
> *And it was commanded them that they should not hurt the grass*
> *of the earth, neither any green thing, nor any tree; but only those*
> *men who have not the seal of God in their foreheads. 5 And to them*
> *it was given that they should not kill them, but that they should*
> *be tormented five months: and their torment was as the torment of*
> *a scorpion, when he strikes a man. 6 And in those days shall men*
> *seek death, and shall not find it; and shall desire to die, and death*
> *shall flee from them."*

There is way we can make these creatures anything other than
what John says they are. They issue from the abyss, which is
consistently described in Scripture as the prison house of evil
spirits and they are given clear boundaries concerning their power.
They are obviously not real locusts, because real locusts are eaters
of vegetation, whereas these are commanded to leave the grass and
trees alone. Real locusts are harmless in themselves whereas these
carry a scorpion's sting and are specifically directed against human
beings. In addition, they are able to discern whom God has sealed
for protection and whom He has not. The language indicates that
they could kill if given permission but their mandate is limited to
physical torment.

The prospect of millions of spirit creatures, like locusts, upon the
face of the earth, capable of stinging like scorpions (and presumably
"un-swattable") is horrible to imagine. Not only is their sting fearful
but their appearance is enough to strike terror into the hearts of
men also.

Verses 7-11:

> *"And the shape of the locusts were like unto horses prepared unto*
> *battle; and on their heads were as it were crowns like gold, and*
> *their faces were as the faces of men. 8 And they had hair as the hair*
> *of women, and their teeth were as the teeth of lions. 9 And they*
> *had breastplates, as it were breastplates of iron; and the sound of*
> *their wings was as the sound of chariots of many horses running*
> *to battle. 10 And they had tails like unto scorpions, and there*

> *were stings in their tails: and their power was to hurt men five months. 11 And they had a king over them, which is the angel of the bottomless pit, whose name in the Hebrew tongue is Abaddon, but in the Greek tongue his name is Apollyon."*

There are eight qualifying clauses in that paragraph. *"like"* is used twice, *"as it were"* twice, and *"as"* is used four times.

1. They looked *"like"* horses prepared for battle.
2. They wore *"as it were"* crowns of gold.
3. They had faces *"as"* the faces of men.
4. They had hair *"as"* women's hair.
5. They had teeth *"as"* lions' teeth.
6. They had breastplates *"as it were"* of iron.
7. The sound of their wings was *"as"* chariots.
8. They had tails *"like"* scorpions' tails.

Unlike true locusts, they had a king over them. True locusts don't have a king. The Bible specifically tells us that they have no leader. These do and he is named.

Whatever these creatures were, they were not of this world and they were released from the abyss, as a terrible five-month plague upon a world that had turned its back upon God, a plague so unbearable that people cried out for death but could not find it.

We speak in the past tense because John saw this vision nearly two thousand years ago but we need to remember that they are all part of what the Lord Jesus termed, *"the things that shall be hereafter."*

The prophet Joel was probably describing the same creatures in his prophecy. He writes in Joel 2:4-9

> *"Their appearance is as the appearance of horses; and as horsemen, so shall they run. 5 Like the noise of chariots on the tops of mountains shall they leap, like the noise of a flame of fire that devours the stubble, as a strong people set in battle array. 6 Before their face the people shall writhe in pain: all faces shall gather blackness. 7 They shall run like mighty men; they shall climb the wall like men of war; and they shall march every one on his way, and they shall not break their ranks: 8 Nor shall one thrust another; they shall*

walk every one in his path: and when they fall upon the sword, they shall not be wounded. 9 They shall run to and fro in the city; they shall run upon the wall, they shall climb up upon the houses; they shall enter in at the windows like a thief."

The Sixth Trumpet, Second Woe

Verse 12:

"One woe is past; and, behold, there come two woes more hereafter. 13 And the sixth angel sounded, and I heard a voice from the four horns of the golden altar which is before God"

The Golden Altar was the altar of incense. The Altar of Sacrifice was made of bronze and it stood outside the Holy Place. In the tabernacle, the Golden Altar stood inside the Holy Place, directly before the veil. It was considered to belong to the Holy of Holies but, as we saw earlier, it stood outside to protect the priests who had to minister on it. It was from this altar that, in chapter 8:5, that the fire was hurled to the earth to signal the commencement of these trumpet judgments.

Verses 14-15:

"Saying to the sixth angel who had the, trumpet, 'Loose the four angels which are bound in the great river Euphrates.' 15 And the four angels were loosed, which were prepared for an hour, and a day, and a month, and a year, to slay the third part of men."

Nobody knows who these angels are. We know they are not good angels because God does not keep His elect angels bound. They are demonic in nature but are limited to the mandate given to them by God. They could not release themselves. They had no power to operate other than the power given to them, for a specific period of time. They were assigned to kill one third of the earth's population. A quarter of the population had already died under the fourth seal (Revelation 6:8), which means that over half of the human race will die before the completion of the sixth trumpet judgment!

However, the angels will not accomplish this grisly assignment unaided. They will energize a huge army which will carry out the work. The phrase, *"for an hour, and a day and a month and a year"* seems to imply the precise timing of the plague. God does not work in "approximates". He works in specifics and His timing is absolutely accurate. The decision is not left to the players to make. They are limited to the script and God writes the script.

Verses 16-17:

> *"And the number of the army of the horsemen were two hundred thousand thousand: and I heard the number of them. 17 And thus I saw the horses in the vision, and those who sat on them, having breastplates of fire, and of jacinth, and brimstone."*

Some commentators have seen this description as one of color. Fire is translated as "fiery red", Jacinth, or hyacinth, is translated as "hyacinth blue" and brimstone as "sulphur yellow". If this is accurate (and it probably is) it may possibly describe the national colors of the invading armies.

Verse 17b-19:

> *"And the heads of the horses were as the heads of lions; and out of their mouths issued fire and smoke and brimstone. 18 By these three was the third part of men killed, by the fire, and by the smoke, and by the brimstone, which issued out of their mouths. 19 For their power is in their mouth, and in their tail: for their tails were like unto serpents, and had heads, and with them they do hurt."*

At this point there does seem to be some legitimate excuse to use our imagination. The four angels are obviously demonic beings but the question arises as to whether the armies are demonic or normal forces, motivated and energized by the four angels.

Armies of 200 million in John's day were out of the question. No nation could field an army of that size. Today, such armies exist. China alone has the ability to raise an army that large. If this were to describe modern warfare (and we cannot be sure it did), how would John have described tanks, rockets, bombs and shells? All he had to draw from was his own experience, which would have amounted to the armies of Rome. The streaking missiles of modern warfare and the flame and smoke of high explosives would be completely strange to him. Seeing them in a vision, they might have suggested to him serpents with death in their heads.

The river Euphrates has always been the boundary between the Far East and the Middle East and the Romans were terrified of invasion from the other side.

Revelation 16 speaks of armies of men from the east crossing the Euphrates and moving down into the Bible lands. It will be there that the final battle will be fought. It will not be fought by angels but by men, like you and me.

John said that the fire came from the mouths and tails, but whose mouths and tails is he referring to? Does he mean the horses or the riders? Did the men have tails and breathe fire, or did the vehicles upon which they were riding do the damage? I suspect it was the latter.

Nobody knows the answers to those questions but this second woe could easily be a description of a modern battle, which would kill a third of the population of the earth.

Verses 20-21:

> *"And the rest of mankind who were not killed by these plagues did not repent of the works of their hands, that they should not worship demons, and idols of gold, and silver, and brass, and stone, and of wood: which neither can see, nor hear, nor walk: 21 Nor did they repent of their murders, nor of their sorceries, nor of their fornication, nor of their thefts."*

The problem is that repentance is not an act of the will. It is something that is granted to us as a gift. In Acts 5:31 Peter said that God raised up Jesus in order to *give* repentance to Israel. In Acts 11:18, the assembled brethren glorified God, saying that God had also *granted* the Gentiles repentance unto life. In Romans 2:4, Paul points to the fact that it is the goodness of God that leads us to repentance. Man is incapable of repenting of his own volition. Repentance is a gift of grace.

Those who have the seal of God in their foreheads will be those upon whom God has placed His hand, whether they realize it or not. It is unlikely that the seal will be visible. The forehead is not only the skin of the head. It could also be the frontal lobe of the brain, where we store truth.

This means that even during the Tribulation period there will be grace. Wherever God has dealt in mercy with men and women who deserve judgment because of their sin, there was grace.

High on some buildings facing the Wailing Wall in Jerusalem is a conspicuous banner, written in Hebrew, fluttering in the wind. It says, "MESSIAH IS NEAR!" Israel is expecting Him, and so should we be.

CHAPTER 10

The Little Book

This chapter deals with the period in between the sixth trumpet, in chapter 9 and the seventh trumpet, in chapter 11. It is parenthetical in nature and comprises a separate unite.

Verse 1:

> *"And I saw another mighty angel come down from heaven, clothed with a cloud: and a rainbow was upon his head, and his face was as it were the sun, and his feet as pillars of fire."*

Some have assumed this was Christ Himself, due to the rainbow, sun and fire, which agree with descriptions of Christ earlier in this book. But this angel cannot be Christ for two important reasons:

1. The word *"another"* is the word *"allos"*, which means *"another of exactly the same kind"*. That makes him the same as the angels who have been described previously. In addition, the letter to the Hebrews goes out of its way to tell us that Christ is far above the angels and cannot be compared with them.

2. This angel swore by Him who lives forever and ever and created all things (verse 6). Christ would never use those words because He Himself is the One who has lived forever and ever and is the Creator of all things.

The evidence points to the fact that this is an angel, like the others John had encountered here in Revelation, but that he is certainly a *mighty* angel. Presumably the rainbow, the sun and the pillars of fire speak of the reflected power and glory this angel exhibits.

Verses 2-4:

> *"And he had in his hand a little book open: and he set his right foot upon the sea, and his left foot on the earth, 3 And cried with a loud voice, as when a lion roars: and when he had cried, seven thunders uttered their voices. 4 And when the seven thunders had uttered their voices, I was about to write: and I heard a voice from heaven saying unto me, Seal up those things which the seven thunders uttered, and write them not. "*

Apparently the thunders communicated logical thought, which John understood and was about to record. We have no idea what they said because God did not choose to let us know. John was told to seal up what they had said and to remove it from His record. God has the right to include or exclude whatever He wishes.

In John 12:29, those standing by when God spoke to Jesus thought they heard thunder. Evidently the voice of God is not easily discernable to the human ear unless God chooses to make it understandable.

Verses 5-6:

> *"And the angel which I saw stand upon the sea and upon the earth lifted up his hand to heaven, 6 And swore by him that lives for ever and ever, who created heaven, and the things that are therein, and the earth, and the things that are thereon, and the sea, and the things which are therein, that there should be time no longer."*

"Time no longer", means *"no delay"*. The judgment upon the earth was to be brought to a speedy conclusion.

Verse 7:

> *"But in the days of the voice of the seventh angel (still future), when he shall begin to sound, the mystery of God should be finished, as he hath declared to his servants the prophets."*

The cataclysmic end is now in sight. Throughout all the centuries of the Old Testament God revealed to His prophets that in the last days He would judge sin and bring in righteousness and justice upon the face of the earth. Now that, coupled with His implied promise to the martyred saints in chapter 6, is about to be fulfilled.

Verse 8:

> *"And the voice which I heard from heaven spoke unto me again, and said, Go and take the little book which is open in the hand of the angel which stands upon the sea and upon the earth. 9 And I went unto the angel, and said unto him, Give me the little book. And he said to me, 'Take it, and eat it up; and it shall make your belly bitter, but it shall be in your mouth as sweet as honey'. 10 And I took the little book out of the angel's hand, and ate it up; and it was in my mouth as sweet as honey: but as soon as I had eaten it, my belly was bitter. 11 And he said to me, 'You must prophesy again before many peoples, and nations, and tongues, and kings."*

We find this same principle in other parts of Scripture, such as Ezekiel 3, where the prophet received the same command. Like John, having obeyed he discovered it was as sweet as honey in his mouth but it left him in bitterness. In Jeremiah 15:16, the prophet wrote, *"Thy words were found and I did eat them."* The idea is that of digesting the information and making it one's own.

The Word of God is sweet to those who hunger after it but it contains some bitter things. Those who set out to live by it often have to face bitter things, such as suffering. The devil sees to that. John was already suffering on the Isle of Patmos for the Word of God. He had stood by what the Word said and had suffered in consequence.

John was not an aggressive person by nature. He was more of a mystic than a prophet. He was not an Elijah, he was a melancholy person, who wrote more about love and the divine nature of Christ than the other apostles. However, in this vision he was commanded to write down things that were terrible in their scope and nature, and which would spell the eternal doom of those upon whom the judgments fell. It is interesting that out of all the apostles, John was the one who was selected to record these horrible things.

In verse 11, where the voice says, *"you must prophesy again before many peoples"* (the NIV says *"about* many peoples") it does not mean *"in front of them"* or *"concerning them"* but *"against them."* John was about to pronounce the judgment of God against those who had rejected Him, worldwide. It would be a bitter assignment for a man of John's nature.

This is the truth behind all true preaching. It has a sweet side and a bitter side. The Word of God brings life to some and death to others, depending upon the response of the hearers.

Paul wrote in 2 Corinthians 2:15-16,

> *"For we are unto God a sweet savor of Christ, in them that are saved, and in them that perish: 16 To the one we are the savor of death unto death; and to the other the savor of life unto life. And who is sufficient for these things?"*

Who indeed? The Word is bitter to those who disregard it. These judgments are not against people who delight in the Scriptures. They are against those who reject and disregard the Scriptures.

In this scene, the angel, planting his feet on the earth and on the sea, symbolically claimed possession of those things, i.e. the world, in the name of the King of kings. The next scene records possession being symbolically claimed in a different way, and by a different figure.

CHAPTER 11

The Temple

Verse 1:

> *"And there was given me a reed like a measuring rod: and the angel stood, saying, 'Rise, and measure the temple of God, and the altar, and them that worship in it."*

"Temple" here is "naos" meaning the building containing the Holy of Holies and the Holy Place, not the whole complex.

At present there is no temple there to measure. A Moslem mosque occupies the platform in Jerusalem where Herod's temple once stood. But in 2 Thessalonians 2:4 we are told that a temple will stand there again during the Tribulation period and the book of Ezekiel goes into great detail describing it. Sooner or later a new temple will be built there and worship will be reinstated. The precise location of the new temple on the mount is still a matter of strenuous argument but the fact that it will be built there is not in question. Already, many of the sacred vessels, for use in the new temple, have been made, together with the robes of the priests. They are open to public display. In addition, careful study is being made to ensure that future priests come from the old Levitical families.

There will obviously be enormous repercussions to any suggestion of a Jewish temple being built in a location at present controlled by

Moslems and considered holy by them. Passions, already at boiling point, will be enflamed still further. But it will happen.

Here John is told to measure three things, of which the sanctuary is the first. The second is the altar and the fact that this is mentioned separately suggests this was the bronze altar of sacrifice rather than the golden altar of incense. Focus on the bronze altar indicates the resumption of animal sacrifices during the Tribulation period.

The third thing John was commanded to measure was the congregation within the temple court. A careful account will be kept of those who remain faithful to the Lord.

Verse 2:

> *"But the court which is outside the temple leave out, and measure it not; for it is given to the Gentiles: and they shall tread the holy city under foot forty two months."*

The people will worship in the court that surrounds the altar of sacrifice and the court that John is commanded to reject is the outer court. The Gentiles will tread this, along with the city itself, down for 42 months, or 3 1/2 years.

The Two Witnesses

Verses 3-6:

> *"And I will give power to my two witnesses, and they shall prophesy a thousand two hundred and sixty days, clothed in sackcloth. 4 These are the two olive trees, and the two lamp stands standing before the God of the earth. 5 And if any man will hurt them, fire proceeds out of their mouth, and devours their enemies: and if any man will hurt them, he must in this manner be killed. 6 These have power to shut heaven that it rain not in the days of their prophecy: and have power over waters to turn them into blood, and to smite the earth with all plagues, as often as they will."*

Who, then, are these two witnesses? It is legitimate to speculate but we must keep in mind that nobody knows for sure who they are.

The Bible is silent on the matter and the most brilliant theories are therefore only guesswork. They must never be taken as fact.

As far as guesswork is concerned, there are factors which point to the witnesses' possible identity. On the Mount of Transfiguration, in Matthew 17:3, two Old Testament characters were seen to be talking with Jesus. They were identified as Moses and Elijah. Neither of these men died under normal circumstances. Moses was taken directly by God as he stood on Mount Nebo surveying the Promised Land and Elijah ascended alive into Heaven in a whirlwind. In addition, between them they had been associated with the same phenomena credited to the two witnesses. Elijah had brought down fire from heaven, when he challenged the priests of Baal on Mount Carmel and by prayer he had shut up the heavens in the days of Ahab, so that it did not rain for precisely the same length of time mentioned here. Moses was used by God to strike the earth with plagues and turn the waters into blood.

The prophet Malachi predicted that Elijah would come again before the great and dreadful day of the Lord. In Matthew 11:14 Jesus said that John the Baptist was a type of Elijah and would have fulfilled that prophecy if the people had believed. So in light of these facts, it seems reasonable to suspect that the two witness of Revelation 11 may be Moses and Elijah.

Some favor the theory that Enoch, rather than Moses, will team up with Elijah. This is because he was translated into God's presence without dying. But whichever theory we espouse we must be careful to remember that it is only guesswork. God's Word alone is our authority and it is silent concerning the identity of these men.

What, then, does God's Word say about these witnesses? Verse 3 says they will draw their power from God and prophesy in Jerusalem for 1,260 days. That is, 3 1/2 years.

According to Daniel 9:27, the Antichrist will make a seven-year covenant with Israel at the beginning of the Tribulation period. During that time worship will be restored. However, in the midst of that seven-year period (after 3 1/2 years) he will break his covenant and will bring worship in the temple to an end. From that point to the end of the Tribulation, "desolations are determined".

In view of these facts, the 3 1/2 years referred to in verses 2 and 3 are likely to be the latter half of the Tribulation period. The "consummation", spoken of by Daniel the prophet, will be the Lord's triumphant return. This agrees with Luke 21:24-27, where Jesus says,

> *"There shall be great distress in the land, and wrath upon this people. 24 And they shall fall by the edge of the sword, and shall be led away captive into all nations: and Jerusalem shall be trodden down of the Gentiles, until the times of the Gentiles are fulfilled. 25 And there shall be signs in the sun, and in the moon, and in the stars; and upon the earth distress of nations, with perplexity; the sea and the waves roaring; 26 Men's hearts failing them for fear, and for looking after those things which are coming on the earth: for the powers of heaven shall be shaken. 27 And then shall they see the Son of man coming in a cloud with power and great glory."*

Some claim that this passage refers to 70 AD, when the Romans, under Titus, destroyed Jerusalem, but there is no way it can all be made to apply to 70 AD. Parts can refer only to the final years of the Tribulation period. The two witnesses will prophesy during the most difficult period of all, when the Antichrist himself is actually residing in Jerusalem and the temple is being desecrated.

Verse 4 is more difficult to explain.

> *"These are the two olive trees, and the two lamp stands standing before the God of the earth."*

Partial insight can be gleaned from Zechariah 3 and 4, where two other Old Testament characters are under discussion. During the rebuilding of the temple in Ezra's time, Zerubbabel the prince and Joshua the high priest encouraged the people to finish the work and stand against the discouragement of their day. In his vision, Zechariah saw two olive trees standing beside a golden lamp stand. When asked what they were, he confessed he didn't know. The angel then pronounced those famous words, *"Not by might, nor by power, but by My Spirit, saith the Lord."* In other words, the work could be carried out only in dependence upon the Lord.

Zechariah then asked what the two olive trees represented and he was told, "*These are the two anointed ones who stand beside the Lord of the whole earth*". It would seem from the text that the two anointed ones in that day were Zerubbabel and Joshua. But in Revelation 4 they are said to be the two witnesses who will be prophesying in Jerusalem. The principle is the same in both cases. They will not operate in their own strength but will be commissioned and empowered by the Holy Spirit. Their activities will be God's doing.

Verse 7:

> "*And when they have finished their testimony, the beast that ascends out of the bottomless pit (the abyss) shall make war against them, and shall overcome them, and kill them. 8 And their dead bodies shall lie in the street of the great city, which spiritually is called Sodom and Egypt, where also our Lord was crucified.*"

We all know where our Lord was crucified, so there is no mystery about the identity of the city referred to. Here Jerusalem is described as "Sodom and Egypt". Sodom has gone down in history as the very embodiment of deviant sexual sin. Sexual promiscuity always indicates unfaithfulness and rebellion against God. Here the principle is applied spiritually to the city of Jerusalem, which will have turned away from the Lord and will be paying a fearful price for its sin.

In the Scriptures, Egypt is symbolized as two things: first, bondage. It was in Egypt that the Lord's people were first made slaves and it was from Egypt that God delivered them under Moses. Second, Egypt is used as a type of the world. The people will have turned away from God to materialism and idolatry. Obviously Jerusalem is neither Sodom nor Egypt but spiritually God holds her accountable for the same sins. I wonder what He holds the nations of the western world accountable for today.

In Luke 13:34-35, Jesus said,

> "*O Jerusalem, Jerusalem, which kills the prophets, and stones those who are sent to you; how often would I have gathered your children together, as a hen gathers her brood under her wings, and you would not! 35 Behold, your house is left unto you desolate.*"

And so it was. Apparently, the two witnesses will be hated, not only in Jerusalem, but all around the world. The words they say will cut and sting and when they are eventually overthrown there will be rejoicing everywhere. They will prophesy the truth, of course, but the truth is profoundly irritating to those who reject God. The flesh would rather silence the truth than change its ways. Rather than listen to the message the world would rather destroy the messenger.

Verse 9:

> *"And they of the people and kindreds and tongues and nations shall see their dead bodies three days and an half, and shall not allow their dead bodies to be put in graves. 10 And they that dwell upon the earth shall rejoice over them, and make merry, and shall send gifts one to another; because these two prophets tormented them that dwelt on the earth."*

There was a time when people used to puzzle over this passage and wonder how in the world all nations would be able to see the dead bodies of two men lying in the streets of Jerusalem. However, these days we see the dead bodies of all kinds of people on our television screens and think nothing of it.

Not only will this event be universally televised but no doubt the anger of the world will have been whipped up by the media, by relaying what the witnesses had preached. Why, otherwise, would the world rejoice over their death? However, the party will be short-lived. It will last for exactly 3 1/2 days!

Verse 11:

> *"And after three days and an half the spirit of life from God entered into them, and they stood upon their feet; and great fear fell upon them which saw them. 12 And they heard a great voice from heaven saying unto them, Come up hither. And they ascended up to heaven in a cloud; and their enemies beheld them."*

Here will be proof positive that these men are God's servants. The actual revival of their bodies would probably be explained away, just as they tried to explain away the resurrection of Christ. People will probably say, "They weren't really dead; they just swooned." However, their visible, public, televised ascension into Heaven will be unanswerable. And the entire world will see it happen.

In addition, the event will be accompanied by a violent shaking of the earth, which will cause many casualties and great damage.

Verse 13:

> *"And the same hour was there a great earthquake, and the tenth part of the city fell and seven thousand people were slain in the earthquake: and the remnant was terrified, and gave glory to the God of heaven. "*

It is interesting to notice that here there is some response from the people. The survivors were terrified and gave glory to God. However, in chapter 9 and again in chapter 16, where similar catastrophes occur we are told that the survivors did not repent.

The truth to learn here is that there is a difference between glorifying God and repenting of one's sin. Words are cheap. The flesh is quite happy to glorify God provided it can hold on to its sin. Repentance is a turning away from sin and we are told very clearly in the Scriptures that repentance is essential for salvation to be real. There is no mention of these people repenting of their sin. They simply recognize these events as having been orchestrated and controlled by God. It doesn't take much imagination to recognize that and it doesn't mean that they became Christians.

This passage also tells us that the people who perish during the Tribulation period will not necessarily be atheists. They will believe in God's existence, just as many unsaved people believe in God's existence today, but they will come short of saving faith because repentance will be missing. Jesus said, *"Unless you repent, you shall all likewise perish."*

The Seventh Trumpet, Third Woe

Verses 14-18:

> *"The second woe is past; and, behold, the third woe comes quickly. 15 And the seventh angel sounded; and there were great voices*

> *in heaven, saying, 'The kingdoms of this world have become the*
> *kingdoms of our Lord, and of his Christ; and he shall reign for ever*
> *and ever. 16 And the four and twenty elders, who sat before God on*
> *their seats, fell upon their faces, and worshipped God, 17 Saying,*
> *We give thee thanks, O Lord God Almighty, who is, and was and is*
> *to come; because you have taken to yourself your great power, and*
> *have reigned. 18 And the nations were angry, and your wrath has*
> *come, and the time of the dead, that they should be judged, and that*
> *you should give reward to your servants the prophets, and to the*
> *saints, and those who fear your name, small and great; and should*
> *destroy those who destroy the earth'."*

So here is evidence that once again we have come chronologically to the end of the Tribulation period, just as we did at the end of chapter 6. It seems almost as if, instead of one chronological narrative that begins in chapter 4 and ends in chapter 22, it describes the same period several times, but with each pass it provides greater detail. The tenses of several important statements tell us that the time has now come in this passage for events to take place that will clearly occur after the Lord returns in His glory.

For instance, in verse 15, the heavenly host says, *"The kingdoms of this world HAVE BECOME the kingdoms of our Lord."* That will not take place until after the Tribulation has come to an end. In verse 18, they say, *"Your wrath HAS COME"* and the time for the nations to be judged. That also takes place at the end of the Tribulation (Matthew 25:31-46).

Verse 19:

> *"And the temple of God was opened in heaven, and there was seen*
> *in his temple the ark of his testament: and there was lightning, and*
> *voices, and thunder, and an earthquake, and great hail."*

Throughout the Old Testament, the Ark of the Covenant was just a symbol. It had no entity of its own, no power and no authority. It simply stood for the presence and power of God among His people. More explicitly, it stood for the person and ministry of the Lord Jesus Christ.

When Jesus came, He fulfilled the type and rendered the Ark obsolete. He was by definition, "Immanuel", which means "God with us". Up until that time, the Ark represented "God with us" but now Jesus had taken its place. Now the real thing had come, God no longer needed to manifest Himself in a symbol. *"In Him (Jesus) dwelt all the fullness of the Godhead, bodily."* This being so, it is interesting to see Heaven opened and the Ark of the Covenant standing within it.

What was the symbol doing in Heaven when the type had been fulfilled? We don't know, but one suggestion might be that although the Antichrist will have desecrated the temple on earth, the temple in Heaven is seen to be as holy as ever. We must remember that the Ark stood not only as a symbol of Christ but also of the covenant that God had made with Israel concerning their sin and His faithfulness. It was the *"Ark of the Covenant"*.

No man could fulfill that covenant; it could be fulfilled only through Christ. Here, the great symbol of God's faithfulness is revealed at the time of history's most blatant period of sin and rebellion, unmovable, untouchable, and unshaken by Satan's most strenuous efforts to dethrone it. It stands unscathed. God remains calmly victorious, regardless of the very worst that His enemies can throw against Him.

When difficult times come along, visualize the heavens open and the Ark of God revealed, rock firm in its unshakable reliability; a symbol of God's righteousness and Christ's ministry on our behalf, and let it give you courage!

CHAPTER 12

The Woman (Israel)

Verse 1:

> *"And there appeared a great wonder (sign) in heaven."*

The word "wonder" (KJV) should be "sign". This is important because it tells us that unlike many other things in this book we are not to take it literally. In other words, we must look for its meaning because it signifies something else.

Verses 1-2:

> *"And there appeared a great sign in Heaven; a woman clothed with the sun and the moon under her feet and upon her head a crown of twelve stars: 2 And she being with child cried, travailing in birth, and pained to be delivered."*

The Red Dragon (Satan)

Verses 3-4:

> *"And there appeared another wonder (sign) in heaven; and behold a great red dragon, having seven heads and ten horns, and seven crowns upon his heads. 4 And his tail drew the third part of the*

stars of heaven, and did cast them to the earth: and the dragon stood before the woman who was ready to be delivered, to devour her child as soon as it was born."

The Man-Child (Christ)

Verse 5

"And she brought forth a man child, who was to rule all nations with a rod of iron: and her child was caught up unto God, and to his throne."

Immediately, several questions come to mind. Who is the woman, who is the man-child and who is the dragon? The easiest way to untangle the problem is to begin at the end and work backwards. First, then, who is the man-child in verse 5?

He is described as one who was brought forth to rule all nations with a rod of iron and was caught up to the throne of God. Obviously, only one child ever born into this world could satisfy these credentials and that was Jesus. Four times in the Scriptures, reference is made to one who will *"rule with a rod of iron"* and every time it describes Messiah's reign at the end of this age. (See Psalm 2:9, Revelation 2:27, Revelation 19:15). So the "man-child" is the Lord Jesus Christ.

The great red dragon stands before the woman to devour her child as soon as He is born. Verse 9 tells us specifically that the dragon represents Satan. When Lucifer rebelled against God, a large company of the heavenly angels rebelled with him and became *his* angels. Jesus refers to these in Matthew 25:41, where He speaks of *"the Lake of Fire reserved for the devil and his angels."*

If the child is Christ and the dragon is Satan, it would be natural to assume that the woman must be Mary. After all, it was she who gave birth to the Christ child. However, verse 1 makes it clear that the woman is not Mary. Verse one pictures her as *"clothed with the sun and the moon under her feet and upon her head a crown of twelve stars."*

Mary was a humble peasant girl, who was never promised glory like that. Men have glorified her since and added all kinds of things that the Scriptures never mention. However, the best clue to the woman's identity is found in Genesis 37:9-11.

> *"And he dreamed yet another dream, and told it to his brethren, and said, Behold, I have dreamed a dream more; and, behold, the sun and the moon and the eleven stars made obeisance (bowed down) to me. 10 And he told it to his father, and to his brethren: and his father rebuked him, and said unto him, What is this dream that you have dreamed? Shall I and your mother and your brethren indeed come to bow down ourselves to you to the earth? 11 And his brethren envied him; but his father observed the saying."*

On that occasion there were only eleven stars because Joseph was the twelfth. The stars represented the twelve sons of Israel. In Revelation 12:1, all twelve are represented because Joseph is not speaking. Jesus, the *man*, was the son of Mary but Jesus the *Messiah* was the son of David, and through David, of Israel. Here, the woman is Israel, under bondage to the Romans and groaning for the promised Messiah. Centuries before, Isaiah had prophesied,

> *"For unto us a child is born, unto us a son is given: and the government shall be upon his shoulder: and his name shall be called Wonderful, Counselor, The mighty God, The everlasting Father, The Prince of Peace. 7 Of the increase of his government and peace there shall be no end, upon the throne of David, and upon his kingdom, to order it, and to establish it with judgment and with justice from henceforth even for ever. "*(Isaiah 9:6-7)

This scene in Revelation 12 is a picture of the age-old conflict between Satan and God. We see it in Genesis 6, where the corruption of the human race, which began in the Garden when Adam sinned, reached such a point of hopelessness that God was obliged to destroy the entire race in the Great Flood and begin again with Noah and his family. We see it again in Exodus 1, where Pharaoh decreed the death of all Hebrew male children but God intervened and the nation continued. It surfaces again in the book of Esther, where all Israel faced extinction at the hand of the Persians but was saved by Mordecai, who exposed the plot to queen Esther. Later still, Satan did his best to destroy the baby Jesus, when Herod ordered all the male children around Bethlehem to be killed. God warned Joseph of the danger and Herod failed in his attempt. Through the centuries, Satan's attack narrowed but it always aimed at the "seed of the woman" in Genesis 3. First, he attacked the race as a whole; then he attacked the nation from which Messiah would come. Then he attacked the district where Messiah was born and finally Jesus Himself. It was not coincidence that the Nazarenes attempted to throw Jesus over a cliff, nor that the storm threatened to swallow the ship in which Jesus slept.

When Satan finally saw the lifeless body of Jesus taken down from the cross and placed in the cold tomb, he must have rubbed his hands in glee! At last he had succeeded! But just imagine his dismay on the resurrection morning, when the full truth of his defeat became clear!

After His death and resurrection, the Lord Jesus was caught up into Heaven, to the throne of God, exactly as verse 5 describes.

However, here in Revelation, there is a mix-up of time frames. The birth of the Lord Jesus and the devil's attempt to kill Him took place two thousand years ago but the events described in the remainder of chapter 12 clearly refer to a time still future.

Verse 6:

> *"And the woman fled into the wilderness, where she hath a place prepared of God that they should feed her there a thousand two hundred and sixty days."*

1260 days are 3 1/2 years, which obviously coincide with the period during which the two witnesses, described in the previous chapter, will prophesy and the Antichrist will carry on his reign of terror.

In Daniel 7:25, the Antichrist is described as a little horn, that grows out of one of the ten kingdoms sharing power in the last days. It says,

> *"And he shall speak great words against the most High, and shall wear out the saints of the most High, and think to change times and laws: and they shall be given into his hand until a time and times and the dividing of time."*

Put that together (singular +plural + a half) and you get 3 1/2 years. Again, in chapter 12 of Daniel's prophecy, we find another reference that reads:

> *"Then I Daniel looked, and, behold, there stood two others, one on this side of the bank of the river, and the other on that side of the bank of the river. 6 And one said to the man clothed in linen, who was upon the waters of the river, 'How long shall it be to the end of these wonders?' 7 And I heard the man clothed in linen, which was upon the waters of the river, when he held up his right hand and his left hand unto heaven, and swore by him that lives for ever that it shall be for a time, times, and an half; and when he shall have accomplished to scatter the power of the holy people, all these things shall be finished.* (Daniel 12:6-7)

Back in Revelation 11:2, John was told not to measure the outer court of the temple because it was given to the Gentiles, who would trample it down for 42 months (3 1/2 years). Finally, in Revelation 11:3, power is given to God's two witnesses to prophesy for 1260 days.

In view of these references, it is very clear that here in Revelation 12 we leap from the time when Jesus ascended into Heaven to the throne of God to the last half of the Tribulation period, which is still future. This kind of leap happens frequently in the prophetic Scriptures.

It is fascinating to see how God, who thinks nothing of jumping over thousands of years as if they were nothing, should , at the same time, have His timetable so finely tuned that the exact days and months when these events will take place are pinpointed with minute accuracy.

Here, in verse 6, the woman (Israel) will flee into the wilderness during the second half of the Tribulation period and will find refuge from the Antichrist. This seems to fit perfectly with the words of the Lord Jesus in Matthew 24:15-22:

> *"Therefore, when you see the abomination of desolation, spoken of by Daniel the prophet, stand in the holy place, (whoso reads, let him understand:) 16 Then let those who are in Judea flee into the*

mountains: 17 Let him who is on the housetop not come down to take any thing out of his house: 18 Neither let him who is in the field return back to take his clothes. 19 And woe to those who are with child, and to those who nurse in those days! 20 But pray that your flight is not in the winter, nor on the Sabbath day: 21 For then shall be great tribulation, such as was not since the beginning of the world to this time, no, nor ever shall be. 22 And except those days should be shortened, there should no flesh be saved: but for the elect's sake those days shall be shortened.

The "abomination of desolation, spoken of by Daniel the prophet" refers to the mid point of the 7-year Tribulation, when the Antichrist will enter into the rebuilt temple in Jerusalem and set himself up as the object of worship. Paul also refers to this event in 2 Thessalonians 2:4, where he prophesies that the Antichrist will *"sit as God in the temple of God, showing himself that he is God."*

Some claim that Daniel referred to the Syrian king named Antiochus Epiphanes, who desecrated the temple around BC 170 and triggered the Maccabean revolt. But here, Jesus, speaking nearly two centuries after the time of Antiochus, clearly refers to it as being still future.

The warning is very clear. "When you see the Antichrist go into the temple and set himself up there as God, then run for your life! Don't stop for anything. Don't waste time getting your belongings. Woe to those whose speed is hindered by pregnancy or small children. The window of escape will be extremely narrow and only those who act immediately will make it to safety. But some *will* make it because the Bible says they will and God will personally feed them for the remainder of that terrible time."

Verse 6 again:

"And the woman fled into the wilderness, where she hath a place prepared by God, that they should feed her there a thousand two hundred and threescore days."

Not very far over the border of Israel and Jordan lies Petra, the rose red city of the Nabateans. It was originally occupied by the Horites and was later conquered by the Edomites, the descendents of Esau. Then the Nabateans occupied it until it eventually fell to the Greeks and finally to the Romans. The Greeks gave it its name, "Petra". The Hebrews always knew it as Selah.

After the fall of Jerusalem, in AD 70, Petra was lost to the outside world. It seemed to disappear. Then, in 1812, Berkhart rediscovered it. Many believe that this city, hewn into the living rock and approached by a narrow, easily defended canyon, is the place that God has prepared for the remnant of Israel. No Scripture confirms this but tradition is very strong. Jordan, an Islamic country, which controls Petra, is at present on fairly good terms with Israel.

Daniel 11:41 says:

> *"He (the Antichrist) shall enter also into the glorious land (Israel), and many countries shall be overthrown: but **these shall escape out of his hand**, even Edom, and Moab, and the chief of the children of Ammon."*

It is significant that the city of Petra is situated in the ancient land of Edom. God has decreed that this area, together with Ammon, further north, will not fall to the Antichrist but will remain free.

Nobody knows for sure that Petra will be the place of refuge for Israelites during the Great Tribulation, but it is certain that God has prepared a place and He knows exactly where it is. When the time comes, He will reveal its location to the remnant and they will flee there to safety.

War in Heaven

Verse 7:

> *"And there was war in heaven: Michael and his angels fought against the dragon; and the dragon fought and his angels, 8 and prevailed not; neither was their place found any more in heaven. 9 And the great dragon was cast out, that old serpent, called the Devil, and Satan, which deceives the whole world: he was cast out on to the earth, and his angels were cast out with him."*

Michael is mentioned a number of times in the Scriptures. In Daniel 10:13 he is described as *"one of the chief princes"*. In Daniel 12:1, he is said to be *"the great prince, who stands for the children of your people"* (the Jews). In Jude 9, he is described as *"the archangel"* and here in Revelation 12 he is doing battle with the forces of evil.

I have often wondered how angels fight! What do they use for weapons? How do they know who has won? Do they have casualties? We shall not know these things until we reach Heaven. But the conflict is there. It is real enough and the stakes are very high.

It has been pointed out that the text of this passage reveals the fact that Michael, not the dragon, initiates the conflict. Michael declares war, indicating that God's time for the cleansing of the heavens had arrived and Michael moved in to carry it out. There was never any question as to the outcome.

The question might be asked, *"What is Satan doing in Heaven?"* The Scriptures confirm that at present he seems to have some kind of access to God. Job chapter 1 makes that clear. That passage reveals two other important things: 1. He is answerable to God for all his actions. 2. He can act only by God's permission. He is not a free agent.

In the Bible, "heaven" is frequently used in the plural (heavens). This refers to the atmospheric envelope surround the earth, not to the dwelling place of God.

Verse 10:

> *"And I heard a loud voice saying in heaven, now is come salvation, and strength, and the kingdom of our God, and the power of his Christ: for the accuser of our brethren is cast down, who accused them before our God day and night. 11 And they overcame him by the blood of the Lamb and by the word of their testimony; and they loved not their lives unto the death. 12 Therefore rejoice ye heavens, and you who dwell in them. Woe to the inhibiters of the earth and of the sea! For the devil has come down to you, having great wrath, because he knows he has but a short time."*

He has 1,260 days, to be precise!

This actually constitutes the "Third Woe". Anger, cruelty, violence and bloodshed are not characteristics of Heaven. They do not describe God but they do describe Satan. That is why conditions on the earth during the final stage of this age will be so dreadful. Satan will be unleashed and will vent his frustration and fury on the earth's inhabitants, especially on the people of Israel.

Verse 13:

> "And when the dragon saw that he was cast to the earth, he persecuted the woman, who brought forth the man child. 14 And to the woman were given two wings of a great eagle, that she might fly into the wilderness, into her place, where she is nourished for a time, times, and half a time, from the face of the serpent."

Modern expositors have explained "the wings of an eagle" quite glibly as a massive air-lift. They state this categorically, as if there were no doubt about it. In addition, American expositors have naturally claimed that it will be an American airlift!

However, there is nothing to base this claim upon except imagination. It is not clear that *any* nation will have forces stationed around the world during the Tribulation period, ready to play "Good Samaritan" to those who fall foul of the Antichrist. Goodness, even secular or political goodness, will be in short supply during that time. Certainly, it is possible that verse 14 describes an airlift of some kind but it doesn't have to do so.

When God brought Israel out of Egypt they didn't have airlifts, yet He said to them in Exodus 19:4:

> *"You have seen what I did to the Egyptians, and how **I bore you on eagles' wings**, and brought you unto myself."*

Verse 15:

> *"And the serpent cast out of his mouth water as a flood after the woman, that he might cause her to be carried away of the flood. 16 But the earth helped the woman, and the earth opened her*

> *mouth, and swallowed up the flood which the dragon cast out of his mouth."*

Once again, various theories have been offered to explain this paragraph. John makes no attempt to explain it; he merely reports what he saw. He saw a big dragon belching water. Then he saw the earth mopping up the water, so it would do no harm. Some say the water is real - a real flood; others, that it represents armies, still others, that it represents artillery. The truth is, nobody knows.

When the Egyptian armies came against Babylon, in Jeremiah's time, he wrote, *"Egypt rises like a flood and his waters are moved like the rivers, and he says, 'I will go up and will cover the earth. I will destroy the city and the inhabitants thereof."* (Jeremiah 46:8)

One thing is clear, namely that whatever force the flood represents, God intends to thwart it! He will protect His people from destruction. That should be sufficient.

Verse 17:

> *"And the dragon was angry with the woman, and went to make war with the remnant of her seed, who keep the commandments of God, and have the testimony of Jesus Christ."*

Frustrated by his failure to capture the remnant fleeing to the wilderness, the Antichrist will turn on those remaining in the land, and there will follow a holocaust more intense than anything seen in World War ll. The 144,000 witnesses will be among those who remain faithful and we are told that an innumerable multitude of others will pay the price for their faith during that time. However, their triumph will remain untainted.

These passages should not frighten us, but impress upon us that God is in control and that the greatest powers are totally ineffective in the face of His power.

CHAPTER 13

The Beast from the Sea

Verse 1:

> *"And I stood upon the sand of the sea, and saw a beast rise up out of the sea, having seven heads and ten horns, and upon his horns ten crowns, and upon his heads the names of blasphemy."*

This is what John saw in his vision but the symbol is not unique to this passage. In Revelation 12:3, John saw a dragon, and verse 9 of that chapter identified the dragon as Satan. That dragon also had seven heads and ten horns but it was not the same beast as we see in this chapter. The beast in chapter 13 is in harmony with (and is empowered by) Satan but it is obviously not Satan himself. This beast will appear upon the earth in the end times as Satan's masterpiece.

To human eyes, this beast will be a man. He will have a name and will be familiar to the people of his generation. However, to God he will be a "beast", due to his ferociousness and cruelty. Paul described him in 2 Thessalonians 2:8-9 as "that wicked one". He said:

> *"Then shall that wicked one be revealed, whom the Lord shall consume with the spirit of His mouth and shall destroy with the brightness of His coming; even him who is after the working of Satan, with all power and signs and lying wonders."*

So although the beast will not be Satan himself, there will certainly be a very obvious connection between the two. The similarity between the dragon in chapter 12:3 and the best in 13:1-2 is two obvious to be coincidental. Both have seven heads and both have ten horns, but whereas the dragon in chapter 12 has seven crowns upon his heads, the beast in chapter 13 has ten crowns upon his horns!

In the prophetic Scriptures, there is a significant difference between heads and horns. Heads belong to the bodies themselves and do not change. They contain the brain, the mind, the intelligence, and usually speak of the kings themselves. Horns, on the other hand, can be broken and removed. They speak of power and origin rather than of intelligence. Horns usually grow from something else, whereas heads come with the body and do not multiply.

In order to discover what these symbols mean we have to go back to the Old Testament. It is almost impossible to understand Revelation without a working knowledge of the book of Daniel.

Daniel 7:1

> *"In the first year of Belshazzar king of Babylon Daniel had a dream and visions of his head upon his bed: then he wrote the dream, and told the sum of the matters. 2 Daniel spoke and said, 'I saw in my vision by night, and, behold, the four winds of heaven strove upon the great sea. (Mediterranean). 3 And four great beasts came up from the sea, different from one another."*

We shall see that each of these beasts in Daniel's vision represented a world empire and earned the title of "beast" because of their savagery and total contempt for human dignity.

Verse 4 says that the first was like a lion, and had eagle's wings.
Verse 5 says that the second was like a bear, which raised itself on one side, and had three ribs in its mouth.
Verse 6 says that the third beast was like a leopard, with four wings on its back and four heads.

Then in verse 17 we are told what these creatures represented:

> "*These great beasts, which are four,* (we've just looked at three of them) *are four kings, which shall arise out of the earth.*"

It is well known that the kingdom ruling the world at the time of Daniel was Babylon and that it's emblem was a winged lion. The next kingdom to dominate the world was Medo-Persia, a confederacy of two nations. It conquered Babylon and spread its influence over a vast area of the world in the 5th and 4th centuries BC.

Of the two allies, Persia was stronger than Media and so the bear raised itself on one side (the Persian side). In rising to power, three nations that made up the old Babylonian empire (Babylon, Lydia and Egypt) were subdued. The three ribs in the bear's mouth symbolize them.

Persia's time of glory was also limited and eventually it fell to Greece, under the brilliant leadership of Alexander the Great. Greece is symbolized by the leopard, due to the speed with which its armies moved, in contrast to the slow and ponderous movements of the Persian armies. The four heads and four wings represent the four parts into which the kingdom was split upon the death of Alexander.

However, it is the fourth kingdom in Daniel's vision that interests us most in this study.

Daniel 7:7:

> "*After this I saw in the night visions, and behold a fourth beast, dreadful and terrible, and strong exceedingly; and it had great iron teeth: it devoured and broke in pieces, and stamped the residue with its feet: and it was diverse from all the beasts that were before it; and it had ten horns.*"

Elsewhere in the book of Daniel five kingdoms rather than four are listed ands the fourth kingdom is more clearly isolated than it is here in this verse. Here in verse 7, the fourth and fifth kingdoms merge and it is difficult to distinguish between them. The fourth beast, with great iron teeth, was the Roman Empire. It exceeded in strength and exercised a vice grip upon the world at the time of Jesus Christ.

In Biblical prophecy there is a mysterious connection between the old Roman Empire and the final future kingdom of the beast. Nobody knows for sure what that connection will be. Some think it will be a territorial connection, meaning that the revived Roman Empire will cover the same territory as old one did. Others think it will be a spiritual connection. We are not told precisely but whatever the connection is, the Bible pictures the kingdom of the Antichrist growing out of the Roman Empire, even though the Roman Empire itself disappeared centuries ago.

At the end of this present age, a ten-nation confederacy will be formed, which will produce the final world ruler. It is useless to attempt to identify the nations that will make up the confederacy. All we know is that a confederacy will be formed.

Daniel 7:8:

> *"I considered the horns, and, behold, there came up among them another little horn, before whom three of the first horns were plucked up by the roots: and, behold, in this horn were eyes like the eyes of man, and a mouth speaking great things."*

Now verses 20-22:

> *"And of the ten horns that were in his head, and of the other which came up, and before whom three fell; even of that horn that had eyes, and a mouth that spoke very great things, whose look was more stout than his fellows. 21 I beheld, and the same horn made war with the saints, and prevailed against them; 22 Until the Ancient of days came, and judgment was given to the saints of the most High; and the time came that the saints possessed the kingdom."*

Daniel had asked for an interpretation of the vision and the angel was about to tell him.

Verses 23-25:

> *"Thus he said, 'The fourth beast shall be the fourth kingdom upon earth, which shall be different from all kingdoms, and shall devour*

the whole earth, and shall tread it down, and break it in pieces
(The Roman Empire). *24 And the ten horns out of this kingdom
are ten kings that shall arise: and another shall rise after them;
and he shall be different from the first, and he shall subdue three
kings. 25 And he shall speak great words against the most High,
and shall wear out the saints of the most High, and think to change
times and laws: and they* (the saints of the most High) *shall be
given into his hand until a time and times and the dividing of time*
(3 1/2 years)."

So according to Daniel's prophecy, the end times will be marked by
a confederacy of ten nations, from which the final ruler will arise
and reign until Christ returns in glory to set up His kingdom.

Back now to Revelation 13.

Verse 1:

*"And I stood upon the sand of the sea, and saw a beast rise up out
of the sea, having seven heads and ten horns, and upon his horns
ten crowns, and upon his heads the name of blasphemy. 2 And the
beast which I saw was like unto a leopard, and his feet were as the
feet of a bear, and his mouth as the mouth of a lion: and the dragon
gave him his power, and his throne, and great authority."*

Here, in one beast, John saw a mixture of all those observed by
Daniel, except that the order was reversed. Daniel lived at the
time of the Babylonian domination (the winged lion) and from his
viewpoint he looked *forward,* first to the bear of Medo-Persia, then
to the leopard of Greece and finally to the terrible beast with iron
teeth, which was Rome. John, on the other hand, standing at the
far end of the succession, at the time of Rome, looked *back* from a
different viewpoint. He looked back through history, first, to the
leopard of Greece, then to the bear of Medo-Persia and finally back
to the winged lion of Babylon.

Verse 3:

"And I saw one of his heads as it were wounded to death; and
his deadly wound was healed: and all the world wondered
after the beast."

We are not told what the seven heads represent, and none of the theories I have read are very convincing. Some suggest that they represent seven of the emperors who ruled the old Roman Empire. Others suggest they represent a succession of rulers over the confederacy of the last days. Many claim that the head that was wounded to death represents the beast himself and that either he is assassinated in some kind of public fashion and comes back to life, or that he is a resurrected individual, such as Nero or Judas Iscariot.

The problem with that interpretation is that only God has the power to give life and such a resurrection would have to be His doing. God could do that but it seems unlikely.

Some scholars consider that the restored head represents the Roman Empire itself. The word translated "deadly" means that death will have occurred. It will have been a real death, and the emphasis seems to be on the miracle of revival, similar to that of the two witnesses in chapter 11.

For what it is worth, and despite the difficulties, I personally feel more comfortable with the scenario of a successful assassination of the beast followed by a public revival. It seems to be this miraculous revival of an obviously dead man that makes the world "wonder after" the beast. It establishes him in the world's eyes as an extraordinary person. And certainly he will be no ordinary man; he will be the devil incarnate, in much the same way as Jesus was God incarnate. Just as the magicians were able to duplicate some of the plagues that God sent through Moses, so he will be able to duplicate some of the acts of God on the earth.

In 2 Thessalonians, Paul calls these acts, *"lying wonders"* and it will be by means of these that the beast will deceive the nations.

Verses 4-8:

> *"And they worshipped the dragon which gave power unto the beast (Satan): and they worshipped the beast, saying, Who is like unto the beast? Who is able to make war with him? 5 And there was given to him a mouth speaking great things and blasphemies; and power was given unto him to continue forty and two months (3*

> *1/2 years). 6 And he opened his mouth in blasphemy against God, to blaspheme his name, and his tabernacle, and those who dwell in heaven. 7 And it was given unto him to make war with the saints, and to overcome them: and power was given him over all kindreds, and tongues, and nations. 8 And all who dwell upon the earth shall worship him, whose names are not written in the book of life of the Lamb slain from the foundation of the world."*

Notice that verse 7 states *"It was **given** to him to make war with the saints,"* and *"power was **given** him over all nations."* We might reasonably assume that Satan would give him that power but we should remember that Satan himself is limited to what ever God allows him to have. When Pilate said to Jesus, *"Do you not know that I have power to crucify you or power to release you,"* Jesus looked at him and said, *"You would have no power at all against me if it were not **given** to you from above."* Pilate was Satan's man but he did not gain his power to crucify Jesus from below; he was given it from above.

God will not relinquish authority during the Tribulation period. Were He to do so, the 144,000 witnesses would be the first to go and no flesh would be saved. God will still be in charge but He will give Satan just enough rope to hang himself.

Verse 9:

> "If any man has an ear, let him hear."

That is the final warning. After that comes disaster. The next verse is a little confused in the King James Bible. It should read something like this:

> *"If anyone is for captivity, into captivity he will go. If anyone is to be killed, with the sword he will be killed."*

The Beast from the Earth

Verse 11:

> "And I beheld another beast coming up out of the earth; and he had two horns like a lamb, and he spoke as a dragon."

The word *"another"*, is *"allos"*, which means *"another of the same kind"*. The second beast will be exactly the same in essence as the first beast, even though he will look different. Outwardly, he will appear to be lamblike but inwardly, he will be a dragon.

Verse 12:

> *"And he exercises all the power of the first beast before him, and causes the earth and them which dwell therein to worship the first beast, whose deadly wound was healed."*

The function of the second beast (who will be another man) will be religious in nature. He will be the worship leader during that part of the Tribulation period. His job will be to compel the earth's population to worship the antichrist. This is another reason to discount the theory that the first beast represents the Roman Empire. People don't worship empires; they worship a person. Therefore, the "death wound" will have to be personal also. This second beast is known as "The False Prophet". Thus, there will be a duo of final leaders, the Antichrist (called "The Beast") and the False Prophet.

We now have a satanic trinity imitating the Trinity of God. Satan impersonates the Father, the Beast impersonates the Son (complete with death and resurrection) and the False Prophet impersonates the Holy Spirit. Lucifer once said, *"I will be like the Most High"*, and here is his supreme effort to deliver on his vow.

Verse 13:

> *"And he does great wonders, so that he makes fire come down from heaven on the earth in the sight of men, 14 And deceives them that dwell on the earth by the means of those miracles which he has power to do in the sight of the beast; saying to them that dwell on the earth, that they should make an image to the beast, which had the wound by a sword, and lived. 15 And he had power to give life unto the image of the beast, that the image of the beast should both speak, and cause that as many as would not worship the image of the beast should be killed."*

138

We should be careful to not think of this in the same light as "The Wizard of Oz", who turned out to be nothing but a mechanical imposter. This individual is real, supernatural, terrifying. Worship will become a matter of life or death, just as it was in the days of Daniel, when Shadrach, Meshach and Abed-Nego were thrown into the fiery furnace for refusing to worship the image of the king.

Verses 16-18:

> *"And he causes all, small and great, rich and poor, free and bond, to receive a mark in their right hand, or in their foreheads: 17 that no one might buy or sell, save he who had the mark, or the name of the beast, or the number of his name. 18 Here is wisdom. Let him who has understanding count the number of the beast: for it is the number of a man; and his number is six hundred threescore and six."*

In the Scriptures, the number seven speaks of completion, or perfection. Number six is just one short of that. Three is the number of God. Thus a trinity of sixes (666) would be a fair symbol for Satan's attempt to be like the Most High. Verse 18 is particularly interesting. *"Let him who has understanding **count** the number of the Beast: for it is the number of a man."*

How could you "count" the number of a man's name, and in what way could 666 be his number? Theories abound, but Dr. Henry Morris has, perhaps, the most logical and believable solution. He points out that in the English language and in most European languages there would seem to be no answer to these questions. However, in the Greek language there might be an answer. In Greek, each letter also stands for a number. Numbers and letters are the same, which means that each letter has a numerical value. If you were to write down the numerical value of the letter that make up any Greek word or name and then add them together, you could "count" the number of that name or word.

For instance, the numerical value of the Greek word for Jesus comes to 888. Each of His other names (Lord, Christ, etc.) also add up to multiples of 8. The first Adam was made on the 6th day, whereas Jesus arose from the dead on the first day of the week, or the 8th day.

The warning seems to be that if some political leader should appear on the world scene, exercising great authority, the numerical number of his name, when transliterated into Greek, should be counted. If it adds up to 666, his identity is revealed.

It's interesting to note that Lyndon. B. Johnson added up to 666, but he wasn't the Antichrist because he didn't live that the right time!

Much has been written about the mark. Some have said it will be actual identifying mark, others, an electronic chip slipped under the skin. However, its actual identity is shrouded in mystery and nobody can say for sure what form it will take.

There are some important things we should bear in mind before deciding that some suspicious electronic wizardry is the mark of the beast. *First*, before the mark of the beast is imposed, the Beast will have to be installed as the world ruler. *Second*, the False Prophet will be heading up a world religion, which will be clearly understood by everyone. The world's population will clearly understand that it is supposed to worship the beast, on pain of death. *Third*, the worship of the beast will not be demanded until halfway through the Tribulation period, and *fourth*, by that time the church will have been gone for 3 1/2 years.

CHAPTER 14

The Lamb and the 144,000 on Mount Zion

Verses 1-5:

> *"And I looked, and, lo, a Lamb stood on the mount Zion, and with him a hundred forty and four thousand, having his Father's name written in their foreheads. 2 And I heard a voice from heaven, as the voice of many waters, and as the voice of a great thunder: and I heard the voice of harpers harping with their harps: 3 And they sung as it were a new song before the throne, and before the four living creatures, and the elders: and no man could learn that song but the hundred and forty and four thousand, who were redeemed from the earth. 4 These are they who were not defiled with women; for they are virgins. These are they which follow the Lamb wherever he goes. These were redeemed from among men, being the first fruits unto God and to the Lamb. 5 And in their mouth was found no guile: for they are without fault before the throne of God."*

Some claim that this scene takes place in Heaven and that this 144,000 is a different group from that in chapter 7. Others say the 144,000 are the same and that Christ is being presented at the beginning of His millennial reign. Both views have weaknesses. There is no reason to assume this scene is in Heaven. John does not say he was in Heaven; but that he heard a voice *from* Heaven. There is also no indication that this 144,000 is different from the first. Both groups are said to have been sealed by God and therefore protected from the wrath of the Beast. It seems logical to suppose that this scene is merely the flip side of what we have seen in chapters 12 and 13. In those chapters we were shown the evil, oppression and cruelty of Satan upon the earth. By contrast, this chapter reveals the purity, power and victory of those who trust in the Lamb during the same period.

The False Prophet has decreed that all who will not worship the Beast will die but God has decreed that the 144,000, whom He has sealed, will not be harmed. The lines are drawn. Here, the sealed saints of God are centered in Jerusalem (Mount Zion is one of the hills upon which Jerusalem is built), with the Lamb in their midst. They work by His commission and in His power, in defiance of the Beast, who is unable to touch them. They are in touch with Heaven. The music of Heaven rings in their ears; a song is in their hearts and on their lips, which is incomprehensible to those who populate the earth around them. It cannot be learned. It is the song of the Lamb and it springs from His presence in the midst of these people.

The words *"defiled by women"* (verse 4) have raised questions in many minds. They point out that marriage was instituted by God and used in the Scriptures as a picture of Christ's relationship with the church. They are right. There is nothing defiling before God about the union of a man and his wife.
Marriage is not in view here. The time pictured here in Revelation is unique. There never was and there never will be any other period in the history of the world to compare with it. These witnesses will not be ordinary people. They will be 100% committed to the Lord and they will not be free to have any other responsibilities to distract their attention. In any case, with evil flooding the world on an unprecedented scale, it would be difficult to find a godly wife. So the idea of defilement here has nothing to do with a legitimate relationship between a man and a woman. It has to do with the time in which they live.

Another characteristic of these witnesses is total honesty (no guile). They will live on a completely different wavelength from the rest of the inhabitants. They will remain true to the Lord in every way.

Verses 6-7:

> *"And I saw another angel fly in the midst of heaven, having the everlasting gospel to preach unto them that dwell on the earth, and to every nation, and kindred, and tongue, and people, 7 Saying with a loud voice, Fear God, and give glory to him; for the hour of his judgment is come: and worship him that made heaven, and earth, and the sea, and the fountains of waters."*

Notice the wording of verse 6. The angel had the everlasting Gospel to preach to those who dwell on the earth, to **every** nation and kindred and tongue and people. This will be the fulfillment of the Lord's statement in Matthew 24:14, where He said, *"This Gospel of the Kingdom shall be preached in all the world, for a witness to all nations, and then shall the end come."* And in the very next verse Jesus speaks of the *"Abomination of desolation, spoken of by Daniel the prophet"*, which marks the mid-point in the Tribulation period.

Some have used Matthew 24:14, to "prove" that the Gospel must be preached to all the world in this age before the Lord can return. But that is a mistake. Jesus places it clearly at the mid point of the Tribulation period, when the Antichrist sets himself up in the temple and demands worship. It does not apply to the present age at all. The Lord could return at any time. We do not delay him; He is not waiting for us to do anything. The time of His coming is entirely decided by Him. However, during the second half of the Tribulation, the Gospel of the Kingdom will be preached to the entire world and then the "end" (the end of the age) will come.

Much of the material found in the remainder of this chapter is expanded more fully in later passages. We shall therefore identify the general themes here but save a deeper explanation for later chapters. Four themes are introduced, setting the scene for the later exposition.

The Mystery of Babylon

Verse 8:

> "And there followed another angel, saying, Babylon is fallen, is fallen, that great city, because she made all nations drink of the wine of the wrath of her fornication.

This subject is explained in chapters 17 and 18. Suffice it to say at this point that most, if not all, of the pagan systems of idolatry can be traced back to Genesis 10 and 11, when Nimrod, the grandson of Noah, founded the city of Babylon (ancient Babel). There, the mystery religions of the world began, and from there they spread across the world.

At present, the city of Babylon does not exist as a center of world commerce. Saddam Hussein did his best to rebuild it, but whether or not it will ever become the great end-time center of trade and power described in Revelation 17 and 18, remains to be seen. The *influence* of ancient Babylon exists today and it will come to a head during the Tribulation period, when it will be crushed forever.

In Isaiah 21:9, the prophet said much the same thing. He said,

> *"Babylon is fallen, is fallen; and all the graven images of her gods he hath broken unto the ground."*

Idolatry is considered by God to be the ultimate unfaithfulness. Here it is called "fornication" because the sanctity of spiritual betrothal to God is violated by it. Here, in Revelation 14:8, Babylon is said to have fallen *"because she made all nations drink of the wine of her fornication"*. Her worldwide influence, drawing men away from God, will terminate in her utter destruction.

The Eternal Punishment of the Lost

Verses 9-11:
> *"And the third angel followed them, saying with a loud voice, If any man worship the beast and his image, and receive his mark in his forehead, or in his hand, 10 The same shall drink of the wine of the wrath of God, which is poured out without mixture into the cup of his indignation; and he shall be tormented with fire and brimstone in the presence of the holy angels, and in the presence of the Lamb: 11 And the smoke of their torment ascends up for ever and ever: and they have no rest day nor night, who worship the beast and his image, and whosoever receives the mark of his name."*

Here, eternal punishment is set against sins peculiar to men and women during the Tribulation period. These sins include worshipping the beast and his image and receiving his mark on their person. These sins can be committed in principle during the present age but only during the Tribulation will people be able to commit them in fact. Only then will there be an image to worship or a physical mark to receive.

However, the context of the passage makes it clear that there will be an element of choice offered to the people during the Tribulation period. Matthew 24 confirms that the Gospel will be preached during that period and in Revelation 7 a command was issued from Heaven by an angel, to the effect that the judgments should not begin until 12,000 from each of the twelve tribes of Israel have been sealed by God. At the beginning of this chapter they were brought before us again, in their relationship with the Lamb. We saw that there was a strong suggestion that their mission was to preach to every nation, kindred, tongue and people, saying *'Fear God, give glory to Him, for the hour of His judgment has come. And worship Him, who made Heaven and earth and the sea and the fountains of waters.'*

It does not actually say that the 144,000 will do the preaching. It says that an angel flew in the midst of Heaven, *"having the everlasting Gospel, which was **to be preached** to those who dwell on the earth."* Obviously, somebody has to do the preaching and we know that angels don't preach to men. Thus, the only people who will be able to do the preaching during that time will be the 144,000, specifically chosen and sealed by God for that purpose.

As we have seen, in Matthew 24, Jesus describes events during the Tribulation. Not only does He say that the Gospel will be preached throughout the world during that time, but in verse 13 He promises, *"He who endures to the end* (the end of the Tribulation) *shall be saved"*

The demand of the False Prophet, for all people to worship the beast and receive his mark, will come at the beginning of the final 3 1/2 years of the Tribulation. That is when the population will have to decide whether to worship the beast or not; whether to receive his mark or not; but by that time they will have heard the Word of God.

This tells us that God will judge responsible individuals when He returns in glory. He will give them fair warning. They will have heard the Gospel and will have accepted or rejected what they heard. However, verses 10 and 11 make it clear that rejection of the message and acceptance of the mark of the beast will result in torment, day and night, with no rest, for ever! That is not a pleasant thought but it is a clear reality.

Some people like to explain away the idea of hell. I remember a chaplain in the army, who told us that hell is not a real place, that it exists only in people's minds, and that God is too loving to send anyone to a literal hell. He told us that all men would make it to Heaven by one road or another. Well, that took quite a lot of weight off our minds because we all had a sneaking suspicion that if hell really did exist we were probably heading toward it! Unfortunately, the chaplain's doctrine didn't agree with what the Bible teaches. In the New Testament, the Lord Jesus personally made eleven out of twelve references to hell and twelve out of nineteen references to hell fire. He used similar expressions more frequently than any other person in the New Testament and He always spoke of hell as a reality.

If hell were not a reality, why did Jesus come and die on the cross? He died to save us from going there and the men and women who receive the mark of the beast during the Tribulation will have consciously rejected that truth. Their doom will therefore be sealed.

The same principle holds true today. The message is available to all who desire it but thousands reject or ignore it, and consequently they face exactly the same doom as is described here.

The Eternal Reward of the Saved

Verses 12-13:

> *"Here is the patience of the saints: here are they that keep the commandments of God, and the faith of Jesus. 13 And I heard a voice from heaven saying unto me,' Write: Blessed are the dead who die in the Lord from henceforth: Yea, saith the Spirit that they may rest from their labors; and their works follow them."*

With the same certainty that judgment will come to those who reject the message of Christ, reward is equally certain to those who receive it. *"Patience"* means *"endurance"*. But notice how the endurance is demonstrated (the last part of verse 12): by obedience and faith. That is how endurance is always demonstrated. Jesus said, *"If you love me, **keep my commandments** (obedience)"* and John wrote, *"This is the victory that overcomes the world, even our **faith**."* Faith makes obedience possible and obedience makes faith effective. Separate them and you will have failure. Obedience without faith is legalism and faith without obedience is audacity.

At the end of verse 13 we find a promise, namely, rest and riches in Heaven. The earthly "works" of faith show up in Heaven as "treasure". Notice the general formula here: Receiving the mark of the beast will result in physical life but spiritual death. Refusing the mark of the beast will result in spiritual life but physical death.

In Matthew 16:25-26 Jesus said,

> *"For whosoever will save his life shall lose it: and whosoever will lose his life for my sake shall find it. 26 For what is a man profited, if he shall gain the whole world, and lose his own soul? Or what shall a man give in exchange for his soul?"*

The Final Battle of This Age

Verse 14-20:

> *"And I looked, and behold a white cloud, and upon the cloud one sat like the Son of man, having on his head a golden crown, and in his hand a sharp sickle. 15 And another angel came out of the temple, crying with a loud voice to him who sat on the cloud, Thrust in your sickle, and reap: for the time has come for you to reap; for the harvest of the earth is ripe. 16 And he who sat on the cloud thrust in his sickle on the earth; and the earth was reaped. 17 And another angel came out of the temple which is in heaven, he also having a sharp sickle. 18 And another angel came out from the altar, who had power over fire; and cried with a loud cry to he who had the sharp sickle, saying, Thrust in your sharp sickle, and gather the clusters of the vine of the earth; for her grapes are fully ripe. 19 And the angel thrust in his sickle into the earth, and gathered the*

> *vine of the earth, and cast it into the great winepress of the wrath of God. 20 And the winepress was trodden outside the city, and blood came out of the winepress, even to the horses' bridles, by the space of a thousand and six hundred furlongs."*

Now this event will also be treated much more fully in later chapters but it is introduced here. The scene is the land of Israel and time is the final showdown between the forces of God and the forces of the beast. The nations of the world will have their armies assembled at this time, for reasons we shall attempt to trace later. At that time, Christ will suddenly return in power and great glory.

The word translated *"ripe"* in verse 15 means *"withered"* or *"overripe"*. The same word is used in Mark 3:1, where a man with a withered arm is described. The words *"fully ripe"* in verse 18 describe grapes bursting with juice and at the pinnacle of their prime. It is the time of harvest, spoken of by Jesus in Matthew 13:38-42, where He said,

> *"The field is the world; the good seed are the children of the kingdom; but the tares are the children of the wicked one. 39 The enemy who sowed them is the devil; the harvest is the end of the world; and the reapers are the angels. 40 As therefore the tares are gathered and burned in the fire; so shall it be in the end of this age. 41 The Son of man shall send forth his angels, and they shall gather out of his kingdom all things that offend, and those who do iniquity; 42 And shall cast them into a furnace of fire: there shall be wailing and gnashing of teeth."*

At the end of verse 20 we see the battle's scope. The entire land of Israel will be involved. A furlong is 220 yards, so 1,600 furlongs is roughly 200 miles. That is longer than the nation of Israel from the north of Dan to beyond its southern border. Actually, Edom and Bozrah are both named in connection with this event and they both lie within present-day Jordan. In Isaiah 63:1-4 the prophet asks two questions and receives two answers from God.

The first question is, *"Who is this who comes from Edom with dyed garments from Bozrah, He who is glorious in His apparel, traveling in the greatness of His strength?"* The answer is, *"I who speak in righteousness, mighty to save."*

The second question is, *"Why are your garments red, your appearance like one who treads in the wine vat?"* The answer is, *"I have trodden the winepress alone and of the people there was none with me. I will tread them in my anger and trample them in my fury, and their blood shall be sprinkled upon my garments, and I will stain all my raiment; for the day of vengeance is in my heart and the year of my redeemed has come."*

Obviously it is Christ who is speaking here. He is coming from Bozrah, an ancient city in Jordan.

Joel speaks of the same event in his prophecy (3:11-13). He writes:

> *"Assemble yourselves, and come, all ye heathen, and gather yourselves together round about: thither cause thy mighty ones to come down, O LORD. 12 Let the heathen be wakened, and come up to the valley of Jehoshaphat: for there will I sit to judge all the heathen round about. 13 Put in the sickle, for the harvest is ripe: come, get you down; for the press is full, the fats overflow; for their wickedness is great."*

There is no known valley that was ever called "Jehoshaphat" but the name means *"God has judged"*. Joel probably chose this name to describe the place where God will judge those who range themselves against Him.

In Ezekiel 38:16, the prophet wrote:
> *"And you shall come up against my people of Israel as a cloud to cover the land; it shall be in the latter days, and I will bring you against my land, that the heathen may know me, when I shall be sanctified in thee, O Gog, before their eyes."*

Finally, in Revelation 16:16 we read,

> *"And he gathered them together into a place called in the Hebrew tongue Armageddon."*

That is where we get the phrase, "The battle of Armageddon". It is actually a campaign, rather than a battle. Armageddon describes the wide valley of Jezreel, on which so many battles have been fought in history. Many nations have used this valley as an invasion route and have been fought there. King Josiah was killed there. Today it is a fertile valley, producing much of the food for the nation.

However, although the valley of Jezreel is more famous than other sites, and although it gives its name to the final campaign, it is actually only a small portion of the whole. Certainly it will be full of soldiers and great bloodshed will take place there, but the whole land will be involved and Jerusalem will be in the middle of it.

Even now we see the pieces being moved into place. The United Nations and the European Community are strongly biased against Israel. Millions of Arabs have sworn to remove her from the map. She is strong and able to fight but the odds against her are so great that without God's intervention she would be unable to withstand a united attack such as is described here.

CHAPTER 15

The Seven Last Plagues

Verse 1:

> *"And I saw another sign in heaven, great and marvelous: seven angels having the seven last plagues; for in them is filled up the wrath of God."*

The words *"filled up"* in the Authorized Version mean, *"finished"* or *"completed"*. This was to be the final set of judgments before the coming of Christ in glory. In them, the anger of God will be completed.

This is a somewhat relative term because the judgments do not actually end with these plagues. There is still the Great White Throne judgment to come, and after that the Lake of Fire. But these judgments will complete God's wrath upon the nations living on the earth.

We should remember that the movement of the book of Revelation is ordered by three series of divine judgments upon the earth. First we saw seven **seals**, broken one by one by the Lord Jesus in chapter 6:1-17 and 8:1. Second, we saw the seven **trumpets**, which emerged from the seventh seal, in chapters 8:1 - 9:21 and 11:15-19. These included three **woes**, all of which were judgments of exceptional severity. Now, after several intervening scenes, the final seven judgments are about to fall, completing God's anger upon a hostile world.

Verse 2:

> *"And I saw as it were a sea of glass mingled with fire: and them that had gotten the victory over the beast, and over his image, and over his mark, and over the number of his name, stand on the sea of glass, having the harps of God."*

One commentator suggested that the sea of glass was intended to reflect the glory of God. We don't know. In chapter 4:6, we saw a similar sea of glass before the throne, described as being clear like crystal, and it was located immediately before the throne of God.

In Exodus 30:17-21, a laver, containing water, was placed between the altar and the Holy Place, where the priests were to wash themselves when going in to service. The altar spoke of the cross of Christ because it was there that the sacrifice was offered and the Holy Place spoke of God's presence. The significance of the laver was that of cleansing.

In 1 Kings 7, where Solomon's temple is described, and everything in it is very much larger than their counterparts in the tabernacle, the laver is described as a *"sea"*. Here, the actual throne in Heaven is in view and the sea of glass before it suggests the holiness, truth and purity of God. It also speaks of His forgiveness and cleansing. Because the sea of glass is clear like crystal, nothing is covered up by it.

Here, it is said to be "mingled with fire", which seems to be the same as justice of God proceeding from His holiness. God is perfect truth and there can be no truth without justice. Denying justice obscures the truth and perverts the principles of righteousness. Because God is perfect righteousness and absolute truth, justice must prevail in His kingdom.

Standing on the sea, John saw those who had prevailed over the beast, who had refused to worship his image or receive his mark. Only the NIV says they were *"beside"* the sea. All other translations agree that it should be *"on"* the sea.

Obviously, the group standing on the sea was the tribulation saints. They had evidently paid for their faith by giving their lives and it is significant that their death is synonymous with their victory. Men view death as defeat but God looks upon it as victory, a total escape from the control of one's enemies.

Jesus said in Matthew 10:29 *"Do not fear those who can kill the body but are unable to kill the soul. Rather, fear Him who is able to destroy both soul and body in hell."* Man has no power over the saved soul. The soul of the believer is safe and secure in the hands of the Savior. *"My sheep hear my voice, and I know them, and they follow me. And I give to them eternal life, and they shall never perish; neither shall any man pluck them out of my hand."* (John 10:27-28)

These people had perished as far as the world was concerned, but they were alive in God's presence. And when the time comes for those who killed them to stand trial before the Lord, these victims will be there, alive and well, to give evidence against them. Men can give us a rough time. They can even take our lives from us, but in doing so they actually project us into a place of blessing, far beyond human ability to grasp.

Verse 3:

> *"And they sang the song of Moses the servant of God, and the song of the Lamb, saying, 'Great and marvelous are thy works, Lord God Almighty; just and true are thy ways, thou King of saints.'"*

What was the *"song of Moses"*? Some say the song came from Exodus 15:1-2, but that seems to speak of Israel's victory over Pharaoh at the time of the Exodus.
Others say it came from Deuteronomy 32, which recites the history of Israel in its dealings with God. In Deuteronomy 31:19 God introduces the song and the reason for writing it.-

> *"'Now therefore write this song for you, and teach it the children of Israel: put it in their mouths, that this song may be a witness for me against the children of Israel. For when I have brought them into the land which I swore to their fathers, that flows with milk and honey; and they have eaten and filled themselves, and grown fat; then will they turn to other gods, and serve them, and provoke*

> *me, and break my covenant. 21 And it shall come to pass, when many evils and troubles have befallen them that this song shall testify against them as a witness; for it shall not be forgotten out of the mouths of their seed: for I know their imagination which they go about, even now, before I have brought them into the land which I promised.' 22 Moses therefore wrote this song the same day, and taught it the children of Israel."*

Verse 29 (Moses speaking now):

> *"'For I know that after my death you will utterly corrupt yourselves, and turn aside from the way which I have commanded you; and evil will befall you in the latter days; because you will do evil in the sight of the LORD, to provoke him to anger through the work of your hands'. 30 And Moses spoke in the ears of all the congregation of Israel the words of this song, until they were ended."*

That prophecy certainly came true. The nation did turn to idols, it did rebel against God, it has suffered more than any other nation in the history of man and it will face the terrible events during the tribulation period in the end times.

If this is the song that will be sung of that occasion (and we have no way of knowing that it is), these singers will have come out of the latter evil about which Moses spoke.

However, the song itself, which begins in chapter 32, does contain some wonderful truths. For instance, verse 4 reads:

> *"He is the Rock, his work is perfect: for all his ways are judgment: a God of truth and without iniquity, just and right is he."*

And the song closes at the end of that chapter with eventual victory promised for Israel.

> *"Rejoice, O ye nations, with his people: for he will avenge the blood of his servants, and will render vengeance to his adversaries, and will be merciful unto his land, and to his people."*

In spite of Israel's rebellion, God was planning to be merciful to them in the end.

We have no way of knowing which song John heard the Tribulation saints sing, but it is significant that it was a song *of Moses*. Moses represented the Law and these were saved people. Moses represented Israel in her covenant relationship with God. The choice seems to speak of the Jewish nature of the Tribulation period.

It was prophesied by both Daniel and Jeremiah to be a time of *"Jacob's trouble"*, Jacob being the founding member of the nation. Gentiles would suffer also but Israel would be at the center of the conflict.

We should not overlook the fact that the Tribulation martyrs sang the *"song of the Lamb"* also.

Verse 4:

> *"Who shall not fear thee, O Lord, and glorify thy name? For thou only art holy: for all nations shall come and worship before thee; for thy judgments are made manifest."*

The Lord's holiness is absolute. That's what makes Him so terrible. Despite the rebellion of mankind through the ages, there will come a day when all nations will bow before Him and all nations will give Him the glory due His name. Paul said,

> *"At the name of Jesus every knee shall bow, of things in heaven, and things on earth, and things under the earth; 11 and every tongue shall confess that Jesus Christ is Lord, to the glory of God the Father."* (Philippians 2:10-11)

Fear of God is in short supply today, but one day it will return in full measure, when the nations see Him face to face.

Preparation for the Bowl Judgments

Verses 5-7:

> *"And after that I looked, and, behold, the temple of the tabernacle of the testimony in heaven was opened: 6 And the seven angels came out of the temple, having the seven plagues, clothed in pure white linen, and having their breasts girded with golden girdles. 7 And one*

155

> *of the four living creatures gave to the seven angels seven golden*
> *bowls full of the wrath of God, who lives for ever and ever."*

Can you imagine what it would be like to be given a bowl to carry filled with the wrath of the Everlasting God? Talk about hazardous material! The environmentalists haven't seen anything yet!

The "Tabernacle of the Testimony" was the Holy of Holies, the tent enfolding the Testimony. The Testimony was the Law of Moses, written by the hand of God on the tables of stone. These were kept inside the Ark of the Covenant, which, in turn, stood within the Holy of Holies, called here "the Temple". It was the place where God dwelt.

What happened here was that the four angels, who we first met in chapter 1, were called into God's presence Then John saw them come out of the Holy of Holies again, and as they did so, one of the four living creatures (seraphim) gave each of them a golden bowl filled with God's wrath.

Verse 8

> *"And the temple was filled with smoke from the glory of God, and*
> *from his power; and no man was able to enter into the temple, until*
> *the seven plagues of the seven angels were fulfilled."*

When the Creator of the entire universe is angry, it is terrible indeed!

CHAPTER 16

THE BOWL JUDGMENTS

Verse 1:

> *"And I heard a great voice out of the temple saying to the seven angels, Go your ways, and pour out the vials of the wrath of God upon the earth."*

We are not told whose voice John heard, but since the temple had been filled with smoke and nobody was able to enter it, we must assume that the voice was the voice of God Himself. If so, this was a terrible sentence directly from the throne of the universe upon mankind.

Gold, in the Scriptures, frequently speaks of divinity, especially in connection with the furniture and vessels of the sanctuary, which is the setting here. These judgments are divine. They are directly from God upon a race that has turned away from Him.

The First Bowl Judgment

Verse 2:

> *"And the first went, and poured out his vial upon the earth; and there fell a noisome and grievous sore upon the men who had the mark of the beast, and upon those who worshipped his image."*

The NIV says that they were *"ugly and painful sores."* The NASB says they were *"loathsome and malignant"* and the New King James describes them as *"foul and loathsome"*. Thus the first plague is a personal, physical affliction upon the bodies of those who are the object of God's wrath. Naturally, our thoughts go back to Moses and Aaron in Egypt, where the sixth plague was a similar affliction, but there it is described as *"festering boils"*.

The Second Bowl Judgment

Verse 3:

> *"And the second angel poured out his vial upon the sea; and it became as the blood of a dead man: and every living soul died in the sea."*

All translations other than the Authorized Version place the word *"as"* before *"dead man"* rather than before *"blood"*. This is important because *"as blood"* would mean that it was like blood but was actually something else, whereas *"blood as of a dead man"* would mean that it was real blood of a particular nature.

The evidence seems to point to the second rendering, namely, that it was real blood, like that of a dead man. When a man dies, his lungs cease to provide oxygen to the bloodstream and so the blood undergoes a change. It becomes a dark, purplish color. It also coagulates and becomes thick and sluggish. Here, the horror of the second plague can hardly be imagined. The sea will change from its clear green brightness into a thick, sluggish, stinking ooze, in which nothing can live. Floating on the surface will be millions of decomposing fish and aquatic animals. After the first Trumpet was sounded, in chapter 8, a third of sea was turned into blood and a third of the life in it died. Here, the curse and resulting death is universal and complete.

The Third Bowl Judgment

Verse 4-7:

> *"And the third angel poured out his vial upon the rivers and fountains of waters; and they became blood. 5 And I heard the*

angel of the waters say, Thou art righteous, O Lord, who is, and was, and shall be, because thou hast judged thus. 6 For they have shed the blood of saints and prophets, and you have given them blood to drink; for they are worthy. 7 And I heard another out of the altar say, Even so, Lord God Almighty, true and righteous are your judgments."

This was similar to the first plague in Egypt, where *"all the waters that were in the river were turned to blood and the fish in the river died and the river stank. And the Egyptians could not drink of the water of the river, and there was blood throughout the land of Egypt."*

How long people could survive with only blood to drink is open to question. They would have to be very thirsty indeed to drink it at all. One thing is stressed. The third plague is a "suitable judgment" upon those who will have shed the blood of God's people like water.

The Fourth Bowl Judgment

Verses 8-9:

"And the fourth angel poured out his vial upon the sun; and power was given unto him to scorch men with fire. 9 And men were scorched with great heat, and blasphemed the name of God, who has power over these plagues: and they repented not to give him glory."

The sun is essential to life on earth. Without it there would be almost total darkness, frigid temperatures and no seasons. It would easy enough for God to heat up the sun, or jog the earth a little nearer in its orbit, or drawer aside the protective atmospheric canopy for a while. The climate would immediately change. Whatever means God uses, the effect is clear; searing heat, which would affect every phase of life on the earth.

As Malachi wrote in Malachi 4:1:

"For, behold, the day comes that shall burn as an oven; and all the proud, yes, and all that do wickedly, shall be stubble: and the day

> *that comes shall burn them up, saith the LORD of hosts, that it*
> *shall leave them neither root nor branch."*

That may refer to the final destruction of the earth, but it could also indicate Revelation 16:8-9. Dr. Henry Morris points out that such a universal heat would almost certainly melt the great ice caps in the Arctic and Antarctic. These two areas have sufficient ice stored in them to raise the level of the oceans some two hundred feet. Obviously this could cause untold damage and loss of life around the world.

Yet, despite the obvious source of all this misery, the earth's population will not repent. They will be blinded to the fact that the calamities are the result of their own sin. Instead of repenting and crying out for mercy, they will blaspheme God.

The Fifth Bowl Judgment

Verses 10-11:

> *"And the fifth angel poured out his vial upon the seat of the beast;*
> *and his kingdom was full of darkness; and they gnawed their*
> *tongues for pain, 11 And blasphemed the God of heaven because of*
> *their pains and their sores, and repented not of their deeds."*

"The seat of the beast" does not refer to the rear portion of the beast's anatomy. It refers to his throne. Until now, the plagues have been general in nature. They seem to have fallen upon the people in general. Possibly the beast and his lieutenants will have escaped the worst of the effects. However, this plague is personal. It falls specifically on the throne room, on the seat of the beast's government, and although his whole kingdom is affected, it singles him out personally. This paragraph gives the impression that the plagues will be, at least to a certain extent, concurrent. Darkness does not produce pain, and the sores belonged to the first plague, so apparently these judgments are accumulative, each adding to those before it.

Despite all these horrors, the population still refuses to acknowledge God. Instead, they will curse Him in their pain.

The Sixth Bowl Judgment

Verse 12:

> *"And the sixth angel poured out his vial upon the great river Euphrates; and the water thereof was dried up, that the way of the kings of the east might be prepared."*

The river Euphrates rises in the mountains of Ararat, in Eastern Turkey, and flows south through Iraq, into the Persian Gulf. On its east side is first, Iran (Persia) and beyond that the teeming populations of China, India and Burma. In John's day, the Euphrates formed the eastern boundary of the Roman Empire. It also marked the eastern boundary of the land God promised to Abraham in Genesis 15:18. *"From the river of Egypt to the great river, Euphrates"* belongs to Israel.

Just as God dried up the Jordan in the days of Joshua, and parted the Red Sea under the rod of Moses, so He will one day dry up the great river Euphrates to facilitate the movement of vast armies from the east on their way to Israel. It will be a journey from which none of them will return.

Verse 13:

> *"And I saw three unclean spirits like frogs come out of the mouth of the dragon, and out of the mouth of the beast, and out of the mouth of the false prophet. 14 For they are the spirits of demons, working miracles, which go forth unto the kings of the earth and of the whole world, to gather them to the battle of that great day of God Almighty."*

The kings of the east will not mobilize on their own volition. They will be drawn, lured, to their doom by demonic intrigue.

John saw the demons as frog-like creatures. They were not frogs but looked to him a bit like frogs and they issued one each, from the dragon (Satan), from the beast (the Antichrist) and from the False Prophet, for the specific purpose of luring the armies of the world to the land of Israel.

Armageddon

Verse 15:

> *"Behold, I come as a thief. Blessed is he who watches, and keeps his garments, lest he walk naked, and they see his shame. 16 And he gathered them together into a place called in the Hebrew tongue Armageddon."*

The word "battle" in verse 14 does not mean a single action, such as the battle of Waterloo or the battle of Gettysburg. It means a whole campaign. The NASB translates it correctly as "war". It is commonly referred to as the "battle of Armageddon" but it will take place over a period of time and will involve a number of engagements.

The end is now in sight. The nations are moving their armies to the appointed place, covering the entire land of Israel but in particular the Plain of Jezreel. At this point they don't realize the danger they are in.

"Armageddon" takes its name from Megiddo, an ancient city-state located on the plain of Jezreel. Today, Megiddo is a "tell" (a hill or mound) that rises abruptly from the plain. Excavations there have revealed remains of many civilizations, one on top of the other, dating back to the earliest times. When Jesus was growing up in Nazareth, He was familiar with this future battleground because Nazareth is located on a hillside overlooking its eastern border and commanding panoramic views of the plain. Today, the plain of Jezreel is a fertile agricultural area, given over to intensive farming.

The Seventh Bowl Judgment

Verse 17:

> *"And the seventh angel poured out his vial into the air; and there came a great voice out of the temple of heaven, from the throne, saying, It is done. 18 And there were voices, and thunders, and lightnings; and there was a great earthquake, such as was not since men were upon the earth, so mighty an earthquake, and so great."*

The final bowl judgment brings about a cataclysmic disruption of nature. Electric storms, affecting the entire globe will be triggered and an earthquake of unprecedented violence will erupt.

The eruption beneath the Indian Ocean in December 2004 created unimaginable damage and loss of life to the surrounding nations but it will pale in comparison with this final earthquake. John says it will be more violent than any in recorded history. The resulting devastation will be phenomenal and although loss of life is not mentioned in the text, its scope will obviously be beyond estimate. Huge tsunamis will engulf coastal areas on every shore and the chaos and disruption caused to inland cities will be equally devastating.

God Himself said, *"It is done"*. What was done? The judgment of God upon a sinful world was complete. His words are reminiscent of Jesus' cry from the cross: *"It is finished"*. Matthew tells us that a great earthquake also followed the Lord's pronouncement. We usually think of it from our viewpoint and say that His words signified that the atonement was completed. It was, of course, but the atonement was complete only when God's judgment upon sin had been satisfied.

Verse 19:

> *"And the great city was divided into three parts, and the cities of the nations fell: and great Babylon came in remembrance before God, to give to her the cup of the wine of the fierceness of his wrath. 20 And every island fled away, and the mountains were not found. 21 And there fell upon men a great hail out of heaven, every stone about the weight of a talent: and men blasphemed God because of the plague of the hail; for the plague thereof was exceeding great."*

The city is described but not named. Therefore all kinds of theories abound concerning its identity. Some say it is Jerusalem, others say it is Rome; still others say it is Babylon, but nobody knows. Its description (*"great city"* - which Jerusalem is not), followed immediately by a reference to Babylon, seems to support the belief that it may be the city of Babylon, but nobody knows for certain.

Whichever it is, it will be split into three parts by an earthquake, unprecedented in history. Cities throughout the world will fall; islands will move out of their places, mountains will disappear. This will be "the big one" that everyone talks about.

A talent is the equivalent to more than a hundred pounds in our measurement, so the hail that falls during this event will be lethal. Yet men will still not repent. Instead, they will blaspheme God and curse Him fro bringing such catastrophes upon the earth.

We must remember that true repentance is a gift from God. It is not something we do at will. It is a work of grace. In Acts 5:31 Peter spoke of repentance as something God will *give* to Israel. And in Acts 11:18, when Peter told the assembly in Jerusalem about the conversion of Cornelius, they recognized that God had *granted* repentance to the Gentiles. These people in Revelation 16 had evidently had their opportunity and now it was too late. They had finally crossed the line and now the ability to repent was denied them.

The Roman governor, Felix, heard Paul preach in Caesarea and *"as he reasoned of righteousness, and temperance and judgment to come, Felix trembled and answered, 'Go your way for this time. When I have a convenient season I will call for you.'"* But Felix was sent elsewhere by his Roman masters and the "convenient season" apparently never came.

King Agrippa also heard Paul preach. He said, *'Almost you persuade me to be a Christian'"* "Almost" is not at all. "Almost" carries the sound of thunder with it and the smell of brimstone. *"I almost caught the train"* means *"I missed it"*! "Almost" indicates an understanding but an unwilling heart.

CHAPTER 17

The Doom of Babylon

There is a remarkable order to everything God does. The material universe is controlled by laws, so complex and so exquisitely organized that nobody taking the effort to investigate could fail to acknowledge a supreme intelligence behind them. Those who claim that the universe evolved randomly, or that it happened by chance, should not be surprised if their credibility is questioned.

Just as this order is present in the realm of nature, so it is present also in the Scriptures because both came from the same hand. As in the physical realm, this structure is not always immediately noticeable but it is there, nonetheless.

As an example, the seven bowl (vial) judgments, which we examined in the previous chapter, fall into five groups, each consisting of cause and effect. The third judgment is characterized by things *heard* and the sixth judgment is characterized by things *seen*. The first and second judgments form a pair, as do the fourth and fifth, and like the seventh, they consist of the same two parts, namely cause and effect.

By way of explanation, the first bowl (16:2) produces sores on the bodies of men. The second (16:3) turns the sea into blood. They form a pair, not by subject but by structure. The fourth bowl (16:8) produces searing heart and the fifth (16:10) produces darkness, making another pair by structure.

The third and sixth judgments each fall into three parts and carry extra characteristics. When the third bowl (16:4-7) is poured out, John hears voices coming from heaven, and when the sixth is delivered (16:12-16) John sees demonic activity emanating from the two beasts and the dragon. They also are a structural pair.

Finally, with the seventh bowl (16:17-21) Babylon is brought into view in preparation for chapters 17 and 18. Some have discerned no order in the book of Revelation but in fact it has a very well defined order.
It builds on the ancient prophecies of the Old Testament, particularly those given to Daniel during the Babylonian captivity in the 5th century BC.

One theme in particular, which runs through the body of Scripture relating to the end times, is the presence of a hideous beast, having seven heads and ten horns. Each time he comes into view, further details are added to his description but there can be no mistaking his distinctive characteristics.

We see him first in Daniel chapter 7, where he is described as "dreadful and terrible and exceedingly strong". No further details are given there, except that he had ten horns, which represent a confederacy of ten nations, from which a little horn will emerge, who will speak great things, persecute the saints and finally be destroyed by "The Ancient of Days", who is obviously God Himself.

Later in Daniel 7, the beast is identified as the last world kingdom and the little horn as the final ruler of that kingdom. He will exercise absolute control over the realm of men for three and a half years at the end of this age.

The next reference to the beast comes in Revelation 12:3, where he is described as "a great red dragon". This time, seven heads are added to the seven horns and seven crowns upon those heads. This time the beast is identified as Satan himself. That must not mislead us. The whole setup at the end of the age will be satanic in nature. The antichrist will not actually be Satan, but he will be energized by Satan and will rule by Satan's power. Thus, we should expect to see common characteristics between Satan and those he places in power.

Next, the beast appears in Revelation 13:1, where a further detail is added. Not only is he described as having seven heads and ten horns but now "upon his heads are the names of blasphemy". Open and flagrant opposition to God and His people is beginning to manifest itself.

Here, in Revelation 17:3, the beast shows up again. Now he does not simply wear blasphemy on his horns but he is said to be "full" of it. The word "full" was originally used to describe the lading of a ship, where the holds of the ship are said to be full of cargo. As time passed, it came to indicate saturation. Thus, in Matthew 23:25 Jesus accused the Pharisees of being "full of extortion and excess", meaning their hearts and minds were saturated with that attitude. Two verses later, Jesus said they were like whitewashed tombs "full" of dead men s bones and all uncleanness. Here, the beast is said to be "full" or saturated through and through with the names of blasphemy.

However, the primary focus of this chapter is not on the beast itself but on the woman who is riding it. Obviously she is in control of this hideous creature. So let's go back to the beginning of the chapter and follow the movement through.

Verse 1:

> *"And there came one of the seven angels which had the seven vials, and talked with me, saying unto me, Come hither; I will show unto thee the judgment of the great whore that sits upon many waters: 2 With whom the kings of the earth have committed fornication, and the inhabitants of the earth have been made drunk with the wine of her fornication."*

One of the angels who had poured out the judgments upon the earth comes to John and issues an invitation. The invitation is for John to witness the judgment of one whom the angel calls "the great whore or prostitute, who sits upon many waters." Obviously the word "whore" is used figuratively. The woman is not really a harlot because in verse 18 she is identified specifically as a city. The word "harlot" or "prostitute" signifies one who has many partners, not out of love but for material profit. The idea of "many waters" seems to indicate the widespread nature of her clientele. This idea is confirmed in verse 2, where both the kings of the earth and the inhabitants of the earth are said to have had relationships with her.

The Woman and the Beast

Verse 3-4:

> *"So he carried me away in the spirit into the wilderness: and I saw a woman sit upon a scarlet colored beast, full of names of blasphemy, having seven heads and ten horns.4 And the woman was arrayed in purple and scarlet color, and decked with gold and precious stones and pearls, having a golden cup in her hand full of abominations and filthiness of her fornication."*

Whoever this woman is, she is powerful, rich, and her position on the beast's back indicates her domination in the end times. The golden cup speaks of this horrible combination of great wealth, great power and great degradation.

Verse 5 then goes a step further and gives the woman a name:

> *"And upon her forehead was a name written, MYSTERY, BABYLON THE GREAT, THE MOTHER OF HARLOTS AND ABOMINATIONS OF THE EARTH."*

"Mystery" stands alone. She is a mystery or secret that has been kept from men. *"Babylon the Great"* identifies her origin. *"The Mother of Harlots"* means that she is the source of harlotry or deviation from God, and *"abominations"* indicates that she is the source, or mother, of idolatry on the earth. This is not the designation she would give herself. It is the designation given to her by God. In man's eyes, she is beautiful and desirable. He sees only the wealth, power and beauty, but in God's eyes, she is the mother of all harlots and the source of all idolatry.

Verse 6:

> *"And I saw the woman, drunk with the blood of the saints, and with the blood of the martyrs of Jesus: and when I saw her, I wondered with great wonder (astonishment)."*

Not only is the woman wealthy and powerful, and not only does she sit astride the beast that has existed from earliest times, but she is besotted, drenched, with the blood of two groups, namely, the saints and the martyrs of Jesus.

The martyrs of Jesus are those who have died for their faith during the church age. They had to know Jesus before they could be His martyrs. These people were Christians. The saints, on the other hand, are not necessarily Christians. Saints are people who are holy, or set apart for God. All martyrs for Jesus are saints, but not all saints are martyrs for Jesus. Not all saints know Jesus. Peter tells us that it was "holy men of God who spoke as they were moved by the Holy Ghost" in the Old Testament. A holy man or woman is a "saint". That is the word's meaning. The Jewish writers and prophets of the Old Testament, such as Isaiah, Jeremiah, and Daniel were saints, but they didn't know Jesus because Jesus didn't come until a later age.

So the *"saints and the martyrs of Jesus"* together make up all those, throughout all the ages, who have paid for their faith with their lives. And the woman on the beast has been behind all of their persecution. In addition, "abomination" in the New Testament invariably indicates idolatry. She is therefore the mother of all idolatry.

The fact that she is defined here as a "mystery" and as "the mother of harlots" reveals that she is, in fact, not a physical person but a spiritual force. This brings us to another conclusion. Underlying all fronts and facades, which have veiled the conflict between God and Satan through the centuries, is one truth. Although the battle has been fought on many different fronts and under all manner of disguises, it is a *religious* conflict. It all boils down to the question of who people worship. Satan's craving from the beginning has been to be worshipped as God.

Why Babylon? Was not Babylon a city? *Political* Babylon was a city but *spiritual* Babylon is far more than that. It was, and continues to be, the fountainhead of all false religions. All religions that do not recognize the Biblical record are false. Evolution versus creationism, for instance, is a religious issue. Science is used as a smoke screen to cover an antagonism toward God. At its very center is the issue of whether or not the Bible is to be recognized as the truth. If it is, then the God of the Bible must be worshipped as sovereign and Jesus Christ must be recognized as His only representative and mediator. If the Biblical record is recognized as the truth, so must the fact that all men are born sinners and therefore are separated from a holy God and are in desperate need of a Savior. If the Biblical record is recognized as the truth, then so must the fact that God Himself became a man and provided salvation in Jesus Christ. And if the Biblical record is recognized as the truth, then so must the fact that Christ arose from the dead, is at this moment at the right hand of God in Heaven and will one day return in glory, to put down evil and set up His kingdom.

Any system that seeks to discount that record, in *any* particular, is aligning itself with the woman of Revelation 17, who sits astride the beast in the end times.

We usually identify Babylon with Nebuchadnezzar because he developed it and embellished the city in the 5th century BC. But the woman's identification with Babylon goes back far beyond that. In addition she is identified as a "mystery", something kept secret from the beginning of time and her influence embraces the entire globe. Nebuchadnezzar was indeed a great king and his Babylon influenced other nations, but there were great civilizations existing in and before the time of Nebuchadnezzar never heard his name.

By the time John wrote this book, Babylon had long since ceased to be of any consequence at all. So how could all nations and all the inhabitants of the earth have "drunk from the wine of her fornication?"

For Babylon's origin we have to go back to Genesis chapter 10, where we discover that Nimrod, the grandson of Ham, founded Babel, along with several other cities in what the Bible calls "the land of Shinar". Daniel 1:2 confirms that ancient Shinar was ancient

Babylonia. Nimrod also founded Assyria and its capital, Nineveh. Micah 5:6 calls Assyria "the land of Nimrod".

Nimrod was not a nice person. The Bible calls him a "mighty hunter" but evidence points to the fact that he hunted men rather than animals. He was, in fact, the first dictator, enslaving men, and it was under his regime that the first alternatives to the worship of God were established.

When God confounded the language, after Nimrod had built a tower designed to reach up to heaven, the mystery religions of Babel began to spread across the world. The race began a second time after the Great Flood. Everyone was wiped out during the Flood, except for Noah, Ham, Shem, Japheth and their wives. Nimrod was only two generations removed from Ham, which means that the entire population of the earth was, at that time, centered around Babel until the confusion of the language caused disperse, taking with it the idolatrous beliefs of Nimrod. Noah had taught them the faith of God but by the time of Nimrod, false religions were rife.

As Dr. Henry Morris wrote, "This monstrous system of evolutionary, polytheistic, pantheistic, spiritistic, astrological idolatry has permeated practically every culture in the world in form or another. Even modern evolutionary scientism is nothing but this same ancient paganism in more sophisticated garb. All religions and philosophies, except those founded on special creation, as revealed in Genesis, worship and serve the creation more than the Creator and thus are under the condemnation of God. They are either humanistic, worshipping man as the highest attainment in the cosmic process, or super-humanistic, worshipping spirit beings as still higher attainments of the same evolutionary process."

The world's trend away from it Creator is not an accident and it is not new. It has been engineered over many thousands of years by this power, described here as a woman, a harlot, whom the Bible pictures sitting astride the beast in the last times and actually controlling him for a brief while. Just as the best is symbolic, so is the woman. As the dragon empowers the beast, so the beast supports the harlot. The woman makes the beast appear outwardly attractive and thus renders it easier for him to attain the power he desires. And instead of following the true bride and the heavenly

Jerusalem, the population of the earth in the last days will follow the harlot, the false bride, the deceiver.

Through the centuries, the harlot has appealed to the baser, fleshly aspect of human nature. As verse 4 suggests, she has provided temples, images and incense to dull the senses. She has provided gold and color and silver and precious stones to delight the eye, and in many cases, even temple prostitution to satisfy the lusts of men. In most cases, the state has endorsed the religion and, in some cases, imposed it upon the population. The fact that she is pictured in verse 6 as being *"drunk with the blood of the saints, and with the blood of the martyrs of Jesus"* confirms that force has been routinely used throughout the ages to compel men and women worship her way. Multitudes have drunk from the harlot's poisonous golden cup and instead of finding the peace they sought; they discovered only darkness and death.

In the end times, all religions will be brought together under one head. The only safe position to take is that of Biblical integrity accepting the Bible as the Word of God and standing firmly upon what it says, without trying to rewrite it or explain it away. Let it say what it says and believe what it says. How gracious God is to give us the truth, on which to base our lives!

Many, who have read Dave Hunt's book, *"The Woman Rides the Beast"*, and other authors with similar views, believe that the woman of Revelation 17 signifies the Roman Catholic Church. Hunt is only one of many teachers who have shared this opinion from the earliest times. However, there are two main difficulties with this view.

First, if the woman is the mother of all idolatry from Babel until now, she has to be responsible for Shintoism, Hinduism and the worship of Baal and Molech and Dagon in the Old Testament. She has to be behind the worship of the Greek deities, before Rome came to power, the gods of the Incas in South America and the many heathen practices in the jungles of Africa. She also has to be the author of the many cults and isms that flourish in the world today. It doesn't take much scholarship to decide that the Roman Catholic Church cannot possibly be held responsible for all those things. Therefore, she cannot be the "mother" of them.

Second, idolatry began in Babel at the dawn of history, whereas the papal church came into being at the beginning of the 4th century AD, when the Roman emperor, Constantine, embraced Christianity. That being so, she could not possibly be the source of something that began several thousand years before she came into being.

However, it is impossible to avoid the enormous body of evidence that points to the Catholic Church as being not the source but the expression of the woman's influence throughout the church age, and as playing an ultimate role in the kingdom of the beast during the Tribulation period.

Reference to purple and scarlet worn by the woman, and the great wealth owned by her bears a significant resemblance to Catholicism's pomp and glory today. Also, the Catholic Church's terrible history of torture and bloodshed throughout the ages, against any who dared to oppose her doctrine, is a matter of record. In addition, the idolatry, which is inherent in her makeup, is obvious to anyone who takes the trouble to investigate.

At the time when Constantine saw his vision of a burning cross in the sky and purportedly embraced Christianity, he was head of the mystery cults, which had their origin in ancient Babylon. They were entirely pagan in nature and had come to Rome via Pergamos in Asia Minor, when Babylon was destroyed. As head of these mysteries, several facts characterized the emperor Constantine, and the emperors before him.

First, he held the title, "Pontifex Maximus" (or "pontiff" as the pope is called today, which means "great bridge". It was a pagan title, used by all the heads of the Etruscan mysteries in Babylon and it was passed to the Roman emperors through Julius Caesar in 74 BC. In 63 BC Caesar was made supreme pontiff of the Babylonian order, and thus became the head the Babylonian priesthood.

Second, Constantine wore the fisherman's ring, which had nothing to do with Peter, but was connected with the fish god, Dagon.

Third, he wore a miter on his head, which originally looked more like a fish than it does today, and was also connected with the god, Dagon (the god worshipped in Nineveh).

When the emperor Constantine embraced Christianity, he became the head of the church, but also retained all the pagan offices and titles, which were his by succession. Consequently, the early Roman church became a mixture of Christian and heathen practices, which still exist, are accepted (innocently) by the great lay congregation of the Roman church to this very day. The vast majority of Roman Catholics have no idea of their true heritage. They are told, and believe, that their church is "the one true church", dating back to, and receiving its authority from, the apostle Peter, when in fact it dates back to the emperor Constantine, who combined the heathen doctrines of the Babylonian mysteries with tenets of Christianity three centuries after Christ died.

The doctrine of purgatory, the sale of indulgences, the infallibility of the pope, the worship of Mary, the use of holy water, the religious celibacy of both priests and nuns, the priestly absolution of sin, together with a whole lot of other doctrines, do not come from the Bible. They cannot be found in the Bible. They are all pagan in origin. Over time, those who were not grounded sufficiently in the Bible to see their error gradually accepted them as valid articles of the Christian faith.

Obviously there were many Christians in the early church who recognized this infiltration of pagan practices and beliefs and opposed them. For three hundred years the church had remained pure and had paid dearly for its faith at the hands of the secular, authorities. Now the persecution came from the same powers, only now they were semi-Christianized. The Roman emperors, who, for three centuries had mercilessly persecuted the church, were now at its head, leading it.

In AD 378, the title and office of head of the Babylonian order were transferred from the emperor, Gratian, to Damasus, the bishop of Rome. Soon the rites of Babylon were brought to the fore and a new, unbiblical version of Christianity was imposed upon the church. Many Christians were not willing to accept it, with the result that true believers continued to suffer horribly, only now their oppressors were those who pretended that their title and authority went back to Peter and claimed to be the "one true church".

Through the centuries that followed, millions of Bible believing Christians died at the hands of the Roman Catholic authorities, on charges of heresy. The only heresy they were guilty of was their unwillingness to accept the idolatry imposed upon them by the usurpers in Rome.

In light of these historical facts, I believe that the Roman Catholic *system* is the *expression* of the woman of Revelation 17, though she could not possibly be the original source of world-wide idolatry, which began in ancient Babylon, long before she came into being.

Verse 7:

> *"And the angel said to me, 'Why do you marvel? I will tell you the mystery of the woman, and of the beast that carries her, which has the seven heads and ten horns. 8 The beast that you saw was, and is not; and shall ascend out of the bottomless pit, and go into perdition: and they that dwell on the earth shall wonder, whose names were not written in the book of life from the foundation of the world, when they behold the beast that was, and is not, and yet is.'"*

A number of questions immediately confront the person who tries to untangle this riddle. Does the best represent a person or a kingdom? Does the present tense refer to John's day or to the end times?

If the beast referred to here is a person, the antichrist, he almost has to have existed before. He existed once (*"he was"*), did not exist, in the days of John (*"is not"*) but will exist in the end times (*'will ascend out of the abyss"*). This would give credence to the view that some hold, namely, that he will be the reappearance of some well-known character from the past, such as Judas or Nero. It would be a fruitless exercise to try to find out who he might be because there is no way to check out the validity of our guesses.

If, on the other hand, the beast is a kingdom, as it appears to be in chapter 13, then it would be the revival of a political system that existed in the past.

Suppose, for example, it represented Babylon. In John's day, the glory and power of Babylon lay in the past (*"it was"*). John could also say with confidence, *"it is not"*. But according to Revelation 14:8, and again in chapter 18, Babylon will be reestablished in the end times (*"it will be"*).

However, there seems to be a much deeper significance than just a political system. One gets the unmistakable sense that we are dealing with a spiritual entity here, because whatever is revived will have spent the time between its original destruction and its return in the bottomless pit (the abyss). The bottomless pit is always a designation with demonic overtones. Demons are kept there. In chapter 9, the scorpion-like creatures of the fifth trumpet rise out of the abyss. In chapter 20, we learn that Satan will be confined there during the millennium. So whatever or whoever this beast is, it will be demonic in nature.

Verse 9:

> *"And here is the mind that has wisdom. The seven heads are seven mountains, on which the woman sits."*

Insert here verse 18 because it belongs in this place:

> *"And the woman which you saw is that great city, which reigns (present tense, "is reigning") over the kings of the earth."*

So here we are told clearly that the woman is a city, the city sits on seven hills, and it reigns over the kings of the earth in John's day. Ancient Babylon did not sit on seven hills. Nor did it reign over the kings of the earth in John's lifetime. Rome, on the other hand, does sit on seven hills and it *did* reign over the kings of the earth when John was alive. For over two thousand years, Rome has been known as the city of seven hills.

Dave Hunt quotes the Catholic Encyclopedia as stating:

"It is within the city of Rome, called the city of seven hills, that the entire area of the Vatican state proper is now confined."

The Catholic theologian, Karl Keating claims that Babylon was a code name for Rome. He writes:

"It is used that way six times in the last book of the Bible and extra-biblical works. Eusebius Pamphilius, writing about AD 303, noted, "It is said that Peter's first epistle… was composed at Rome itself; and that he himself indicates this, referring to the city figuratively as Babylon."

Augustine agreed. He wrote in the 4th century AD:

"Babylon is a former Rome, and Rome is a later Babylon."

So the Catholic theologians themselves identify Rome as Babylon. The reason for this is almost certainly the fact that the mystery cults that originated in Babylon were now firmly entrenched in Rome.

Verse 10:

> *"And there are seven kings: five are fallen, and one is, and the other is not yet come; and when he comes, he must continue a short space."*

Theories abound as to who these kings were, but if the present tense indicates John's day (which seems almost certain to be the case), then perhaps the best place to begin would be with the king who *"is"*. At the time of John's writing, Domitian was emperor. That would mean that five significant kings would have had to precede him. And they did.

Moving back from Domitian, we have five Roman emperors, taking us back to Julius Caesar, who was the first. Working backwards from Domitian, we first have Nero, then Claudius, then Caligula, then Tiberias, and finally, Julius Caesar. All five had fallen. Nero committed suicide, Claudius was poisoned, Caligula was assassinated, Tiberias was poisoned and Julius Caesar was assassinated. So if we apply the angel's words to John's day, five had, in fact, fallen and one "was". The final one had yet to come. He has still not yet come, but when he does, he will "reign for a little season".

Verse 11:

> *"And the beast that was, and is not, even he is the eighth, and is of the seven, and goes into perdition."*

177

If we were to pursue the same line of reasoning further, we would say that the link between the Babylonian cults and the ruler in Rome, beginning with Julius Caesar in 74 BC and continuing under cover for the last 1500 years, will manifest itself again in the last days. The beast will be the last ruler prior to Christ, and as far as we can see, he will reign over a revived Roman empire in the spirit and power of Caligula or Nero. The "great harlot" of verse 1 will be manifested again and will ride the beast for a short period of time. Many consider that the false prophet of chapter 13 will be the leader of this religious power.

Verse 12:

> *"And the ten horns which you saw are ten kings, who have received no kingdom as yet; but will receive power as kings one hour with the beast."*

In Daniel chapter 2, when Nebuchadnezzar dreamed of a great image made of various metals, Daniel interpreted the dream as symbolizing successive world empires, which would rise to power after Nebuchadnezzar had departed. First would come Medo-Persia, then Greece, then Rome, and finally a confederacy of ten nations, symbolized by the ten toes of the image. The head of gold represented Nebuchadnezzar himself and the Babylonian power over which he ruled, and although kingdom would follow kingdom through history, the influence of the Babylonian head would persist. In Nebuchadnezzar's dream, a stone, cut from the mountain without hands, struck the image on its feet and not just the feet but the *whole thing* disintegrated into dust, while the stone grew into a mountain that filled the earth.

Daniel said the stone represented the God of Heaven, who, in the days of these kings, would set up a kingdom that would never be destroyed. That tells us that the ten-toed kingdom of Daniel chapter 2 is the same as the ten-horned kingdom of Revelation 17 and it will come to power at the final end of this age.

The Victory of the Lamb

Verses 13-14:

> *"These (the ten kings) have one mind, and shall give their power and strength to the beast. 14 These shall make war with the Lamb, and the Lamb shall overcome them: for he is Lord of lords, and King of kings: and they that are with him are called, and chosen, and faithful."*

This tells us that "the God of Heaven", spoken of by Daniel is the same as the Lamb introduced in Revelation 5. We know that the Lamb is Jesus. Therefore Jesus is the "God of Heaven".

Verses 15-18

> *"And he said to me, 'The waters which you saw, where the whore sits, are peoples, and multitudes, and nations, and tongues. 16 And the ten horns which you saw upon the beast, these shall hate the whore, and shall make her desolate and naked, and shall eat her flesh, and burn her with fire. 17 For God has put in their hearts to fulfill his will, and to agree, and give their kingdom to the beast, until the words of God shall be fulfilled. 18 And the woman which you saw is that great city, which reigns (present tense) over the kings of the earth.'"*

At the very end of the Tribulation period, a struggle will take place between the religious and political powers. The political power will prevail and the "great Harlot" will be destroyed. God will still be in complete control. Verse 17 tells us that He will cause the ten-nation confederacy to unconsciously perform His will. He will place the desires in their hearts and they will carry out His purpose. This will bring the influence of Nimrod to a final end.

God has used nations as a means to judge other nations many times in history. Assyria, Babylon, Egypt, Greece and Rome were all used to fulfill His purposes, but each of them ultimately paid for their wickedness. Though God used them to carry out His plan, they did not avoid judgment themselves and the ten-nation confederacy will be no exception.

CHAPTER 18

The Fall of Babylon

In chapter 16, when the seventh angel poured out his bowl of judgment, John said:

"There were flashes of lightening ... peals of thunder and ... a great earthquake, such as had not been since man was on the earth ... And the great city was split into three parts, and the cities of the nations fell. And *Babylon the Great* was remembered before God, *to give her the cup of the wine of His fierce wrath.*"

This was all part of the seventh bowl judgment.

Then, in chapter 17, some of the details were filled in. "Babylon the Great" was likened to a woman who rode a hideous beast and was proclaimed by the angel as the mother of all harlots and the source of all idolatry. Using references from the book of Daniel and earlier chapter of Revelation, we were able to identify the beast upon which she rode as the last world empire, under the dictatorship of the antichrist.

The woman, on the other hand, could be traced to ancient Babel (later to become Babylon) where all systems of idolatry and false religions had their origin. Although Babylon lost its political dominance after the 5th century BC, its spiritual influence persisted throughout the ages, until the present day, and will reach its climax during the Tribulation period.

In chapter 17, verse 16, we were told that at some point in the last days, the beast will turn on the woman and destroy her. This will probably occur at the time when the population of the earth, regardless of what religion they have been following until that point, will be forced, on pain of death, to worship the beast and his image.

It is important to grasp a clear picture of these events because by the time chapter 18 opens the religious influence of the woman (called here Babylon the Great) will have been destroyed. Yet the opening words of the chapter demonstrate that the story is not yet over.

Verses 1-2:

> *"And after these things I saw another angel come down from heaven, having great power; and the earth was lightened with his glory. 2 And he cried mightily with a strong voice, saying, Babylon the great is fallen, is fallen, and has become the habitation of demons, and the hold of every foul spirit, and a cage of every unclean and hateful bird."*

This cannot be the same picture as we saw in chapter 17 because John clearly says, *"After these things"* (after the events of chapter 17) *"I saw another angel"* (different from the first).
 This is a new scene, even though the focal point is called by the same name.

From the description in chapter 17, there can be little doubt that "Babylon", there, is an allegorical name for Rome. Both Protestant and Catholic scholars have understood this from earliest times. However, the description given in this chapter suggests a revival of the actual city of Babylon as a great commercial center in the last days.

This immediately brings objections from some, based on the premise that Babylon was destroyed in the Old Testament and that God's Word prophesied that it would never be rebuilt. It would be profitable to check these passages out because they will help us understand the terms in our present study.

Isaiah 13:1:

> *"The burden of (against) Babylon, which Isaiah, the son of Amoz, did see."*

That sets the scene. In the following verses, Isaiah describes the overthrow of Babylon in detail. Then, in verse 19, he writes:

> *"And Babylon, the glory of kingdoms, the beauty of the Chaldees' excellency, shall be as when God overthrew Sodom and Gomorrah. 20 It shall never be inhabited, neither shall it be dwelt in from generation to generation: neither shall the Arabian pitch tent there; neither shall the shepherds make their folds there. 21 But wild beasts of the desert shall lie there; and their houses shall be full of doleful creatures; (jackals) and owls shall dwell there, and satyrs (wild goats) shall leap there."*

The various translations of these verses vary widely. Some say "ostriches" instead of jackals and some say "satyrs" instead of goats, but the sense is about the same in all translations. They all describe a permanent and complete destruction of Babylon, similar to that of Sodom and Gomorrah. Babylon would never be inhabited again.

Jeremiah described a similar scene. In Jeremiah 51:26 we read that even the stones of Babylon would never be used to build other cities. In verse 43 of the same chapter, Jeremiah prophesied that no one would ever dwell there again.

Now these, and other prophecies have been taken by many scholars to refer to the capture of Babylon by Cyrus in 541 BC, on the night of Belshazzar's feast. However, when we look at the details more closely, it becomes obvious that the prophecies of Isaiah and Jeremiah were not fulfilled at that time and, in fact, to this point never have been fulfilled.

Cyrus took the city by stealth. He diverted the river that ran through Babylon and entered under the gates along the dried up riverbed. On that occasion, the city fell so quietly that some of the inhabitants did not know until the third day that their city had fallen. Virtually no damage was done to Babylon at that time.

Sixty-three years later, in 478 BC, the Persian king, Xerxes, plundered and damaged the great temple of Bel in Babylon but did not touch the city. Nearly 150 years after that, Alexander the Great found Babylon strong and flourishing. He had no need to fight for the city because the inhabitants welcomed him gladly. Alexander intended to make Babylon his capital. He began to rebuild the temple of Bel. He employed thousands of workers to clear away the rubbish in preparation for the work but died before the actual building could take place.

Following Alexander's death, Babylon's fortunes waned considerably and eventually it was reduced to only a shadow of its former glory. Many Jews remained there, the descendents of those who had been taken by Nebuchadnezzar. By the 5th century AD, Babylon was spoken of as a Jewish city, boasting three universities. At the end of the 5th century AD, the Babylonian Talmud was published, which was recognized as authoritative throughout the Jewish world.

Over the centuries, many towns and villages have been built with the stones taken from Babylon. Babylonian stamped bricks can be found in Baghdad to this day.

Isaiah 13:6 continues the condemnation of Babylon, but it does not fit with the days of Isaiah and Jeremiah.

Isaiah 13:6-13:

> *"Howl; for the day of the LORD is at hand; it shall come as a destruction from the Almighty.*
> *7 Therefore shall all hands be faint, and every man's heart shall melt: And they shall be afraid: pangs and sorrows shall take hold of them; they shall be in pain as a woman in labor: they shall be amazed one at another; their faces shall be as flames. 9 Behold, the day of the LORD comes, cruel both with wrath and fierce anger, to lay the land desolate: and he shall destroy the sinners thereof out of it. 10 For the stars of heaven and the constellations thereof shall not give their light: the sun shall be darkened in his going forth, and the moon shall not cause her light to shine. 11 And I will*

> *punish the world for their evil, and the wicked for their iniquity; and I will cause the arrogance of the proud to cease, and will lay low the haughtiness of the terrible. 12 I will make a man rarer than fine gold; even a man than the golden wedge of Ophir. 13 Therefore I will shake the heavens, and the earth shall remove out of her place, in the wrath of the LORD of hosts, and in the day of his fierce anger."*

Those events have not yet happened. They certainly did not happen in the days of Cyrus and they have not happened since, but they *will* happen in the end times, in what is called in prophecy "The Day of the Lord". Twice in this passage this is specifically stated. Thus, the events prophesied by Isaiah and Jeremiah are still future.

Zechariah also speaks of this time.

Zechariah 5:5:

> *"Then the angel who talked with me went forth, and said to me, Lift up now your eyes, and see what this is that goes forth. 6 And I said, What is it? And he said, This is an ephah that goes forth."*

Some translations have "basket" instead of "ephah" but an ephah was a measure in Old Testament times and it speaks of trade.

Verse 7:

> *"He said moreover, This is their resemblance through all the earth. 7 And, behold, there was lifted up a talent of lead: and this is a woman that sitting inside the ephah. 8 And he said, 'This is wickedness'. And he thrust her down into the ephah; and he threw the weight of lead upon the mouth of it."*

The talent was another important measure in ancient times and here the talent is used as a kind of lid. When it was lifted from the ephah, Zechariah saw a woman whom the angel symbolized as "wickedness". When the woman started to get up the angel pushed her down into the ephah and slammed the lid back on to keep her there.

Verse 9:

> *"Then lifted I up my eyes, and looked, and, behold two women came out, and the wind was in their wings; for they had wings like the wings of a stork: and they lifted up the ephah between the earth and the heaven. 10 Then I said to the angel who talked with me, 'Where do these carry the ephah?' 11 And he said to me, 'To build it a house in the land of Shinar: and when it is ready it shall be set there on its own base.'"*

We have already seen that "Shinar" was an ancient designation for Babylonia and in Scripture the stork is considered an unclean bird. Here, the two women, having stork's wings carried the ephah (the symbol of trade), containing the woman, (the symbol of wickedness) back to Babylon to establish it on its own base. It is suggestive of the fact that the city of Babylon will be rebuilt in the last days and swiftly become the world's commercial center.

Now back to Revelation 18.

Verse 3:

> *"For all nations have drunk of the wine of the wrath of her fornication, and the kings of the earth have committed fornication with her, and the merchants of the earth have grown rich through the abundance of her luxury."*

Apparently, huge sums of money will change hands through Babylon's exchanges in the last days. That, in itself, will not be immoral, but here the angel calls it fornication. This indicates that rulers and merchants in the end times will engage in a godless lust for wealth and totally disregard ethics concerning trade.

Verses 4-5:

> *"And I heard another voice from heaven, saying, 'Come out of her, my people, that you be not partakers of her sins, and receive not of her plagues, 5 for her sins have reached to heaven, and God has remembered her iniquities."*

As always, God will give any who belong to Him, and presumably there will be some, an opportunity to leave Babylon before the final catastrophe takes place. Just as He brought Lot out of Sodom and Rahab out of Jericho, so He will ensure that His people are free from the city before the judgment falls.

Verses 6-7:

> *"Render to her even as she rendered to you, and repay her double according to her works: in the cup which she has filled, fill to her double. 7 In the measure she has glorified herself, and lived luxuriously, so much torment and sorrow give her: for she has said in her heart, 'I sit a queen, and am no widow, and shall see no sorrow.'"*

This seems to be prayer by somebody but by whom, we are not told. However, God answers it in the next verse.

Verse 8:

> *"Therefore shall her plagues come in one day, death, and mourning, and famine; and she shall be utterly burned with fire: for strong is the Lord God who judges her."*

Obviously the overthrow of the final Babylon will not be slow and stealthy, as it was before. It will be a sudden, cataclysmic judgment that will take everyone by surprise.

Lament for Babylon

Verse 9:

> *"And the kings of the earth, who have committed fornication and lived luxuriously with her, shall bewail and lament for her, when they shall see the smoke of her burning, 10 standing afar off for the fear of her torment, saying, 'Alas, alas that great city Babylon, that mighty city! For in one hour is your judgment come!' 11 And the merchants of the earth shall weep and mourn over her; for no man buys their merchandise any more: 12 The merchandise of gold, silver, and precious stones, of pearls, fine linen, purple, silk, and scarlet, all kinds of citrus wood, and all kinds of vessels*

> *of ivory, and all kinds of vessels of most precious wood, of brass,*
> *iron, and marble, 13 And cinnamon, and incense, and ointments,*
> *and frankincense, wine, oil, fine flour and wheat, cattle, sheep, and*
> *horses, chariots, slaves, and the souls of men. 14 And the fruits*
> *that your soul lusted after have departed from thee, and all things*
> *that were rich and goodly have departed from you, and you shall*
> *find them no more."*

Kings and merchants alike will mourn Babylon's demise, mainly because the source of their income will have been taken away. Material prosperity has always been of immense value to the world. This is reflected today in some of the sentences given to those who interfere with it. Sentences imposed upon people who embezzle money are often more severe than those given to people who commit more physical or moral crimes. Money appears to be more important than people even today.

Verses 15-19:

> *"The merchants of these things, who were made rich by her, shall*
> *stand afar off for the fear of her torment, weeping and wailing, 16*
> *And saying, 'Alas, alas that great city, that was clothed in fine*
> *linen, and purple, and scarlet, and decked with gold, and precious*
> *stones, and pearls! 17 For in one hour such great riches came to*
> *nothing'. And every shipmaster, and all who travel in ships, and*
> *sailors, and as many as trade by sea, stood afar off, 18 And cried*
> *when they saw the smoke of her burning, saying, 'What city is*
> *like unto this great city!' 19 And they threw dust on their heads,*
> *and cried, weeping and wailing, saying, 'Alas, alas that great city,*
> *wherein all who had ships were made rich by her wealth! For in*
> *one hour is she made desolate."*

Three times, the incredulous statement is made, "**In one hour** your judgment has come", "**in one hour** such great riches have come to nothing", "**in one hour** she is made desolate". They were dismayed and terrified by the sudden destruction of this great center of business, with which the whole world did business. Man's greatest achievements are nothing before the power of God.

Nevertheless, the mourning of the earth is cause for rejoicing in Heaven.

Rejoicing in Heaven

Verse 20:

> *"Rejoice over her, thou heaven, and you holy apostles and prophets; for God hath avenged you on her."*

The Babylon of chapter 17 is a *religious* system, which has saturated the world throughout the years of her history, but here it is revealed that the *commercial* system of Babylon has also been at work from the beginning. The prophets and apostles lived in different ages, under different dispensations, yet here it infers that all of them are victims of the same system. Isaiah warned the people in his day not to focus on material wealth and neglect the Lord, and the danger of being drawn away from God by the lust for material goods is still a problem today. Apparently, the root cause of the world's persecution of the prophets and the apostles was not only the woman riding on the beast in Revelation 17 but also the materialistic system (Zechariah's woman in the ephah) described in Revelation 18.

Verses 21-23:

> *"And a mighty angel took up a stone like a great millstone, and cast it into the sea, saying, 'Thus with violence shall that great city Babylon be thrown down, and shall be found no more at all. 22 And the sound of harpers, and musicians, and of pipers, and trumpeters, shall be heard no more at all in you; and no craftsman, of whatsoever craft he be, shall be found any more in you; and the sound of a millstone shall be heard no more at all in you; 23 And the light of a lamp shall shine no more at all in you; and the voice of the bridegroom and of the bride shall be heard no more at all in you: for your merchants were the great men of the earth; for by your sorcery were all nations deceived."*

Unlike the overthrow of Babylon by the Persians, this description fits perfectly with the prophecies of Isaiah and Jeremiah. It is a permanent, sudden, total destruction of Babylon. The stone hurled into the sea represented the city itself. It was how Babylon will perish, in one terrible moment.

Verse 24:

> *"And in her was found the blood of prophets, and of saints, and of all that were slain upon the earth."*

In Babylon was found the blood of ALL those who had been slain in the world. This again speaks, like chapter 17, of the fact that this system was responsible for the blood of all those through the ages, who have died for their faith.

Jeremiah 51:47-49 helps us to understand this.

> *"Therefore, behold, the days come, that I will do judgment upon the graven images of Babylon: and her whole land shall be confounded, and all her slain shall fall in the midst of her. 48 Then the heaven and the earth, and all that is therein, shall sing for Babylon: for the spoilers shall come to her from the north, saith the LORD. 49 As Babylon has caused the slain of Israel to fall, so at Babylon shall fall the slain of all the earth."*

It will be a worldwide judgment, concentrated in one city because it is representative of the whole trend of worldwide materialism through the centuries. The prophets and saints mentioned here represent Israel. The number of Israelites killed through the centuries must number tens of millions of people, but God has kept the record. He knows each one, and here is the reckoning. God told His people, way back at the dawn their existence, *"To me belongs vengeance and recompense. Their foot shall slide in due time. The day of their calamity is at hand and the things that shall come upon them shall come quickly."* (Deuteronomy 32:35). Paul paraphrased that verse in Romans 12:8, *"Vengeance is mine, I will repay, saith the Lord"*. God is keeping track and although it looks as if the world is getting away with its sin, it is not. A reckoning will come eventually and when it does, it will be so severe that the destruction will be complete. Neither the religious system nor the commercial system will ever rise again.

CHAPTER 19

Verse 1:

"And after these things"

- (After the destruction of religious and commercial Babylon in chapters 17 and 18) -

> *"After these things I heard a great voice of many people in heaven, saying, Alleluia; Salvation, and glory, and honor, and power, unto the Lord our God: 2 For true and righteous are his judgments: for he has judged the great whore, who corrupted the earth with her fornication, and has avenged the blood of his servants at her hand. 3 And again they said, Alleluia And her smoke rose up for ever and ever. 4 And the four and twenty elders and the four living creatures fell down and worshipped God who sat on the throne, saying, Amen; Alleluia. 5 And a voice came out of the throne, saying, Praise our God, all you his servants, and you who fear him, both small and great. 6 And I heard as it were the voice of a great multitude, and as the voice of many waters, and as the voice of mighty thundering, saying, Alleluia: for the Lord God omnipotent reigns."*

The reason for this great outburst of praise is evidently the destruction of religious and commercial systems, called collectively here, "The great harlot". The same demonic spirit that founded and fed the world's idolatry through the ages is also accountable for the world's insatiable lust for material things. Both have resulted in rebellion against God and both have generated a hatred for God's Word and God's people. Consequently, they have resulted in much bloodshed through the centuries.

The Marriage of the Lamb

Verses 7-9:

> *"Let us be glad and rejoice, and give honor to him: for the marriage of the Lamb has come, and his wife hath made herself ready. 8 And to her was granted that she should be arrayed in fine linen, clean and white: for the fine linen is the righteousness (righteous acts) of saints."*

In Bible times, marriage had three stages. First, there was the betrothal. This was often contracted between the parents before the children were old enough act for themselves. The contract was legally binding and a down payment (dowry) was paid to the bride or her representative. Later, when the parties had reached marrying age, the actual marriage took place.

Suddenly, the bridegroom, accompanied by his friends, would go unexpectedly to the house of the bride and take her back to his own house.

The final stage would be the marriage itself, followed by the marriage supper, in much the same way as a reception follows our weddings today. By this time, the "bride" would be the "wife" of the bridegroom.

In the New Testament, the church is pictured as the bride of Christ. By "church" is meant the body of believers, regardless of which denomination they may belong to, or what they may call themselves. The church is a collective body, made up of every person who has trusted Jesus Christ as his or her Savior.

John the Baptist referred to Christ as the "bridegroom" and to himself as "the friend of the bridegroom" (John 3:29). The Lord Jesus identified Himself as the bridegroom, when answering the criticism of the Pharisees in Luke 5:34-35, and in His parables, the

Lord twice referred to Himself as the bridegroom (Matthew 22:1-14 and Matthew 25:1-13). Later, in 2 Corinthians 11:2, Paul wrote, *"I espoused you to one husband, that I may present you as a chaste virgin to Christ."* The most detailed passage on the subject is found in Ephesians 5:23-32, where the marriage union is specifically presented as a picture of Christ's relationship with the church.

The threefold contract described above is true of this relationship and it is in view here in Revelation 19. *First,* the betrothal stage began before the foundation of the world, when the bride was chosen and set apart for the bridegroom (Ephesians 1:4). In John 17:6-9, the Lord Jesus refers several times to the fact that believers were given to Him by the Father.

In time, each individual member comes to know Christ in a personal way and enters into a saving relationship with Him. At that time, the "earnest" (dowry) of the Holy Spirit is given to every believer. He not only empowers and guides and guards the believer during his or her life on this earth, but is the divine pledge of future inheritance (Ephesians 1:14). It is interesting to note that the old Greek word for "earnest" is now the Modern Greek word for "engagement ring".

Second, the Lord will come unexpectedly for His bride and take her back to His house. Jesus said in John 14:2-3:

> *"In my Father's house are many mansions. If it were not so I would have told you. I go to prepare a place for you. And if I go to prepare a place for you, I will come again and receive you unto myself; that where I am, there you may be also."*

Third, the marriage itself will take place in the Lord's house and be followed by the marriage supper. Here in verse 7 this third stage is in view.

Verse 7 again:

> *"Let us be glad and rejoice, and give honor to him: for the marriage of the Lamb has come, and his wife hath made herself ready."*

The church is His wife now, because the marriage has taken place. That means that the Judgment Seat of Christ, mentioned in 1 Corinthians 3 and 2 Corinthians 5, will have taken place and be over. The church will have been purged and rewarded. Only the "gold silver and precious stones" of 1 Corinthians 3 will remain. The "hay, wood and stubble" of dead works will have gone for ever. Thus, in verse 8, we read:

> *"And to her was granted that she should be arrayed in fine linen, clean and white: for the fine linen is the righteousness (righteous acts) of saints."*

The word, "righteousness" in that verse is plural ("righteousness-es") meaning acts deemed righteous in God's site. They will not necessarily be deeds considered righteous in our sight, but those things done in accordance with His will, in His strength. The "hay, wood and stubble" of 1 Corinthians 3 will no doubt include "good" things that were done in our own strength, without relying on Him.

Verse 9:

> *"And he said to me, 'Write, Blessed are they who are called to the marriage supper of the Lamb'. And he said to me, 'These are the true sayings of God'. 10 And I fell at his feet to worship him. And he said to me, 'See you do it not: I am thy fellow servant, and of your brethren who have the testimony of Jesus: worship God: for the testimony of Jesus is the spirit of prophecy."*

Marvelous though he was, the angel was still only a created being, who owed his existence, beauty and wisdom to the One who had created him. In that, he was the same as John, because they both served the same master. Although they were different in many other ways they worshipped and focused in the same direction.

The phrase, "testimony of Jesus" draws attention to the humanity of the Savior. The antichrist will bring the age-old denial of Christ's divinity to ultimate head. That Jesus was God in human form is the very heart of the Gospel. Many of the cults deny that Jesus is God. Therefore it will be the focus of satanic opposition. Yet that fact is called here, "the spirit of prophecy". In 1 John 4:3, written by the same author (John) several years before he saw this vision in Revelation, John pin-pointed the single factor by which the spirit of the antichrist might be discerned. Anyone who denied that Jesus, the Messiah (Christ), had come in the flesh was not of God. Anyone who saw Jesus would recognize that Jesus was a real man, but John's thrust was that the man, Jesus, was God incarnate.

The Coming of Christ in Glory

Verses 11-16

> *"And I saw heaven opened, and behold a white horse; and he who sat upon him was called 'Faithful and True', and in righteousness he judges and makes war. 12 His eyes were as a flame of fire, and on his head were many crowns; and he had a name written, that no man knew, but he himself. 13 And he was clothed with a robe dipped in blood: and his name is called 'The Word of God'. 14 And the armies in heaven followed him on white horses, clothed in fine linen, white and clean. 15 And out of his mouth goes a sharp sword, that with it he should smite the nations: and he shall rule them with a rod of iron: and he treads the winepress of the fierceness and wrath of Almighty God. 16 And he hath on his vesture and on his thigh a name written, KING OF KINGS, AND LORD OF LORDS."*

The word "crowns" in verse 12, is not "stephanos" the victor's wreath, given to Him in chapter 6:2, but "diadem", the crown of a king. Here He wears many of them, which goes along with His title, "King of kings and Lord of lords." He is coming to reign. According to Isaiah 63:1-2, He will enter the kingdom at the extreme southern end (Bosrah, or Edom) and will ride northward to Jerusalem, ending up in the valley of Jezreel. Just as the sword coming from His mouth is a figurative, symbolic term, so will probably be the bloodstained garments. However, the death toll will not be figurative, as the massed armies of the world turn to face Him.

Verse 17:

> *"And I saw an angel standing in the sun; and he cried with a loud voice, saying to all the birds that fly in the midst of heaven, Come and gather yourselves together for the supper of the great God; 18*

> *That you may eat the flesh of kings, and the flesh of captains, and the flesh of mighty men, and the flesh of horses, and of those who sit on them, and the flesh of all men, both free and bond, both small and great."*

This is not a pleasant picture but the race has been heading toward this point for thousands of years. The combined might of the most advanced military machines of all time will prove utterly powerless before the spoken word of Jesus Christ. (The sword coming from His mouth signifies the spoken word).

"The word of God is alive and powerful, sharper than any two-edge sword", and there will be no greater demonstration of that in the history of the human race than this scene on the plain of Armageddon, when Jesus speaks the word and his enemies die in their millions!

Doom of the Beast and False Prophet

Verse 19:

> *"And I saw the beast, and the kings of the earth, and their armies, gathered together to make war against him who sat on the horse, and against his army. 20 And the beast was taken, and with him the false prophet who wrought miracles before him, with which he deceived those who had received the mark of the beast, and those who worshipped his image. These both were cast alive into a lake of fire burning with brimstone."*

There will be no battle, as we think of battles. The forces of this world will not grapple physically with the armies of Christ. There will be no prolonged exchange of firepower or actual engagement. There will simply be a paralysis, a terrible inability to function in the presence of this One who comes as King of kings and Lord of lords.

John records no dialog, in the sense of an exchange of words. There will be no pause for negotiations, no call to surrender. The time for that will have passed. There will remain only the carrying out of the sentence, and that will be done speedily.

There are tremendous implications in what is *not* said here. After all the action of the past seven years, and the fearful authority wielded by the beast and the false prophet over the earth's population, this will be almost an anticlimax. There will be no pomp, no ceremony; just a simple statement:

> *"The beast and the false prophet were taken and cast into a lake of fire".*

Such is the overwhelming power of God, vested in Christ. Before Jesus left His disciples, He told them, *"All power is given to me, in heaven and on earth."* Here that power is demonstrated with terrifying simplicity.

The Lake of Fire is mentioned a number of times in Scripture. In Matthew 25:41, where Jesus judges the nations, immediately following this scene in Revelation 19, Hew says to those who fail to meet His criteria for mercy,

> *"Depart from me, you cursed, into everlasting fire, prepared for the devil and his angels."*

Where it is, when it was prepared and what form it will take, is not clear. It seems obvious that fire, as we know it here on earth, cannot be indicated. Physical fire could have no power over spirits. In any case, physical fire ceases when the material upon which it feeds is exhausted. This fire is eternal. It never ceases, and apparently does not devour what is placed in it.

Some people have the mistaken idea that the devil will rule over hell, but that is far from the truth. He and his angels will be consigned there, as final retribution for their sin. We can rest assured that the punishment will be equal to the enormity of their crimes.

For the moment, Satan is not in view here in Revelation 19:20, but his two representatives (the beast and the false prophet) will precede him to that place. This will be no "O.J. Simpson trial". God's justice will be swift and absolute. The guilt of these men will be beyond argument; their sentence will be a matter of record, and it will be carried out immediately. There will be no appeals, no plea-bargaining, no clever arguments to blur the facts, no smoke screens. There will be a simple execution of justice.

As for the millions of men assembled on the plains of Israel, Christ will merely say the word and they will die.

Verse 21:

> *"And the remnant was slain with the sword of him that sat upon the horse, which sword proceeded out of his mouth: and all the birds were filled with their flesh."*

The word of God is irresistible because it is the pronouncement of God's will. He is omnipotent. In the beginning, the earth was formed by the word of God. He spoke the universe into existence from nothing. He said, *"Let there be..."* and there *was!* John 1, Colossians 1 and Hebrews 1 all confirm that the creation was carried out through the Second Person of the Trinity, and here we see Him coming in power and glory. By the same irresistible word that spoke the universe into existence He will wipe out the combined might of the nations ranged against Him.

CHAPTER 20

Satan Bound

As we open chapter 20, an age has come to an end and a new age is about to begin. This new age is known as The Millennium, and it will be quite different from the age in which we now live. However, before it can begin there is a very important matter that will have to be seen to.

Verses 1-3

> *"And I saw an angel come down from heaven, having the key of the bottomless pit and a great chain in his hand. 2 And he laid hold of the dragon, that old serpent, which is the Devil, and Satan, and bound him a thousand years, 3 And cast him into the bottomless pit, and shut him up, and set a seal upon him, that he should deceive the nations no more, till the thousand years should be fulfilled...'*

"Devil" (diabolos) means *"accuser, slanderer."* The word is actually used as a common noun in 1 Timothy 3:11, 2 Timothy 3:3 and Titus 2:3 to describe those who would divide others by passing false information. Satan earned that name when he slandered God in the Garden, and he still undermines the truth of God's Word in the minds of millions today. He tells them it is unreliable, inaccurate, just a collection of fables.

According to Revelation 12:9-10, Satan is also *"the accuser of the brethren"* before God. In John 8:44, Jesus called him *"the father of lies"*. The name "Satan" simply means "adversary". He withstands and opposes every worthwhile cause and everything God holds dear. Unlike his puppets, the beast and the false prophet, Satan will not be consigned to the lake of fire immediately. That will be his final destination but his career will yet have a little while to run. He will be taken and confined to the abyss, or bottomless pit, for the duration of the millennium, namely, for one thousand years.

Some have objected to the idea of a spirit being chained and literally confined but I have no problem with it. God is able to do both those things if He wishes. After all, John doesn't say these are *metal* chains. Peter and Jude both speak of fallen angels being bound with chains of darkness and being confined while awaiting final judgment. Jude calls them everlasting chains. We must never make the mistake of limiting God on the basis of our own inability to understand spiritual things. Here, God's word says that Satan will be chained and confined to the abyss for a thousand years, and we must accept what it says, even though we cannot understand the details.

John says Satan will be taken, bound, cast into the abyss, shut in and sealed. Nothing could be clearer than that.
Seals have played a prominent role in this book. We have read about seals denoting security, protection, secrecy and ownership. Here, Satan's imprisonment is seen to be under the seal of God. The tomb of Jesus was sealed with the seal of Pilate and it was broken within three days. This seal will not be broken until God decides.

Now the last part of verse 3:

> *"… and after that he must be loosed a little season."*

After what? After the millennium. Satan will have to wait on death row for a thousand years before his final case comes up.

Verse 4:

> *"And I saw thrones, and they who sat upon them, and judgment was given to them: and I saw the souls of those who were beheaded*

for the witness of Jesus, and for the word of God, and who had not worshipped the beast, nor his image, nor had received his mark upon their foreheads, or in their hands; and they lived and reigned with Christ a thousand years."

This is a specific reference to what are termed, "The Tribulation Saints", those who respond to the preaching of the 144,000 witnesses set aside by God in chapter 7.

We should remember that there is a significant difference between the church and the tribulation saints. The church is composed of all those throughout the ages who have received Jesus Christ as their Savior. Denomination is immaterial in deciding who makes up the church. The Bible says that the church will be removed from the earth before the Tribulation begins (1 Thessalonians 4:16-18). In 1 Thessalonians 4:17, the phrase, *"so shall we ever be with the Lord"*, guarantees that the church will be with Christ when He returns and will continue to be with Him during the millennial kingdom. 2 Timothy 2:12 also confirms that the church will reign with Christ.

However, this passage refers to those who will die for their faith after the church has been removed. It ensures them also a place in the millennial kingdom.

Verse 5:

"But the rest of the dead lived not again until the thousand years were finished. This is the first resurrection. 6 Blessed and holy is he who has part in the first resurrection: on such the second death has no power, but they shall be priests of God and of Christ, and shall reign with him a thousand years."

The question now arises, "Who are 'the rest of the dead'?" Let's work it out. *First,* we know that the Old Testament saints will be alive at this time because, according to Ephesians 4:7-10 they were taken to Heaven from Sheol at the time of the Lord's resurrection and ascension. *Second,* the New Testament saints, the Christians throughout the church age, will be alive because, according to 1 Corinthians 15:50-54 they will have been resurrected and changed before the Tribulation begins. *Third,* the Tribulation saints will be alive because verse 4 of this chapter states that they will be resurrected when Christ returns in glory, at the end of the Tribulation.

So, who is left? *"The rest of the dead"* will be those of all ages who have died in unbelief. They will not be resurrected until the end of the millennium, when the "Great White Throne Judgment" takes place.

At this point it would be profitable to fill in some of the blanks between the end of chapter 19 and the seventh verse of chapter 20. In order to do this we must leave Revelation for a while and examine other sections of Scripture. Since all books of the Bible are equally part of God's Word, we shall not break any rules by doing this.

God's Master Plan

Let us first briefly trace through the development of God's plan.

As Revelation 19 closes an age comes to an end. It began in Genesis 3, when Adam forfeited his dominion over the earth and Satan became "the god of this world." Yet from the outset, even before the drama in the garden had been concluded, God laid down a blueprint, which decided the path history, would take until its final close.

In Genesis 3:15, speaking to the serpent, God said,

> *"I will put enmity between you and the woman, and between your seed and her seed; it (the seed of the woman) shall bruise your head, and you (the serpent) shall bruise his heel."*

Immediately, the struggle began. The enmity persisted throughout the years of the Old Testament and on through the New. The battle for souls continued, and will continue, until the very end.

But God's plan was on schedule. In Genesis 12, God chose a *man*, Abram, and separated him from his people. Through Abraham's miracle son, Isaac, God created a *nation* and promised it a *land*. This nation would be the "woman" of Revelation 12, the nation of Israel.

Later, through David, God established a *throne* and Israel became a *kingdom*. Then, in the fullness of time,

> *"God sent forth **His Son**; made of a woman, made under the law, to redeem those who were under the law, that we might receive the adoption of sons."*

Through His mother, Mary, Jesus was the *"seed of Abraham"* and of the line of David. He was the *"seed of the woman"* promised by God in the garden. Thirty-three years later, the serpent *"bruised His heel"*. As serpents do, he struck low and Jesus died on the cross. But it was all part of God's plan. As the writer to the Hebrews points out, Jesus became a partaker of flesh and blood *"so that ...*

> *". .through death, He might destroy him who had the power of death, that is, the devil; and deliver those who through fear of death were all their lifetime subject to bondage."*

Satan's seeming victory was short-lived because, on the third day Jesus rose from the dead and ascended to the throne in Heaven, taking with Him those who had been awaiting redemption since the beginning of time. Salvation was now available to any who would claim it by faith, but the battle between the serpent and the "seed of the woman" continued unabated. Not only did it affect God's chosen people but it involved the land God had given to them.

Throughout history, Israel has been the scene of countless wars and invasions. Assyrian, Babylonian, Persian, Mede, Egyptian, Greek, Roman, Turkish, Arab, Syrian French and British armies have all crossed her borders and left their blood on her soil. The city of Jerusalem has suffered under them all. As Jesus predicted in Luke 21:24, she was "trodden down by the Gentiles" for over two thousand years.

Then, in 1948, less than ten years after Satan's most vicious attempt to destroy the Jewish people under Nazi Germany, Israel became a nation again and the scene was set for the final drama, which we have been studying in this book.

In chapter 19 we reached the climax, when the "seed of the woman" (Jesus Christ) came in power and great glory to "bruise the serpent's head", to set up His kingdom and to reign in Jerusalem upon the throne of David, in fulfillment of Gabriel's promise to Mary in Luke 1:32-33.

It is that this point that other Scriptures supply details that are omitted in Revelation.

In Zechariah 12:9 we read,

> *"And it will come to pass in that day, that I will seek to destroy all the nations that come against Jerusalem."*

We have already seen that the armies of many nations will hopelessly surround Jerusalem when the Lord returns.

Zechariah 14:2 gives a vivid description.

> *"For I will gather all nations against Jerusalem to battle; and the city shall be taken, and the houses rifled, and the women ravished; and half of the city shall go forth into captivity, and the residue of the people shall not be cut off from the city."*

There will seem to be no hope, but at the final moment, when it seems all hope has gone, the scene described in Revelation 19:11-18 will take place. The heavens will open and Christ will appear at the head of His armies.

As Jesus said in Matthew 24:29-30,

> *"Immediately after the tribulation of those days shall the sun be darkened, and the moon shall not give her light, and the stars shall fall from heaven, and the powers of the heavens shall be shaken: 30 And then shall appear the sign of the Son of man in heaven: and then shall the tribes of the earth mourn, and they shall see the Son of man coming in the clouds of heaven with power and great glory."*

Zechariah 14:3-4 continues:

> *"Then shall the LORD go forth, and fight against those nations, as when he fought in the day of battle. 4 And his feet shall stand in*

> *that day upon the mount of Olives, which is before Jerusalem on the east, and the mount of Olives shall cleave in the midst, toward the east and toward the west, and there shall be a very great valley; and half of the mountain shall remove toward the north, and half of it toward the south."*

The Mount of Olives lies on the east side of Jerusalem, with the Kidron valley running north south between the two. When the Lord's feet touch the Mount of Olives, the valley that is created will run east-west, at right angles to the Kidron valley, rather like a cross, and directly opposite the Easter Gate of the city. This is the gate through which Jesus rode as king in Matthew 21, and which opened directly into the temple area. Today it is blocked up, but in any case, the original Eastern gate now lies below ground level.

Ezekiel 43:1-2 supplies more details.

> *"Afterward he brought me to the gate, even the gate that looks toward the east: 2 And, behold, the glory of the God of Israel came from the way of the east: and his voice was like a noise of many waters: and the earth shone with his glory."*

At the moment, there is no "way of the east". If you were to stand before the Golden, or Eastern Gate today and look east, you would see only the Mount of Olives on the other side of the Kidron valley, just a short distance away. Therefore it becomes clear that "the way of the east" from which Jesus will approach Jerusalem will be the east-west valley created when He steps on the to the Mount of Olives.

Ezekiel 43:4-5:

> *"And the glory of the LORD came into the house by the way of the gate whose prospect is toward the east. 5 So the spirit took me up, and brought me into the inner court; and, behold, the glory of the LORD filled the house."*

The Lord will once more enter Jerusalem by way of the Eastern Gate, only this time He will take His place in the Holy of Holies of the rebuilt temple. Notice that the angel took Ezekiel into the inner court of the temple, but the glory of the Lord was not there. From the inner court, Ezekiel was able to see the glory of the Lord filling the *"house"*, the temple itself.

Zechariah 12:10 supplies further information:

> *"And I will pour upon the house of David, and upon the inhabitants of Jerusalem, the spirit of grace and of supplication: and they shall look upon me whom they have pierced, and they shall mourn for him, as one mourns for his only son, and shall be in bitterness for him, as one that is in bitterness for his firstborn."*

And Zechariah 13:1-2:

> *"In that day there shall be a fountain opened to the house of David and to the inhabitants of Jerusalem for sin and for uncleanness. 2 And it shall come to pass in that day, saith the LORD of hosts, that I will cut off the names of the idols out of the land, and they shall no longer be remembered: and also I will cause the prophets and the unclean spirit to pass out of the land."*

In Romans 11:25, Paul told his readers that *"blindness in part is happened to Israel, **until the fullness of the Gentiles be come in."*** That means that the spiritual blindness which has prevented Israel, as a whole, from seeing Christ as its promised Messiah, was imposed by God for a specific period of time, namely, until the dominance of the Gentile nations had been brought to an end. That will have happened at this point in the story and the blindness will have been removed.

Zechariah 13:6:

> *"And one shall say unto him, 'What are these wounds in your hands?' Then he shall answer, 'Those with which I was wounded in the house of my friends."*

"The house of my friends" is a reference to Israel.

Zechariah 14:9:

> *"And the LORD shall be king over all the earth: in that day shall there be one LORD, and his name one."*

At this point,

1. The battle of Armageddon will be over.
2. The beast and the false prophet will have been consigned to the lake of fire.
3. The devil will have been confined to the bottomless pit.
4. A great valley will have been created east of the Golden Gate.
5. Christ will have entered the city in triumph and will have taken up His residence in the temple.
6. Israel will have recognized Christ as their Messiah and,
7. The land will have been cleansed from idolatry and wickedness.

Everything seems to be ready for the Millennium. But there will remain one more thing to decide before it begins. Who, out of the Gentile nations remaining on the earth will qualify to enter the kingdom?

The answer is found in Matthew 25:31-46.

> *"When the Son of man shall come in his glory, and all the holy angels with him* (that pinpoints the time very clearly as being at the close of the Tribulation period) *then shall he sit upon the throne of his glory: 32 And before him shall be gathered all nations: and he shall separate them one from another, as a shepherd divides his sheep from the goats."*

Christ will have already dealt with the nation of Israel. The remnant surviving the fearful events of the past few years will have recognized Christ for Who and What He is. Their land will have been cleansed and restored and He will be established in their midst. These nations are therefore the Gentile nations gathered before Him. They are not Christians, they are not the church. Most of the Tribulation saints will have died for their faith during the past seven years and been resurrected (Revelation 20:4). They are therefore the unsaved Gentile nations preparing to meet their Judge.

Verses 33-37:

> *"And he shall set the sheep on his right hand, but the goats on the left. 34 Then shall the King say to those on his right hand, Come,*

> *ye blessed of my Father, inherit the kingdom prepared for you from the foundation of the world: 35 For I was hungry, and you gave me food: I was thirsty, and you gave me drink: I was a stranger, and you took me in: 6. naked, and you clothed me: I was sick, and you visited me: I was in prison, and you came to me. 37 Then shall the righteous answer him, saying, 'Lord, when did we see you hungry, and fed you? or thirsty, and gave you drink? 38 When did we see you a stranger, and took you in? Or naked, and clothed you? 39 Or when did we see you sick, or in prison, and came to you? 40 And the King shall answer and say to them, 'Truly I say to you, Inasmuch as you have done it unto one of the least of these my brethren, you have done it unto me."*

We must remember that Jesus came as the *Jewish* Messiah, in fulfillment of the *Jewish* prophets. Salvation was extended to the Gentiles by grace. They were *"grafted in"* to the original tree (Romans 9:4-5, Romans 11:17). Since at this point Jesus will be judging Gentile nations and the Jews will have been restored, it is safe to assume that *"these, my brethren"* are the Jews.

Now verse 41:

> *"Then shall he say also to those on the left hand, Depart from me, you cursed, into everlasting fire, prepared for the devil and his angels: 42 For I was hungry, and you gave me no food: I was thirsty, and you gave me no drink: 43 I was a stranger, and you took me not in: naked, and you clothed me not: sick, and in prison, and you visited me not. 44 Then shall they also answer him, saying, Lord, when did we see you hungry, or athirst, or a stranger, or naked, or sick, or in prison, and did not minister to you? 45 Then shall he answer them, saying, Truly, I say to you, Inasmuch as you did it not to one of the least of these, you did it not to me. 46 And these shall go away into everlasting punishment: but the righteous into life eternal."*

We know that salvation is never granted on the basis of works, but always on the basis of faith in Jesus Christ (Titus 3:5). Here, the issue will not be primarily salvation. It will be a question of who among the Gentile nations surviving at the close of the Tribulation will be allowed to continue into the millennial kingdom. This is clear from verse 34. Apparently their attitude toward Israel during the past seven years will play a very significant part in that decision.

Today, Israel honors the many Gentiles who had compassion on the Jews during the holocaust of the 1930's and 1940's. There is an avenue of trees leading up to the holocaust museum in Jerusalem, and each tree is planted in memory of a Gentile, like Schindler or the Ten Boom family, who risked, and often forfeited their lives in an effort to save Jews from their persecutors. Many of these were Christians but many others were not. The spirit of compassion ran through a cross section of society. That, I believe, will be the spirit, which will dominate this judgment. Those who, during the terrible days of persecution, had compassion on their Jewish neighbors and ministered to them in their need, feeding, clothing, and visiting them, will be rewarded on the final day.

Now back to Revelation 20:5 again:

> *"But the rest of the dead lived not again until the thousand years were finished."*

We have already seen that *"the rest of the dead"* comprise those who will not enter the millennial kingdom. The Old Testament saints will be there, the church will be there, the Tribulation saints will be there and the righteous nations of Matthew 25 will be there. The *"rest of the dead"* will therefore be those of all ages who have died in unbelief, plus those who are disqualified in Matthew 25. They will not rise again until the thousand years have come to an end.

Verse 6 then establishes that the resurrected saints will reign with Christ in the capacity of priests. A priest is one who leads in worship, who represents the people before God and God before the people. Their role will be to carry out the Lord's will administratively in the kingdom, in much the same way as the angels serve God in Heaven today.

The righteous nations of Matthew 25 will not be included in that group because they will not yet be resurrected. They will have entered into the Millennium without dying. They will in fact be the nations over which the Lord will reign. These will lead normal lives, under the most ideal conditions. They will worship, work, build, have children and multiply. Age will be increased, the earth's productivity will be heightened, Satan's influence will have been removed completely and nature will have been restored to its pre-Adamic beauty. The earth will be filled with the glory of God as the waters cover the sea.

The last part of verse 5 and 6:

> *"This is the first resurrection. 6 Blessed and holy is he who has part in the first resurrection: on such the second death has no power, but they shall be priests of God and of Christ, and shall reign with him a thousand years."*

The position of the last clause of verse 5 makes it look as if those who do not live again until the thousand years are past will be the people who figure in the "first resurrection". Actually, just the opposite is true. The first resurrection will comprise those who are resurrected to enter the millennium. This group will include the Old Testament saints, the church and the Tribulation saints.

E.W. Bullinger writes in his commentary on Revelation:

> "Many Scriptures tell of the glories of that thousand years. We can only sum them up, and that briefly:- Those years will be characterized by (1) the absence of Satan; (2) the restoration of the earth: many physical marvels, converting deserts into gardens and causing its wilderness to bloom as the rose; (3) changes in the sun, moon and stars, which affect the climate and fruitfulness of the earth; (4) changes in nature and habits of the wild animals; (5) righteous government, which is today the world's greatest need, and (6) life prolonged and health improved.
>
> When the thousand years end, their blessedness does not end, but increases with the glory of the new heaven and new earth. Men will not cease to live. The nations of the new earth will "consist" and be upheld by the eternal power of the great Creator."

John makes reference six times to a specific period of one thousand years. There is no basis for thinking he is using figurative language.

The text is unambiguous and could be taken to mean something else only by doing violence to the clear sense of the passage.

In the third century AD the Alexandrian school of theology set out to give *all* Scriptures an allegorical or non-literal meaning. Later, Augustine countered this teaching and claimed that while the poetical, historical and theological parts of Scripture should be taken literally, the prophetic portions should be interpreted spiritually. With this view he became the principal source of what is called Arminianism today. Those holding to the Arminian principles believe that there will be no future one thousand year reign of Christ on earth. Unfortunately, Augustine's teaching was accepted without question by the Roman Catholic church and was later embraced by many of the Protestant reformers as well.

However, as Dr. Walvoord points out, the doctrine of a future millennium on this earth is more than a dispute over the 20th chapter of Revelation. It involves a whole system of Biblical interpretation, from cover to cover. It affects the promises to Abraham concerning the land, to David concerning the throne and to Christ concerning His reign. Amillennialism also maintains that God's promises to Israel are no longer in effect but that the church has taken Israel's place. This should be rejected, first, because it does violence to the Scriptures themselves and second, because it suggests that God's promises through Abraham, David, Jeremiah and Ezekiel are unreliable. If those promises were unreliable, what basis would we have to believe any of His others?

If we take the Bible literally and listen to what it says, we have no alternative but to accept the literal future, one thousand year reign of Christ upon this earth, together with the restoration of Israel as the center of His kingdom.

Satan's Release and Overthrow

Verses 7-10

> *"And when the thousand years are expired, Satan shall be loosed out of his prison, 8 And shall go out to deceive the nations which are in the four quarters of the earth, Gog, and Magog, to gather*

> *them together to battle: the number of whom is as the sand of the*
> *sea."*

At first glance it is inconceivable that people who have enjoyed the personal rule of Christ upon a restored earth for a thousand years could be deceived and rally to Satan's cause, as soon as he is released from his prison house. However, when you think about it more carefully, it is really no surprising at all. In verse 3 of this chapter we read, "After the thousand years, Satan must be released for a little while." The emphasis is on the *"must"*.

When we view history it becomes clear that no created being is capable of standing in his own strength. Lucifer, who, though blessed above all other creatures, fell before the onslaught of his own pride, illustrated this. It was illustrated by Adam and Eve, who, rebelled against God though surrounded by the perfection of Eden, by Israel, which, though favored above all other nations, consistently went its own way and by each one of us in our inherent waywardness. Only the intervention of God from outside can create the kind of change which God's nature demands.

Through the centuries it has been popular to blame Satan for man's problems, but for a thousand years at the end of this age, Satan will have been removed from the scene and man will have had the opportunity to demonstrate what he is really like without Satan's influence. He will have been blessed beyond measure. He will have heard, seen, tasted and touched a perfect environment under the direct control of the glorified Christ. He will have experienced this for a thousand years; yet will still rebel as soon as the opportunity presents itself! That is what man is like. That is why Christ had to die.

One nation, Israel, will not be included in that rebellion. The people of Israel will have already paid dearly for their rebellion and God will graciously keep them in His way.

Ezekiel 36:24-28 reads like this:

> *"For I will take you from among the heathen, and gather you out*
> *of all countries, and will bring you into your own land. 25 Then*
> *will I sprinkle clean water upon you, and you shall be clean: from*

all your filthiness, and from all your idols, will I cleanse you. 26 A new heart also will I give you, and a new spirit will I put within you: and I will take away the stony heart out of your flesh, and I will give you a heart of flesh. 27 And I will put my spirit within you, and cause you to walk in my statutes, and you shall keep my judgments, and do them. 28 And you shall dwell in the land that I gave to your fathers; and you shall be my people, and I will be your God."

Verse 36:

"Then the heathen that are left round about you shall know that I the LORD build the ruined places, and plant that which was desolate: I the LORD have spoken it, and I will do it."

"I will do it". This is something God will do by His own power. It will not depend on Israel's ability.

There are indications in Scripture that even during the millennium itself there will be a reluctance on the part of some of the nations to worship. For instance, Zechariah 14:16-19 prescribes penalties for those who fail to do so. So the release of Satan at the end of the millennium and the consequent rebellion among the nations will be a graphic demonstration of the fact that blessing alone does not produce faith. We would think that provided conditions were right, everyone would believe. But that is not so. Even the most intense of blessings over a prolonged period of time will not produce universal faith. Man rebelled under the Law; he has rebelled under grace and he will rebel under the most ideal conditions possible on this earth. Nothing other than the intervention of God Himself can solve that problem.

Ezekiel uses the words *"Gog"* and *"Magog"* to denote the nations which lie north and northeast of Israel, and also of the prince who will rule over those nations. Here they seem to refer to the Gentile nations in general. Magog, of course, was the first son of Japheth and with him were associated his brethren, Gomer, Tubal and Meshech. Ezekiel made these famous in chapters 38 and 39 of his prophecy. Ezekiel also adds Persians, Ethiopians and Libyans to the confederacy. Josephus interprets Magog as the Scythians, who inhabited the area north of the Black Sea.

However, there is no connection whatsoever between the confrontation described here in Revelation 20 and the invasion of Israel prophesied in Ezekiel 38 and 39. The Ezekiel invasion will take place prior to the millennium, during the Tribulation period, whereas this rebellion will take place one thousand years after the Tribulation closes.

According to Revelation 20:8, there will be many people involved in the last rebellion, so many that it will be impossible to count them. There number will be *"as the sand of the sea"*.
Verse 9:

> *"And they went up on the breadth of the earth, and compassed the camp of the saints about, and the beloved city (Jerusalem): and fire came down from God out of heaven, and devoured them."*

That will be the end. There will be no battle. The demise of this great multitude will be quick and thorough. The word *"devoured"* means *"consumed"*, like something that has been eaten and digested. They will disappear from the face of the earth.

Satan's Final End

Verse 10:

> *"And the devil who deceived them was cast into the lake of fire and brimstone, where the beast and the false prophet are, and shall be tormented day and night for ever and ever."*

The Lake of Fire and the fire that devours the rebelling armies are not the same. The fire that consumed the armies will be physical in nature. It will destroy their bodies but not their souls. They will then take their place among "the rest of the dead". The Lake of Fire, on the other hand, is spiritual in nature and will be the final, eternal destination of the lost. The beast and the false prophet will be sent there before the millennium begins (Revelation 19:20) and they will still be there when Satan joins them one thousand years later. This tells us that the Lake of Fire will not devour. Its torment will be eternal and without any hope of reprieve.

The next verse introduces us to the final event before eternity begins.

The Great White Throne Judgment

Verse 11:

> *"And I saw a great white throne, and him that sat on it, from whose face the earth and the heaven fled away; and there was found no place for them."*

The throne would seem to be in Heaven. There is no indication that it is on earth. John has seen other thrones in this book and they have all been in Heaven. In addition, the same Person has occupied them all. The only description given here is that the throne is a white throne and the One who sits upon it is so holy and so glorious that the created universe cannot bear to remain in His presence. No word is spoken. His presence alone is sufficient to make it reel away in terror. *"From whose FACE the heavens and the earth fled away"*! That is the glory of the God we shall one day see.

Verse 12:

> *"And I saw the dead, small and great, stand before God; and the books were opened: and another book was opened, which is the book of life: and the dead were judged out of those things which were written in the books, according to their works."*

This will be *"the second resurrection"*, when the "rest of the dead" (verse 5) will be brought before God for the final judgment. If you are a Christian, you will not be there. Actually, you will be "there", with Christ, but you will not be among those who are standing before the Great White Throne. Those about to be judged will be the unsaved that were not present during the millennium, plus those who rebel at the end of the millennium.

Two books will be used. One will contain each person's "works" and the other will contain a register of those who are saved. The roll call will be extremely thorough. Nobody will be missed. All who have not figured in the first resurrection will have their part in the second.

Verse 13:

> *"And the sea gave up the dead who were in it; and death and hell delivered up the dead who were in them: and they were judged every man according to their works."*

Many people have died in the oceans of this world and have never been recovered. No doubt this group will also include those who died in the Great Flood of Noah's day. "Hell", here, is "Sheol", the place described by Jesus in Luke 16, where the souls of the lost dead have been awaiting final judgment throughout the ages. All will now assemble for the final judgment.

Notice that there is no mention of sin. Sin was paid for at the cross. John wrote in his first letter that the blood of Christ *"is a propitiation for our sin, and not for our sin only, but also for the sins of the whole world."* In other words, the blood of Christ paid for sin, period, whether we take advantage of it or not.

Salvation is offered to "whosoever will". Jesus does not die for you when you receive Him as your Savior. He died already on the cross, and when we believe we simply place our faith in something that happened two thousand years before we were born.

God tells us in His Word that we cannot be saved by our works. Man imagines that he can. He imagines he can make the grade by himself if he tries hard enough. Therefore, he rejects the offer of salvation by grace, which God offers to him as a free gift through Jesus Christ and then he dies. The opportunity has then gone forever.

At the Great White Throne, God wills say, in effect, *"You rejected my offer of grace when you had the opportunity. I gave you My Son; He died for you, to pay for your sin but you rejected Him and chose to rely instead upon your own efforts. OK. Now we will examine your record and evaluate your works."*

Unfortunately, all man's acts of righteousness are as filthy rags in God's sight. They will be worthless before God. But *"every man will be judged **according to his works** and according to the things that are written in the books."*

216

Verse 14:

> *"And death and hell were cast into the lake of fire. This is the second death. 15 And whosoever was not found written in the book of life was cast into the lake of fire."*

The *first* death is physical. We all die, sooner or later, unless the Lord returns first. That is simply the separation of the spirit from the body. The *second* death is spiritual and is the eternal separation of the soul from God. In verse 6 we read, *"Blessed and holy is he who has part in the first resurrection. Over such, the second death has no power."* So for the believer, the judgment is past. He will be forever with the Lord and has nothing to fear. However, for those who stand before ✶ the Great White Throne there will be everything to fear because, by that time, there be no hope.

As we saw in chapter 3, there are various interpretations of the term, "The book of Life". One view is that a person's name is written in it when he or she becomes a Christian. Another is that it is added when a Christian dies. But neither of these seems to fit references to the Book of Life in the Scriptures. Moses suggested that his name might be blotted out of the Book of Life in exchange for the forgiveness of his people - an idea which God rejected. However, it does tell us that his name was already there. In Revelation 3:5, Jesus promised overcomers in the church of Sardis that they would be arrayed in white garments and that He would *"not blot their names out of the Book of Life"*. Once again, their names were already there. In addition, both references tell us that God will blot some names out of the Book. If nobody's name were blotted out God would not keep promising not to do so.

God promises to those who trust Him that they shall never perish. So we have the promise of God that the name of a Christian will never be removed from the Book of Life. This suggests that everybody's name is written in the Book of Life at birth, but that the names of those who die without receiving salvation will be removed at death.

A computer illustrates the principle. If material on a computer is saved before a sudden power cut, it will remain. But if it is not saved before the power goes out, it will be irrevocably lost.

This passage therefore says that your name is, at this moment, written in the book of life, whether you are a Christian or not. But the entry needs to be saved and the only way to save it is to place your trust in the finished work of Jesus Christ. The moment you do that, your name is made permanent. It becomes indelible. If you fail to save the entry and the power (your life) should go out unexpectedly, your name will disappear from the page and you will have to stand before the Great White throne.

Verse 15 again:

> *"And whosoever was not found written in the book of life was cast into the lake of fire."*

This is serious business. There is no more solemn passage to be found anywhere in the Scriptures. There will be no reprieve, no appeal and no parole. The sentence is irreversible and it is forever. Think about it!

One Friday evening, I had finished preparing my message for the following Sunday. I had edited it and was ready to print it. A lot of time and research had been put into this preparation but my mistake was that I had not saved it. When I went to print it, for some reason the computer froze up. I hit everything in sight but all to no avail. Nothing would work and I had no option but to restart the computer, which meant that the power had to be switched off in the process and every single word was lost. For a moment, I just stared that that blank screen in disbelief. I even called people to make sure there was not something I could do to get it back. I couldn't believe that it had all gone! But there was nothing anyone could do to help me. My work was gone, just as if I had never written it. All my good efforts amounted to nothing but a waste of time. That is how it will be with the Book of Life.

Tell me, if the "power" should go out tonight unexpectedly, would your name be preserved? Or would it vanish, as if it had never been there? If that were the case, the lists could be searched and searched but your name would not be there. Even if for 30, 40, 60 years it had been written in that book, it would now be gone and there would be no way of bringing it back! That is the risk we take if we fail to trust God's remedy for our sin, which is the shed blood and broken body of the Lord Jesus Christ.

CHAPTER 21

The New Heaven and Earth

As we move into chapter 21 we find ourselves in an entirely new world. With the last verse of chapter 20 the millennial reign of Christ comes to an end. All enemies, including Satan, the beast, the false prophet, even death and Hades, have been vanquished. Judgment has been concluded and the eternal state has begun.

1 Corinthians 15:25-26 makes the sequence of events clear:

> *"For he must reign, until he has put all enemies under his feet. 26 The last enemy that shall be destroyed is death."*

Revelation 20:14 confirmed this when Death and Hades were cast into the Lake of Fire. That will be the last enemy and with its destruction God's purpose for this present age will have been brought to completion.

We cannot be dogmatic in many of these topics but I personally believe there is a connection between this event in Revelation 20 and Peter's prophecy in his second letter.
In 2 Peter 3:5, Peter, speaking of those who scoff at prophetic truth, writes,

> *"For this they are willingly ignorant of, that by the word of God the heavens were of old, and the earth standing out of the water and in the water."*

That was the "first earth", created by God in Genesis 1.
Then Peter continues:

> *"Whereby the world that then was, being overflowed with water, perished."*

The earth that emerged from the Flood was quite different from that which predated it. Geography was different, atmosphere was different, life span was different and population was different. Peter then turns to the heavens and earth, which are now.

Verse 7:

> *"But the heavens and the earth, which are now, by the same word, are kept in store, reserved unto fire against the Day of Judgment and perdition of ungodly men."*

We discussed the Day of Judgment in the last chapter, together with the perdition of ungodly men. It will take place at the Great White Throne, described in Revelation 20:11-15.

Peter adds (verse 10):

> *"But the day of the Lord will come as a thief in the night; in the which the heavens shall pass away with a great noise, and the elements shall melt with fervent heat, the earth also and the works that are therein shall be burned up."*

Obviously this could not take place during the Tribulation period, as the result of some atomic reaction, as some have claimed, because if it did there would be no earth to restore during the millennium, and no nations to populate the kingdom. It has to take place at the end of Revelation 20.

According to Ephesians 4:8-10, Sheol or Hades (the abode of the lost dead) are located in the center parts of the present earth. This being so, when Death and Hades are cast into the Lake of Fire, the *"earth that now is"* will accompany it, and at that point the present universe and its works will be burned up.

It has been pointed out that the word *"new"*, in both Old and New Testaments, often stands for *"freshening"* rather than *"replacement"*. This has caused some commentators to reckon that God will purge the earth with fire rather than destroy it. That may be so but passages such as those found in Psalm 102 and Hebrews 1 clearly speak of the present earth and heavens *"perishing"* and of Christ *"folding them up and changing them"*. These passages give more credence to the idea of actual destruction and replacement.

Whichever view is correct, and there is no way to be certain, we are not told how God will protect or transfer the earth's righteous population from the dreadful heat of such event to the new earth. I have no problem believing that He will be able to do so.
Now, as we begin Revelation chapter 21, the old heaven and the old earth will have been folded up and cast away and new heavens and a new earth will have taken their place.

Revelation 21:1:

> *"And I saw a new heaven and a new earth: for the first heaven and the first earth were passed away; and there was no more sea."*

This has puzzled many people. Why focus on this one aspect concerning the sea? Here again, we are not told and it is unproductive to devise theories because there is no way of testing their accuracy. John simply makes the statement, *"there was no more sea"* and we must accept it as a fact.

In chapter 22, a river is described, which, according to our human reasoning, must flow into something, but perhaps that law applies only to our present world. It would be a mistake to bind God's eternal kingdom to the physics of this present age. Maybe the rules will change and water will flow up hill and not empty into anything! The God who invented everything we use for reference in time is well able to create a whole new system for eternity.

Verse 2:

> *"And I John saw the holy city, New Jerusalem, coming down from God out of heaven, prepared as a bride adorned for her husband."*

John gives us no description of the new heaven and new earth. His gaze is captivated by the sight of the Holy City, New Jerusalem, coming down from God out of Heaven. He doesn't mention it landing on the earth. He just saw it coming down. Some believe it will remain suspended but that is not made clear.

Of all the apostles, John was most aware of the overall picture. Now in his old age, he had outlived most, if not all, of the other original apostles. He knew the writings of the Old Testament prophets and also of Paul Peter and James. The old Jerusalem was by this time nothing but a heap of ruins, and had been for between twenty and thirty years. But as John gazed upon this new and lovely city, the writings of his forefathers and friends must have rushed back into his mind.

The writer to the Hebrews mentioned it in reference to Abraham. He wrote:

> *"For he looked for a city, which has foundations, whose builder and maker is God."*

And speaking of the multitude that would spring from Abraham through Isaac, he continued,

> *"But now they desire a better country, that is, a heavenly: wherefore God is not ashamed to be called their God: for He has prepared for them a city."*

Peter, in his second letter, wrote:

> *"Nevertheless, according to His promise, we look for new heavens and a new earth, wherein dwells righteousness."*

In the Old Testament, Isaiah had also prophesied this event. In Isaiah 65:17-19 we read:

> *"For, behold, I create new heavens and a new earth: and the former shall not be remembered, nor come into mind. 18 But be glad and rejoice for ever in that which I create: for, behold, I create Jerusalem a rejoicing, and her people a joy. 19 And I will rejoice in Jerusalem, and joy in my people: and the voice of weeping shall be no more heard in her, nor the voice of crying."*

The Psalmist had also been inspired to write of this glorious scene in Psalms 45, 46, 47 and 48. John knew all these Scriptures and as he watch the holy city descending, he must have been filled with wonder and awe, just as we shall be one day when we see it.

John's statement that the New Jerusalem was *"prepared as a bride adorned for her husband"* does not mean that she was dressed up like a bride. It means it was prepared with fastidious care and filled with joy, as a bride is when she prepares herself to meet her bridegroom. Those of us who have married daughters can appreciate the significance of that!

Verse 3:

> "And I heard a great voice out of heaven saying, Behold, the tabernacle of God is with men, and he will dwell with them, and they shall be his people, and God himself shall be with them, and be their God."

The old Jerusalem was always associated with God's special relationship with Israel. But the New Jerusalem will be open to all people on the earth. Hebrews 12:22-24 says,

> *"But you are come to mount Sion, and to the city of the living God, the heavenly Jerusalem, and to an innumerable company of angels, 23 To the general assembly and church of the firstborn, who are written in heaven, and to God the Judge of all, and to the spirits of just men made perfect, 24 And to Jesus the mediator of the new covenant, and to the blood of sprinkling, that speaks better things than that of Abel."*

The original Mount Zion was always associated with David. The actual "City of David", which he took from the Jebusites, was not located on Mount Zion. It was southwest of Zion, overlooking the

Kidron Valley, but David's palace was there and he was buried there. However, this Zion will be God's city. He will be there in person. It will be His dwelling place, surrounded by *"an innumerable company of angels"*.

The *"general assembly and church of the firstborn"* will be there also. That will be you and me. We will be there, provided we have received Christ as Savior. In John 14, Jesus said He was going to prepare a place in the Father's house for those who had trusted Him. Here we catch our first glimpse of that place. This will be the Father's house.

"The spirits of just men made perfect" will be there. They are the Old Testament saints, who had to wait for the atonement to be made before their salvation was rendered complete.

Most important, *"Jesus, the mediator of the new covenant"* will be there.

What of conditions within the city? Verse 4:

> *"And God shall wipe away all tears from their eyes; and there shall be no more death, neither sorrow, nor crying, neither shall there be any more pain: for the former things are passed away."*

The former things are those which categorize this life drawn from Adam. Sickness, pain, death, sorrow, tears, discouragement, disappointment and fear, can all be traced back to the original fall. They are all part of a fallen society in a fallen world. But that will all change. God Himself will remove the cause of the problem and wipe away all tears. The spectacular beauty of the city will be equaled by the utter joy of its population.

Verse 5a:

> *"And he that sat upon the throne said, Behold, I make all things new."*

No trace of the fallen world will remain. If God Himself is going to dwell within this city it has to be perfect in every detail. Perfection can sometimes be hard and clinical but God's perfection embraces every facet of creation. Not only will the city itself be perfect but life within and around it will be perfect also. Beauty will be perfect; love and fellowship will be perfect; music, color, perfume, climate, health and intelligence will be perfect. Nothing immature or blemished will be able to exist in God's dwelling place.

Verses 5b-7:

> *"And he said unto me, Write: for these words are true and faithful. 6 And he said to me, It is done. I am Alpha and Omega, the beginning and the end. I will give unto him who is athirst of the fountain of the water of life freely. 7 He that overcomes shall inherit all things; and I will be his God, and he shall be my son."*

The Lord Jesus introduced Himself twice in one chapter with the same words: *"I am alpha and omega, the first and the last."* He is the source of all things and the finisher or completer of all things. In the beginning God created the universe and set it on its course. Through the centuries, the great ship has ploughed the waves and weathered the storms. At this point it will have reached its destination and God says *"it"* (that is, His purpose) *"is done"*.

In verse 6, God gives the first invitation on the new earth. He promises free access to the fountain of the water of life. What form the fountain takes is not revealed. It is called "water" but obviously it will not be ordinary water. In the next chapter the angel shows John a river of the same substance and there seems to be no reason to spiritualize it into meaning something else. Perhaps the fountain and the river are one and the same. Or perhaps the fountain is the river's source. We don't know, but everything points to the fact that the water of life is a physical, tangible substance of unimaginable value and purity. Yet unrestricted access will be given free to every inhabitant of that great city.

Verse 8:

> *"But the fearful, and unbelieving, and the abominable, and murderers, and whore-mongers, and sorcerers, and idolaters, and all liars, shall have their part in the lake which burns with fire and brimstone: which is the second death."*

Some Christians have trouble with this verse. They may not be murderers or whoremongers or sorcerers but they are fearful sometimes, they have been guilty of lying from time to time, and they feel apprehensive. They think, *"Could this include me after all?"* However, we should remember the sequence of events and conditions of salvation. Those who are Christians in this age will not be saved because they are without sin. Just the opposite is true. Christ came into this world to save sinners. It is *because* we are sinners that we are candidates for salvation. We are saved (by grace) simply by recognizing the fact of our unworthiness, and reaching out to Christ for cleansing and forgiveness. That being so, there will be people in the New Jerusalem from every category in the list in verse 8. Their names will be written in the Book of Life, not because they are good, not because they managed to clean up their own act, but simply because they believed in Jesus Christ while they had the opportunity.

Jude wrote,

> *"Now unto Him who is able to keep you from falling and to present you faultless before the presence of His glory... "*

By the time a Christian walks through the gates of the Heavenly Jerusalem his record, no matter how blemished it once may have been, will have been perfectly clean for at least one thousand years! Perhaps he was once was guilty of fear, idolatry, lying, even murder, but his record will now be spotless. It will have been cleansed because the blood of Jesus Christ cancelled the debt completely.

Who, then, are those referred to in verse 8? They are those who stood before the Great White Throne at the end of chapter 20, and whose names were missing from the Book of Life.

The New Jerusalem

Verse 9:

> *"And there came unto me one of the seven angels which had the seven vials full of the seven last plagues, and talked with me, saying, Come here, I will show you the bride, the Lamb's wife. 10 And he carried me away in the spirit to a great and high mountain,*

and showed me that great city, the holy Jerusalem, descending out of heaven from God."

That immediately raises a question - *"How can a city be the Lamb's wife?"* As Clarence Larkin points out, what makes up a city is not its building, parks and businesses but its inhabitants. It is clear here that the bride and city are identical. Since the New Jerusalem is the home and residence of the bride, it represents the bride. We should remember that the city will be inhabited not only by the church. The saints of all ages, angels and God Himself will also be resident there. No wonder John had difficulty describing it!

This indescribably beautiful place will be "the Father's house" referred to by Jesus at the beginning of John 14. If you are a Christian, this is a description of your future home. It is already yours and one day you will take up residence within it. Read about it, study it and enjoy the anticipation of actually stepping through its gates.

When my sister and I were quite young, my father bought a vacation house in Cornwall. We were living in London at the time. Our parents came and told us about the house. They described it in detail and spoke of the beautiful countryside surrounding it. We were very excited and anticipated actually visiting the place which we so vividly imagined. Eventually the day arrived and we traveled to the place, entered its doors, touched its walls and climbed its stairs. Everything now was so much clearer because we could see it as it was. But the reality did not rob us of the excitement and anticipation we had experienced in looking forward to it.

As believers, we have the right to anticipate the Father's provision and to be excited about our heavenly home. One day we will touch it, explore it, and experience it. We sometimes here that old sneer about people being *"so heavenly minded that they are no earthly good."* Personally I suspect we could afford to be a little more heavenly minded than we are. After all, we are told in Scripture that our citizenship is in heaven and that we should set our affection on things above, rather than things on the earth. We are told to look not for the things that are seen but for the things that are not seen, because the things that are seen are temporal whereas the things that are not seen are eternal. There is nothing wrong in being heavenly minded. This present world has absolutely nothing to offer for the future. It is all destined to be burned up and disappear. Only God can offer real security and we should anticipate our future home with excitement.

So let us take a look at this marvelous place where one day we shall take up our permanent residence. From his lofty vantage point, John saw the city of God descending from God out of heaven.

Now verse 11:

> *"Having the glory of God: and her light was like a stone most precious, even like a jasper stone, clear as crystal."*

We could waste a lot of time trying to pinpoint the exact identity of the stones mentioned in this description. It really doesn't matter which stones John had in mind at all. He was not a geologist. He was simply trying to get a point over. He was describing the *light* here, not the stone. It was *like* a stone. The city radiated light which flashed with a brilliance that reminded John of the most precious gems, clear as crystal, reflecting the rays that came from within. Verse 12:

> *"And had a wall great and high, and had twelve gates, and at the gates twelve angels, and names written thereon, which are the names of the twelve tribes of the children of Israel: 13 On the east three gates; on the north three gates; on the south three gates; and on the west three gates."*

I don't get the impression that the names were written on the angels but upon the gates. Gates are points of entry. Jesus likened Himself to a gate in Matthew 7 and to a door in John 10. You enter in through doors and gates and it was through Israel that God brought salvation to the rest of the world. You are a Christian today because God worked through Israel. Therefore Israel was the gate to salvation.

In the ninth chapter of Romans, Paul speaks of Israel as those *"to whom pertain the adoption, and the glory, and the covenants, and the giving of the law, and the service of God, and the promises. Whose are the fathers and of whom, as concerning the flesh, Christ came, who is over all, God blessed for ever, Amen."* That was the heritage possessed by Israel and no other nation on the face of the earth could claim it. Israel was (is) unique and privileged.

Just as the early history of the United States is actually the history of the rest of the world, so the early history of the Christian faith is the history of God's dealing with Israel. Jesus told the woman at the well, *"Salvation is of the Jews"*, as so it was.

It is therefore entirely fitting that the gates of the eternal city should be associated with those through whom all of the saved inhabitants inside the city found entrance.

Verse 14:

> *"And the wall of the city had twelve foundations, and in them the names of the twelve apostles of the Lamb."*

The apostles were Israelites also but they were unique. All but one walked with Jesus during His ministry and he personally trained them. To them was committed the Great Commission and through them the church was born. We all know that Jesus Christ was the great foundation of the church but humanly speaking the apostles were commissioned to set it going. Paul told the Corinthians, (1 Corinthians 3:10), *"According to the grace that was given to me, as a wise master builder I have laid the foundation."* And in Ephesians 1:11, Paul wrote, *"In whom also we have obtained an inheritance, being predestinated according to the purpose of Him who works all things after the counsel of His own will, that we (the apostles) should be to the praise of His glory, who first trusted in Christ. In whom you also trusted, after you heard the word of truth, the Gospel of your salvation."*

The Apostles were the link between the Old and the new; between the Jew and the Gentile. God used them as the unique link. They began as part of the old dispensation. They were born Jews, born under the law. Then Jesus called them out and they were the first to believe. Then they passed on their faith to us and we believed also. In Ephesians 2:19-22 he was able to say, *"Now therefore you are no longer strangers and foreigners but fellow-citizens with the saints and of the household of God, and are built upon the foundation of the apostles and prophets, Jesus Christ being the chief corner stone."*

231

Israel itself was the gate through which the world was offered salvation and the apostles of the Lamb became the human foundation of that new thing that God was doing, namely, the Church of Jesus Christ.

Verse 15:

> *"And he who talked with me had a golden reed to measure the city, and the gates thereof, and the wall thereof. 16 And the city lies foursquare, and the length is as same as the breadth: and he measured the city with the reed, twelve thousand furlongs. The length and the breadth and the height of it are equal."*

Twelve thousand furlongs equals fifteen hundred miles, roughly the distance from Seattle to the Great Lakes. If this city were to be placed on the United States it would occupy all the land west of the Missouri river. To illustrate it another way, center it over present-day Jerusalem and it would cover all Greece, all Turkey, all Syria, all Iraq, all Jordan, most of Saudi Arabia, all of Egypt, Libya and the eastern half of the Mediterranean Sea! That is a BIG city!!

However, that is not all. Not only will this city measure fifteen hundred miles *horizontally*, but it will also be fifteen hundred miles *high*. Some commentators, such as Clarence Larkin, point out that it doesn't *say* the city is a cube. They suggest that it may be a pyramid. They worry about the ability of the foundations to support something that high. Well, I am neither an architect nor an engineer but I have to question their logic. Their fears may be justified by present day physics but this city will be on the new earth, which will probably have a whole new system of physical laws. I am quite sure God will not create anything that is unable to support its own weight. In any case, it seems to come down from God without resting on anything, which would make the question of weight immaterial.

Verse 17:

> *"And he measured the wall thereof, an hundred and forty and four cubits, according to the measure of a man, that is, of the angel."*

Presumably this means that the angel was the same size as a man. A cubit was eighteen inches from the elbow to the tip of the finger, so we have a measure of eighteen inches. 144 cubits would therefore measure 216 feet. This seems rather small in comparison with the huge proportions of the city itself but we must presume that the people inside the city will be the same size as they always were, which means that even a wall 216 feet high would dwarf those who came in and out of its gates. We are talking about a wall twenty-one stories high and six thousand miles long!

Distance will not have the same significance on the new earth as it does today because according to John, the gates will be five hundred miles apart.

Verse 18:

> *"And the building of the wall of it was of jasper: and the city was pure gold, like clear glass. 19 And the foundations of the wall of the city were garnished with all manner of precious stones. The first foundation was jasper; the second, sapphire; the third, a chalcedony; the fourth, an emerald; 20 The fifth, sardonyx; the sixth, sardius; the seventh, chrysolyte; the eighth, beryl; the ninth, a topaz; the tenth, a chrysoprasus; the eleventh, a jacinth; the twelfth, an amethyst."*

Some of these stones are rather difficult to identify today, and if you read ten different commentaries you will get ten different definitions. Exact identification is not very important. The important factor is the impact, which the city had upon John as it descended.

The wall was *made* of jasper but the foundations were *garnished* with all manner of precious stones. The city within the wall was made of gold, so pure that it looked like glass. We are talking about colors here - beautiful colors: blues and greens, yellows and reds and violets against a background of shimmering gold. They will not be dull or flat colors, but clear and sparkling, like reflections from the finest gemstones.

Verse 21:

> *"And the twelve gates were twelve pearls: every individual gate*
> *was of one pearl: and the street of the city was pure gold, as it were*
> *transparent glass."*

God either keeps some VERY large oysters somewhere or He will
create these pearls especially for the gates. It is also interesting
to remember that pearls come from the sea but on the new earth
there will be no more sea. Regardless of how God will achieve this
phenomenon, these gates will undoubtedly be very beautiful. The
soft luster of fine pearls, together with their rarity, has set them
apart from the very beginning as precious.

Verse 22:

> *"And I saw no temple therein: for the Lord God Almighty and the*
> *Lamb are the temple of it. 23 And the city had no need of the sun,*
> *neither of the moon to shine in it: for the glory of God illuminated*
> *it, and the Lamb is the light thereof."*

The purpose of, first the tabernacle and then the temple, was to
provide a way whereby man could atone for his sins and come
into some kind of fellowship with God. That is why sacrifices and
ceremonial washings were always a part of the tabernacle and
temple services. It was only by the blood of the atonement that man
could approach God.

However, in the New Jerusalem sin will be a thing of the past.
Therefore the temple will not longer have any purpose. God will
be able to move freely among His people without violating His
holiness and His glory will provide a light far more perfect the sun
or the moon could ever provide.

Isaiah prophesied of these things, back in chapter 60 of his book.
He wrote:

> *"Violence shall no more be heard in your land, wasting nor*
> *destruction within your borders; but you shall call your walls*
> *Salvation, and your gates Praise. 19 The sun shall no longer be*
> *your light by day; neither for brightness shall the moon give light*

unto you: but the LORD shall be to you an everlasting light, and your God your glory. 20 Your sun shall no more go down; neither shall your moon withdraw itself: for the LORD shall be your everlasting light, and the days of your mourning shall be ended. 21 Your people also shall be all righteous: they shall inherit the land for ever, the branch of my planting, the work of my hands, that I may be glorified."

Revelation 21:24:

"And the nations of those who are saved shall walk in the light of it: and the kings of the earth shall bring their glory and honor into it. 25 And the gates shall not be shut by day: for there shall be no night there. 26 And they shall bring the glory and honor of the nations into it."

Reference to "nations" and "kings" in that passage has led some to believe that John is reverting back to millennium. However this would do violence to thrust of John's vision. He is no longer speaking of the millennium; he is describing a new heaven and a new earth. There is no reason to believe that there will not be nations and kings on the earth at that time. Millions will live righteously through the millennium and will continue into eternity. There is no mention anywhere of the millennial nations ceasing to exist.

It is clear from the Scriptures that God does not intend to create a new race of people for the new earth. His promise to Israel is that the descendents of Abraham will inherit the earth for a thousand generations. That is at least thirty-three thousand years! God promised Israel, through Isaiah, in Isaiah 66:22, *"For as the new heavens and the new earth, which I will make, shall remain before me, says the Lord, so shall your seed and your name remain."* The nation of Israel will be on the new earth in eternity.

Isaiah 9:6 confirms that *"of the increase of His government and peace there shall be no end, **upon the throne of David,** and upon His kingdom, to order it and to establish it with judgment and justice, from henceforth, **even for ever."***

The nations will live and walk in the light of this great city on the new earth and they will bring their glory to it. How they will travel is not revealed to us but no doubt present methods of travel will be as obsolete then as dugout canoes are today. The gates of the city will always be open to them and refreshment and fellowship and love will always be freely available. A city of that size, radiance and beauty will be visible for great distances and it will draw the people to it like a magnet.

Verse 27:

> *"And there shall in no wise enter into it any thing that defiles, or anything that works abomination, or makes a lie: but they who are written in the Lamb's book of life."*

This does not suggest that there will be people on the new earth that would do any of those things. All of those whose names were not written in the Book of Life were dealt with at the Great White Throne. The thrust here is that the city will be eternally pure, with no hint of things that would spoil it.

CHAPTER 22

Here John continues his description of the New Jerusalem, that one day will be the home of every believer. Questions abound, many of which are difficult to answer because some details are not provided. However, perhaps it would be beneficial to briefly summarize the chronology of what we have studied thus far.

1. At the end of the 7-year Tribulation period, Christ will return to this earth in power and great glory (Matthew 24:29-30).

2. Christians will return with Him. They will have been taken from the earth prior to the Tribulation. 1 Thessalonians 4:17 promises that once we have been taken from this earth, *"so shall we ever be with the Lord"*.

3. Upon His return, the Lord will judge the living nations and decide who will enter the kingdom and who will be excluded (Matthew 25:31-46).

4. At that time, Satan will be bound and confined to the abyss for one thousand years (Revelation 20:1-3) while the Lord Jesus reigns on a restored earth (Revelation 20:6).

5. During that time nature will be changed, violence will be removed and conditions restored to their original Edenic beauty (Isaiah 11:1-9).

6. At the end of the thousand years, Satan will be released from his prison house and will go out to deceive the nations once again. An innumerable multitude will turn to him and prepare to face Christ in war.

7. The Lord will destroy them as they are about to attack Jerusalem and Satan will be taken and cast into the Lake of Fire (Revelation 20:7-10).

8. That will leave the righteous nations on the earth. Some will have gone into the millennium and others will have been born during the millennium. My assumption is that by this time all those who remain on the earth will be saved.

9. At this point, the unsaved dead from all ages will be resurrected and will stand before the Great White Throne. Because their names will not be found written in the Book of Life they will have their place in the Lake of Fire (Revelation 20:11-15).

10. The present heavens and earth will be destroyed and the Lord will create a new heaven and a new earth. The New Jerusalem, described in chapter 21, will descend upon it.

In some way (which we are not told) the righteous nations existing on the earth at the end of the millennium will be transferred to the new earth and continue to live on it. They are referred to several times in this account. They will walk in the light of the city, they will bring their glory to it and its gates will always be open to them. God will provide for them in every way. Although no description is given of the new earth itself, it will obviously be perfect in every detail.

The River and the Tree of Life

Revelation 22:1:

> *"And he showed me a pure river of water of life, clear as crystal, proceeding out of the throne of God and of the Lamb. 2 In the midst of the street of it, and on either side of the river, there was the tree of life, which bore twelve kinds of fruits, and yielded her fruit*

every month: and the leaves of the tree were for the health of the nations."

We came across the water of life in chapter 20:6. There God referred to it as a fountain and promised all who were thirsty free access to it. Here it is a river and we see that its source is the throne of God itself. Apparently it will flow down the center of the main boulevard of New Jerusalem, bordered on either side by an avenue of trees. The trees will be Trees of Life, such as grew in the Garden of Eden. There will be many of them in the holy city, probably on the new earth as well. In all probability there were also many of them in Eden. We speak today of *"the* oak" and *"the* maple", meaning the type of tree rather than their number. It is the same with the Tree of Life. It will bear its fruit every month and its leaves will be for the health of the nations.

It is interesting to see reference to months in eternity. A month is the period of time in which the moon revolves round the earth. Months also suggest seasons. Nowhere do the Scriptures say that the sun and moon will disappear. They simply state that we shall not need them for light. They will probably be present in eternity, for the glory of God rather than for their physical functions. The Bible says, *"The heavens declare the glory of God."* If that is the case, why remove them?

Passages such as Hebrews 1:10-12 and 2 Peter 3:7 indicate that the new heavens in Revelation 21:1, which God will create along with the new earth, will not be another dwelling place for Himself. They will be new stellar heavens, containing galaxies of new stars.

Once again, the nations are referred to in verse 2 and the leaves of the tree of life will be there for their health. We are given no details beyond that. The tree of life was intended to preserve Adam and Eve eternally but apparently they failed to eat of it. After they sinned, God drove them out of the garden, not as a punishment but to prevent them from gaining access to the tree of life in their fallen state. Had they done so, and eaten, there would have been no salvation. God said, *"Now, lest he put forth his hand and take also of the tree of life, and eat, and live for ever, therefore the Lord sent him forth from the Garden of Eden to till the ground from whence he was taken."* (Genesis

3:23-24). He sent him out to prevent him from having access to the tree of life.

Adam failed to eat and *then* he sinned. Consequently, he and all his descendents lost the privilege and Christ had to provide an alternative way of salvation. Here, in Revelation 22, the chaos caused by Adam's fall will have been finally remedied and once again, the nations will have access to what Adam lost

Some claim that the tree of life was not really a tree at all but some sort of principle. But here in Revelation 22 we find it growing again on either side of the river of life and bearing edible leaves and fruit. We are unlikely to find a principle that can be planted in the ground and grown up to provide physical leaves.

Verse 3a:

> *"And there shall be no more curse."*

The curse was placed upon the present earth following Adam's sin. In Genesis 3:17 God said, *"Cursed be the ground for your sake. In sorrow you shall eat of it all the days of your life. Thorns also, and thistles shall it bring forth to you and you shall eat of the herb of the field. In the sweat of your face shall you eat bread, until you return to the ground. For out of it you were taken; for dust you are and unto dust you shall return."*

Thorns, thistles, work and sweat are all symptoms of the curse, and will be unknown on the new earth. Also, since the curse principally affected the world of nature, here is evidence that nature will flourish again.
Trees, flowers and animals will continue but with nothing to mar their beauty; no disease, no violence, no death. Instead, the earth will be filled with the knowledge of the Lord as the waters cover the sea."

Verse 3 again:

> *"And there shall be no more curse: but the throne of God and of the Lamb shall be in it; and his servants shall serve him: 4 And they shall see his face; and his name shall be in their foreheads."*

Another difference between the present world and the next will be that God will be visible and accessible to everybody. In This age none could look upon God and live. Moses wanted to see God's face but was refused the privilege because he would not have been able to bear it. However, in the next world there will be no restrictions.

Verse 5:

> *"And there shall be no night there; and they need no lamp, nor light of the sun; for the Lord God gives them light: and they shall reign for ever and ever. 6 And he said unto me, 'These sayings are faithful and true': and the Lord God of the holy prophets sent his angel to show to his servants the things, which must shortly be done. 7 Behold, I come quickly: blessed is he who keeps the sayings of the prophecy of this book."*

Many people dismiss the book of Revelation, either as incomprehensible or as the imagination of man. All I can say is that it would take a very strong imagination to invent this story and a very high intellect to draw together so many Scriptural themes from all parts of the Bible into final closure. Everything finds its terminus here.

Here the angel confirms to John that the book's message is inspired and affirms that the events prophesied in it, including Christ's soon coming, will take place suddenly. In verse 7, Christ speaks for Himself, *"Behold I come quickly"*. *"Quickly"* is a word that sometimes means *"suddenly"*. In any case, *"shortly"*, by God's reckoning, is not the same as *"shortly"* by ours. A thousand years to us is just a day to God.

Verse 8:

> *"And I John saw these things, and heard them. And when I had heard and seen, I fell down to worship before the feet of the angel who showed me these things. 9 Then said he to me, "See you do it not: for I am your fellow servant, and of your brethren the prophets, and of those who keep the sayings of this book: worship God."*

Throughout this book there is a very obvious nervousness among the angels when people try to worship them. They want nothing to do with it. The reason for this is obviously that they have their perspective straight. They dwell in the presence of God and they know who should be worshipped and who should not. In addition, they witnessed the fall of Lucifer, the greatest of them all, together with a great multitude of their own company, due to the fact that Lucifer desired to be worshipped as God.

Verse 10:

The Final Message

> "And he said to me, Seal not the sayings of the prophecy of this book: for the time is at hand."

Daniel was told to seal up his prophecy because another dispensation was to come between Daniel's time and the events foretold in his vision. That dispensation would be the present church age. Here John was told *not* to seal up the book because there was no intervening dispensation. Nothing stood between John's vision and its fulfillment.

Verse 11:

> *"He that is unjust, let him be unjust still: and he who is filthy, let him be filthy still: and he who is righteous, let him be righteous still: and he who is holy, let him be holy still. 12 And, behold, I come quickly; and my reward is with me, to give every man according as his work shall be."*

John was not to conceal what he heard. He was to proclaim it, even though some would discount the message. Many men and women go on in their sin despite His warnings but the warnings are given, nevertheless. Much of Revelation sounds bizarre but it must still be proclaimed because it is God's Word. Our reaction to the truth does not affect the truth one bit. If we neglect to listen to it, we simply hurt ourselves.

Verse 13:

> *"I am Alpha and Omega, the beginning and the end, the first and the last. 14 Blessed are they that do his commandments, that they*

may have right to the tree of life, and may enter in through the gates into the city."

Access to the tree of life is based upon obedience, just as expulsion from the tree of life was caused by disobedience. Obviously Christ is speaking again. He was there in the beginning, He was *"alpha"*; he was there when paradise was lost. He has been there throughout the struggles of lost mankind and He will be there when paradise is regained. He is *"omega"*.

Verse 15:

> "For outside are dogs, and sorcerers, and whoremongers, and murderers, and idolaters, and whosoever loves and makes a lie."

I have known some very nice dogs in my time. In fact some of them have demonstrated more Christian attributes than some who claim to be Christians! However, this is not about the four-legged type of dog. It is an uncomplimentary reference to unsaved Gentiles, called "dogs" by the Jews. These people will not be lurking outside the city on the new earth. They won't. The reference means that they are outside the family, outside the privilege, they will never be able to cross the divide between where they are and the holy city.

Verse 16:

> *"I Jesus have sent my angel to testify unto you these things in the churches. I am the root and the offspring of David, and the bright and morning star."*

He is the "root" of David, in that He predated David by an eternity. He is the offspring of David, in that in time He entered this world through David's line.

Verse 17:

> *"And the Spirit and the bride say, Come. And let him that hears say, Come. And let him that is athirst come. And whosoever will, let him take the water of life freely."*

Here is an invitation to "whoever will" to come and enjoy the blessings of the new paradise. In Genesis 3, man sinned and was expelled fro the first paradise. Throughout history until this point he has lived outside. Now he has been invited back. The invitation is initiated by the Spirit, then echoed by the bride, then taken up by those who hear. The invitation could not be simpler. *"If you are thirsty you may drink." If you wish to experience forgiveness and restoration, you may. If you wish to walk beside the river of life, the door is open for you."* But you must walk through it. It won't come to you. The invitation is clear. *"If you want it, you must come!"* Come to Jesus Christ!

The Final Warning

Verse 18:

> *"For I testify unto every man who hears the words of the prophecy of this book, If any man shall add to these things, God shall add to him the plagues that are written in this book: 19 And if any man shall take away from the words of the book of this prophecy, God shall take away his part out of the book of life, and out of the holy city, and from the things which are written in this book."*

Jesus includes the whole book of Revelation in this warning, not just parts of it. It is *"the book of this prophecy"* and it is His Word from beginning to end, whether we understand it or not. Some parts we don't completely understand because not all the details are provided. In other cases we may be off in our interpretation but enough is clear for us to grasp a very detailed picture of what is coming on this earth.

Verse 20:

> *"He who testifies these things says, 'Surely I come quickly.' Amen. Even so, come, Lord Jesus. 21 The grace of our Lord Jesus Christ be with you all. Amen."*

The final promise of Christ (verse 20) is the key to the interpretation of the whole book of Revelation. *"Behold, I come quickly"*. This is "The Revelation of Jesus Christ" and without His triumphant appearance at the end of the story nothing else in this book would make sense. John's response is *"Amen ("so be it!")* Even so, come Lord Jesus".

About the Author

Ashley Day began his career as the Administrator of a college of languages in London's West End. Called into the ministry during one of Billy Graham's early London crusades, he and his wife, Edna, left the city and took up an itinerant preaching ministry in the South West of England.

The Days immigrated to the USA in October, 1959, and since then have ministered in Oregon, Missouri, England and Idaho. After returning to England, to pastor the Brookdale Evangelical Church in Devon, Pastor Day was called back to the United States in 1980 to become the Senior Pastor of the Coeur d'Alene Bible Church, where the Days remained until retirement in 2003. He now serves as Pastor Emeritus.

Ashley and Edna Day have been happily married for 53 years and have five children.

Seed-Time Ministries began in 1973 and has been used by the Lord to reach tens of thousands of listeners in the United States, Africa, the Middle East, China and the UK. It exists to provide sound Bible exposition through radio broadcasts, tapes, CDs and printed material.

Printed in the United States
38027LVS00004BA/130-153